The New England Merchants
in the Seventeenth Century

D0814847

The New England Merchants

in the Seventeenth Century

BERNARD BAILYN

Harvard University Press
Cambridge, Massachusetts
and London, England
1979

© Copyright 1955 by the President and Fellows of Harvard College

Printed in the United States of America.

Second printing 1979

Library of Congress Catalog Card Number: 55–5222

ISBN 0–674–61280–9 (paper)

ACC LIBRARY SERVICES AUSTIN, TX

To

My Mother

And to the Memory of

My Father

Contents

Illustrations

Following page 130

Preface

THROUGHOUT THE colonial period the merchants — those who dealt for personal profit in the wholesale import, export, and distribution of goods — were the dynamic economic force in the northern colonies, and they occupied a strategic position in society. By the middle of the eighteenth century the leading merchants were towering figures, and an important part of our Revolutionary history is written in terms of their group interests. But, though united by the demands of a common occupation, they did not form a socially homogeneous unit. Their social differences, in fact, were important elements in the determination of events. The roots of these differences lie entwined in the circumstances of the formative period, when colonial society was emerging from the confusions and dislocations of settlement, receiving its character from the impress of New World circumstances upon uprooted Europeans. The story of this development — the crystallization of the interests and social character of the merchant group in New England — is the theme of the chapters that follow.

In such a study, based upon a reconstruction from scattered and fragmentary records of the lives of several generations of individuals, completeness is an elusive goal. But an attempt has been made to give a realistic account of the interdependence of the merchants' activities. The merchants were first of all businessmen, and consequently their business lives must be related to their social and political concerns. How did their social position and political role affect their entrepreneurial activities? Conversely, in what way did their commercial ventures affect their position in colonial society? Linking the Old World and the New, the New England merchants from the beginning were involved in European affairs. What bearing did events in the Old World have on their undertakings? Of what importance were their personal relationships with Europeans?

In seeking answers to such questions I have had the invaluable guidance of Oscar Handlin. His wise counsel and the example of his remarkable scholarship have helped me over innumerable difficulties. Not only did he read and criticize this book at every stage of its preparation, but in his commentary he conveyed something of his own inspiration which makes of history a subtle, penetrating analysis of society.

Others have also helped in important ways. Arthur H. Cole, Leland H. Jenks, and John E. Sawyer gave me the benefit of their full and careful criticism. The views of John L. Clive and Robert E. Kuenne resulted in a number of improvements. Clifford K. Shipton made readily available to me the typescript of John Hull's Letter Book. Ruth Crandall put at my disposal the results of her own research in the fourteen volumes of the *Suffolk Deeds*. The consideration of Dean Francis Keppel of the Harvard Graduate School of Education made it possible for me to complete the manuscript with a minimum of delay. Margaret F. Fouhy and her willing assistants attended to the final typing with unusual promptness and accuracy. The manuscript was prepared for the press with the skillful assistance of Ann Louise Coffin.

The publication of this book has been made possible by a subsidy from the Research Center in Entrepreneurial History, Harvard University, for which I am most grateful. Sections that have appeared in the *Journal of Economic History* and in *Explorations in Entrepreneurial History* are reprinted with permission.

I am particularly indebted to Lotte Lazarsfeld Bailyn for her criticism, her help on countless details, and her wonderful forbearance.

BERNARD BAILYN

Cambridge, Massachusetts

SINCE THE original publication of this book in 1955 a number of writings have appeared that deal with one or another aspect of the merchants' lives. If I were to rewrite the book now I would want to enlarge or compress sections to take account of them; but I have found no reason to reconsider the general interpretation of the book or the treatment of significant details in it. The book is therefore reissued with only a few corrections of technical errors that slipped by in proofreading.

I have myself, with Lotte Bailyn, accepted the invitation to statistical analysis mentioned on page 229; the results are published in *Massachusetts Shipping, 1697-1714: A Statistical Study* (Cambridge, 1959).

The full text of Robert Keayne's Last Will and Testament, discussed on pages 41-44, has been edited and published in volume 42 of the *Proceedings of the Colonial Society of Massachusetts (Transactions, 1952-1956),* and as a separate volume entitled *The Apologia of Robert Keayne: The Self-Portrait of a Puritan Merchant* (New York, Harper and Row, 1965).

The New England Merchants

in the Seventeenth Century

I

Origins of Trade

IN 1630, along the coast of New England, from the island-fringed fiords of Maine to the beaches of Connecticut, were scattered isolated groups of Europeans, part of the vanguard of six generations of Englishmen who laid the foundation of American society. In the spring of that year on the coast of Maine the crews of a small fleet of fishing vessels were cleaning and packing their catch, trucking with the natives, loafing, or brawling. Farther inland at a few trading posts Indians gathered to exchange furs for cloth, hardware, liquor, or fire-arms. Salem and the Massachusetts Bay region, hitherto the homes of a few dozen people living in almost total solitude, were now the scenes of frantic bustle as several hundred newly arrived settlers threw up tents, lean-tos, and cabins in an effort to prepare for the rigors of a New England winter. At Plymouth, the Pilgrim community, number-ing now a little over three hundred souls, lived in primitive comfort within small frame houses built along two intersecting streets. On the shores of Long Island Sound three or four trading houses indicated that Europeans were opening North America to the civilization of the Old World.

This condition of New England society in 1630 was the result not of the will and intentions of successful colonizers but of a series of failures that stemmed from misconceptions of the economic possibil-ities of the region. New England had caught the attention of a variety of Englishmen interested in settlement, men as different in purpose as Sir Ferdinando Gorges, who had dreamed of a feudal Nova Britannia complete with gentry and *bourgeoisie* and divided into counties, baronies, and hundreds, and the Reverend John White, who had tried to organize a community of pious fishermen whose labor and right-eousness would glorify God and who would bring the Gospel to the savages. For three decades English merchants, presumably cautious men, who built fortunes on their ability to judge investments shrewdly, had thrown away thousands of pounds in futile efforts to exploit New England's resources.

The plans of these men failed. Yet their efforts form the background of later, successful undertakings. Out of the frustration of their thwarted ambitions emerged accurate knowledge of New England; and in the wake of their broken enterprises came the scattered settlers of 1630, among whom were the first New Englanders to engage in commerce.

1

New England might have developed like Virginia, as the preserve of a powerful English business corporation, the monopolist of trade, and the source of public authority. The Plymouth Company, created by the Virginia Company charter of 1606, had received the exclusive right to start settlements anywhere between the Potomac River and the present site of Bangor, Maine. It had responded by establishing in 1607 the ill-fated settlement of Sagadahoc near the mouth of the Kennebec River. Its colonists erected a fort, planted crops, built a "pretty pinnace," and prepared to trade with the natives and to begin exploration. But disaster followed disaster until, by the end of 1608, the last of the settlers, as disillusioned with the prospects of the venture as was the company at home, returned to England. "And this," wrote a contemporary, "was the end of that northerne colony uppon the river Sachadehoc." [1]

Behind this first important failure lay the accidents, if such they were, of the economic geography of England and of a mistaken picture of New England and its native population. The Plymouth Company was financed mainly by men from England's west country. For half a century the inhabitants of Bristol and the port towns of Devonshire and Dorsetshire had led England in exploring the continent discovered by John Cabot and in exploiting the rich fisheries of Newfoundland. Bitterly jealous of "the Engrossing and Restraint of Trade by the rich Merchants of *London*," the westerners were a separate interest in New World settlement, and by 1606 demanded a position at least equal to that of the Londoners in the projected settlement of "Virginia." [2]

Bridging these two groups was that "huge, heavie, ugly man," the Lord Chief Justice.[3] Sir John Popham was at the same time a native of the west country, an important royal officer, and a believer in the social benefits to England of colonizing. He became the link of the west-country merchants to the crown, and his influence on the framing of the Virginia Company charter was decisive.

What was needed in this competitive situation was a scheme for colonization that would allow both Londoners and westerners to participate equally in the colonization of America and that would prevent them from clashing so that their combined efforts might contribute to the national good. The famous document issued on April 10, 1606, satisfied these requirements. The charter of the Virginia Company created two separate companies, one located in London and the other in Plymouth, and opened to them separate though overlapping portions of the North American coast. It specifically forbade the two groups to settle within one hundred miles of each other. Each company was to be directed by a council of thirteen, and over both of these boards was to be a royal council to "have the superior managing and direction . . . of . . . matters that . . . concern the government" of the colonies established in the two precincts.[4]

As an enterprise backed mainly by west-country merchants, Sagadahoc suffered a number of disadvantages. The west-countrymen commanded less capital than the Londoners for ventures promising delayed dividends. The sums subscribed to the Plymouth Company could not have approached the £52,624 12s. 9d. pledged to the London Company by 1619. The City Council of Bristol refused to venture anything unless the undertaking was subsidized by the king, and only thirteen merchants in that town subscribed to the company's joint-stock. Moreover, the governmental structure of the Virginia Company, which had been designed to satisfy the west-country demands for independent action, succeeded in doing exactly the opposite. It weakened the enthusiasm of the very men upon whom success depended. The Deputy Mayor of Plymouth protested the overriding "Councell of dyvers," and Sir Ferdinando Gorges, the leader of western colonization plans, made it clear that the westerners resented the presence of Londoners on the council. For the west-country members, said Gorges, "to be tyed upon all occacions to Poste yt to London, is a matter soe tedeous and chargeable as they are wholie distasted with the ymagination thereof, and . . . they utterlie refuse to proceede any farther." When it was learned how many mere citizens and tradesmen were to have a hand in the direction of the company, "all the gentlemen that before weare willing to be lardge adventurers presentlie withdrew themsealves and by noe meanes will have to doe therein." [5]

Finally, it was as west-countrymen that the Plymouth representatives had accepted, at some critical point in the negotiations for the charter, the northern part of "Virginia" as their portion. It probably seemed more native to them, closer to their old haunts at Newfoundland, an extension of their private colonial world. But it had serious shortcomings. For even with these initial disadvantages flowing from west-country membership, the company might have succeeded eventually if, during the first year, the project had given some signs of returning a reasonable profit. Instead, the merchants learned at great cost that the glowing reports of three exploratory voyages had ignored certain basic conditions affecting the commercial possibilities of New England.[6]

The western merchants proceeded on the assumption that North America, abounding in natural wealth, could be exploited by establishing trading factories to which the natives would bring the local products. Such commerce as the merchants had in mind demanded commodities with high value in proportion to bulk and weight, to be furnished by a native population organized economically and politically. The agents and employees they sent over were not expected to raise products to be exported or to search out native goods deep in the interior. Though these men proved contentious and unruly they accomplished their main task. They built a trading fort not different in kind from those established in Asia.[7] But no goods flowed in to match those of the East India Company; there was, Gorges ruefully reported, "no returne, to satisfy the expectation of the Adventurers." The Indians, instead of coming peacefully to the fort to trade, "shew themselves exceeding subtill and conninge, concealing from us the places, wheare they have the commodityes wee seeke for." The men at Sagadahoc waited in vain for throngs of natives to haul precious piles of goods into the fort to exchange for tinkling bells and snippets of bright cloth.[8]

This fundamental miscalculation in the planning of the settlement as a commercial enterprise doomed it to failure. A series of accidents — Popham's death, the resident leader's inheritance in England, a fire in the fort, and a severe winter — provided the immediate causes of its collapse. There was no possible justification for supplying and repopulating a trading post that promised no profits. The financial backing necessary for setting up colonies in New England would not be forthcoming until it was clearly demonstrated that such invest-ments were profitable.[9]

The Plymouth Company never recovered from this disastrous con-clusion to its grand enterprise. Its assets fell to Sir Francis Popham, son of the Chief Justice, who used the ships and equipment in the only way likely to yield a return. From 1609 to 1614 he sent yearly fishing expeditions to the Maine shores. His men set up crude habitations near their stages on Monhegan Island and may have used the old Sagadahoc Fort as a trading center. By 1614 Popham's frequent visits to those parts had given him a high claim to whatever the Indians had to trade, but his main purpose was to fish, for which neither trade nor perma-nent settlements were necessary. These trips undoubtedly paid their expenses, but by no means could they recoup the Pophams' losses in the Plymouth Company. Sir Francis found the attempt "fruitlesse," Gorges wrote, "and was necessitated at last to sit down with the losse he had already undergone." But others followed where he led and, by 1614, Damariscove Island, Pemaquid Point, and Matinicus Island had become with Monhegan Island the yearly rendezvous for a few English fishermen.[10]

2

In the years that followed it seemed likely that New England would become another Newfoundland, frequented by the crews of fishing vessels but unsettled and undeveloped. Captain John Smith visited New England in 1614 and in his influential *Description of New Eng-land* stressed that the region's main staple "to bee extracted for the present to produce the rest, is fish." In this widely read pamphlet he explained in detail how the proper management of New England's fisheries could become the basis of a thriving colonial economy.

To this industry Ferdinando Gorges turned when, in 1619, he or-ganized the Council for New England. This group of forty nobles and gentlemen was responsible for the second and most extravagant attempt to colonize east of the Hudson River. The "Councill estab-lished at Plymouth, in the County of Devon, for the planting, ruling, ordering, and governing of New England, in America" was invested with possession, under the crown, of America between the fortieth and forty-eighth parallels, that is, from the site of Philadelphia to the Gaspé Peninsula, and from sea to sea. It was not organized as a joint-stock company and, unlike most other colonization projects of the period, was not commercial in nature. The patentees were given the power to establish and govern a population of Englishmen in America. Political authority was to be centered in a governor, assisted by a resident council and appointed officers of state. Two-thirds of all the land was to be divided into counties for the patentees and subdivided into baronies and hundreds. Representatives of these units as well as of the incorporated cities were to meet in an assembly to draw up the laws, but it was the president and council in England "who are to give life to the Lawes so to be made." The minor lords were to hold separate courts to adjudicate "petty matters" among tenants. The merchants were to be organized in their own "government" for economic purposes, as were the tradesmen in the cities. The remaining one-third of the land was to be reserved for public uses, "to be belonging to the State, as their revenew for defraying of publique charge." [11]

These ideas had been shaped to the pattern of Gorges' personality. They were, like that Elizabethan knight, bold, patriotic, old-fashioned, and impractical. If his plans had succeeded, New England would have become a feudal principality, dominated by a new colonial nobility. In such a society the merchants would have formed a carefully circumscribed class, their economic activities channeled into medieval institutional forms.

The impracticality of Gorges' scheme immediately became apparent when the Council considered "how to raise the meanes to advance the plantation." Two plans were suggested. "The one was the voluntary contribution of the *Patentees;* The other, by an easie ransoming of the freedomes of those that had a will to partake onely of the present profits, arising by the trade, and fishing upon the coast." [12] Though there were wealthy and energetic men among the original councilors, their interest was such as to force Gorges to rely mainly upon the "easie ransoming" of the west-country merchants.[13] It was primarily for this purpose that the charter granted the monopoly of the trade and fishing in the area to the Council, thus guaranteeing to it control of what it assumed would be a continuing flow of private commerce into New England. This economic energy Gorges and his friends proposed to harness to the purposes of the new colony.

How this was to be accomplished became clear to the Bristol merchants in September 1621 when Gorges sent them a copy of the Council's "Articles and Orders . . . for the better Government of the Trade and [for the] Advancement of the Plantacion in those parts." [14] This document announced that all trade to New England was to be placed by the Council in the hands of joint-stock companies formed in the five leading west-country ports. These five companies, whose stocks were to be liquidated after each expedition, were to meet in yearly conferences at Tiverton, "to resolve uppon their Mutuall proceedings," which might include the determination of one grand joint-stock for all five companies. Since it had become the task of the Council to maintain the peace and safety of the settlements, forts, warships, and military officers would have to be provided. To pay for this expense one-tenth of the "first Capitall adventure" of these companies was to be sent to the Council. For the salaries of the administrative officers, "one in the hundred of all goods" exported or imported was to be reserved for the Council's treasury. The companies were to assist also in the populating of the country. They were to attempt to furnish New England towns with "all kinds of necessary tradesmen" and to insure that shipmasters left in New England one-fifth of their complement of fishermen, well equipped and provisioned for continuing in their trade. Article 24 reads: "And it is further ordered that every shipp of three score tons shall carry with them twoe Piggs, two Calves, twoe couple of tame Rabbetts, two couple of Hens, and a cocke, which they shall deliver at the Iland of *Menethiggen* [Monhegan]." The directors of the five companies were to set prices for goods bought from the settlers and to send detailed information to the Council concerning all men and ships engaged in New England trade. Disputes within or among the companies were to be settled, the forty nobles and gentlemen decreed, "by us."

Such was the plan by which the Council for New England intended to put its trade monopoly to work. But even before the western merchants discovered what was expected of them, the Council's franchise came under attack. The Virginia Company protested the Council's monopoly of the New England fishery and succeeded in obtaining from the Privy Council an exemption for its fishermen. Moreover, the Virginia Company's treasurer, Sir Edwin Sandys, introduced the subject of the Council's monopoly to Parliament. His arguments in behalf of a free fishing bill, though mainly concerned with the Newfoundland fisheries, opened a long battle that formed part of the Commons' campaign against the royal prerogative.[15]

In his stand against the Council's monopoly, Sandys was soon joined by others more directly concerned in the matter. Warding off Gorges' importunity with the complaint that the "Articles" were "difficult," the Bristol merchants quickly got in touch with their representatives in Parliament. The Merchant Venturers Company, the Bristol men wrote, "in no sorte doe like of the said Articles, being they concerne the establishing and making of a Jointe Company Stocke throughout all the Westerne parts to be ordered and governed by the said President and Counsell." But they wanted to continue in the New England fisheries, and some were even willing to pay the license fees, which Gorges had set at £10 per thirty tons of shipping.[16] Before they did so, however, they wanted to be sure that the Council's monopoly was legal. With this encouragement the Members from the west country continued the agitation started by Sandys' group. By 1624 these forces, combined with others in opposition to the crown, succeeded in listing the Council's monopoly as a major grievance of the realm. The dismissal of Parliament, however, eased the pressure to void the charter, which remained in effect until it was surrendered in 1635.

If the merchants could not destroy the monopoly, they could ignore it; and this they did from the start. The issuance of the Council's charter by no means ended the annual voyages to New England. By September 1621 "interloping" in the reserved province was so flagrant that the Privy Council issued an order against such activity. A year later the "outrages" committed by "sundrie irregular persons" in the reserved territory were considered serious enough for the Council to ask for a royal proclamation in its behalf. But though the proclamation was soon issued and though the Council commanded printed copies of the order in council to be "fixed . . . uppon the mayne Mast of every Shipp," the monopoly could not be enforced.[17]

In the fragmentary records of the Council for New England there is mention of only one important offer of financial support. In 1622 some merchants considered investing £100,000, perhaps for a sub-monopoly of the fisheries. But the arrangement was "respited in regard of the Difficulty of findeing security," [18] and the business of the Council meetings became a continuous search for money. Again and again the patentees were dunned for their promised contributions of £110, but even the threat of dropping their names from the list of applicants for a renewal of the charter had no effect. Some of the members undertook a private venture, but it was so poorly supported that they had to mortgage their ship in order to buy needed provisions and equipment. Finally, in a move that contradicted a major premise of Gorges' rationalization of his purposes, the Council decided to add several merchants to the list of patentees. This innovation, understood at the time to be a significant change, is less important for the money it produced than for the light it throws on the fundamental miscalculations in the elaborate plans of Gorges and his friends.[19]

What would have happened to their scheme of government once large numbers of immigrants had settled in New England can only be surmised; that stage was never reached. The Council hoped to achieve that goal by yoking the activities of the west-country merchants to their own purposes of colonization. There was a sharp distinction from the beginning between the function of the Council and that of the merchants. Unlike the forty patentees who had nothing to lose and everything to gain, the merchants were confronted with an organization empowered to take percentages of their profits, to burden them with regulations, and even to clutter their vessels with animals. They were ordered to contribute heavily but were offered little authority. Instead, as in 1606, they found themselves controlled by men whose interests conflicted with their own. Not only were they asked to order their affairs along lines laid down by courtiers and gentlemen, but they were expected to subordinate their private interests to an unwieldy central apparatus which violated their deeply local loyalties. Moreover, bitter experience in Newfoundland had taught them that colonies along the fishing shores were a threat to the success of their expeditions. Colonists would eventually control the wood and salt supplies and meddle in the management of harbors.

The merchants were able to frustrate the Council's aims because of a simple contradiction in the machinery of control. The Council's monopoly depended upon the coöperation of the merchants themselves. The coastal cruisers, harbor forts, and colonial courts of law necessary to put the monopoly into effect were to be paid for by taxing the fishermen and the five companies. When called upon to help enforce regulations against their own interests, the merchants' strongest weapon was not legislation or violence, but indifference. Deprived of financial vitality the Council exhausted itself in futile search for other sources of capital. In 1623, and again in 1635, it liquidated its only real assets by dividing up its land in America among the patentees.

3

Thus the Council, for all its orders and proclamations, did not affect the thin flow of traffic to New England.[20] The fishermen continued their trips to the Maine shores, and the efforts of the Council's admiral, Captain Francis West, to deal with these "stuberne fellows" came to nothing. Most important, the merchants, no longer concerned with the threat of an enormous joint-stock company controlled by men antagonistic to them, were free to invest as they saw fit in private ventures to Gorges' visionary province. During the 1620's, groups from both London and the west country helped to finance expeditions resulting in the first organized settlements in the area. The inhabitants of these plantations were the Pilgrims, the Old Planters of Salem, the first Maine and New Hampshire colonists, and that wayward band of half-legendary characters, the original settlers of Massachusetts Bay. These people were connected in one way or other with efforts of English merchants to tap· the wealth of New England.

The most important of these groups – the Adventurers to New Plymouth, the Dorchester, New England, and Laconia companies – had in common with some of the lesser concerns[21] the type of organization necessary to effect ideas like those expounded by Smith in his *Description*. The theory was simple and convincing: costs could be reduced and profits greatly increased by sending settlers to New England, where, as self-sufficient residents, they could catch fish, collect furs, and process other products for shipment to the entrepreneurs in England. Relationships between the merchant-adventurers and the colonists varied. In some cases the latter were minor shareholders in the companies; in others, they were employees or personal servants of the adventurers. A common device was to have the total assets of the companies – land, buildings, goods, and cash – owned in common by the shareholders, until after a specified period of time they were divided in proportion to investments. Since the merchants were usually the heaviest investors they claimed the greatest share of the proceeds.

Though differing widely in size, type of settlers, and location, these enterprises had, up to 1630, a consistent pattern of development: the expected profits did not materialize, and the merchants, realizing that further investment would send good money after bad, withdrew their support and attempted to recover as much as they could of their investments. Thereafter, they either ceased to concern themselves about the settlers, or restricted their interest in them to sending over English goods at exorbitant prices.

Disappointed as well as baffled by this conclusion to their undertakings, they probably agreed with those who called the land "good for nothing but to starve so many people as comes in it." [22] The causes of their failures lay rooted in their assumptions and calculations, enmeshed in the conditions of the time.

By 1620 the flush of prosperity that had accompanied the peace of 1604 had faded into depression. Harvests were bad, exports lagged, coin disappeared from the market, and confidence in a dependable future was shaken by continuing war on the Continent and the rumblings of civil storms at home. The lack of money was an absorbing problem to which some of the best minds in England were directed; and in 1621 the economic situation was discussed in detail in a series of Parliamentary debates. The upheaval in England's economic life was further increased in the middle of the decade when war brought a constant threat of depredation to merchant shipping. Under these circumstances, large commercial ventures to America, speculative under normal conditions, became gambles that could be justified only by immediate and sizable profits. The pressure of this need was increased by the unpredictably soaring costs of launching plantations. Try as they might "to saf theyre Monys" by skimping on provisions and renting rather than buying ships, the merchants could not avoid the mounting overhead charges of equipment and supplies.[23] Either the plantations produced quick yields or the adventurers would drop the project at the first opportunity.

The planters were from the start well aware of their responsibilities to the merchants and, while they condemned "the vain expectation of present profit" as "the overthrow and bane . . . of Plantations," they did their best to satisfy it.[24] But the very intensity of the merchants' desire stood in the way of its gratification. Hope for the economic success of the settlements rested in part on the assumption that the settlers would immediately become self-sufficient. Under the best conditions a wait of several months was required before the first crops were harvested, during which time the whole food supply had to be sent from home or bought from Maine fishermen. Conditions were usually against the quick raising of a food supply. Proper soil had to be found, the ground cleared, and the techniques of raising Indian corn acquired. Men engaged in raising the first crops on virgin soil could not fish or erect trading posts at the same time. The period of agricultural adjustment constantly exceeded expectations, and in 1628 prospective adventurers were warned, "Let no man goe without 18 moneths provision." [25]

More destructive to the merchants' timetable of profits was the need of the colonists to explore and resettle in places best fitted for agriculture, trade, and fishing. Though they knew in general where to settle, the first colonists landed where tides or chance winds happened to direct their ships. Without detailed information about the best points of contact for the peltry trade or the shores closest to the fishing waters, they were either forced to send out "discoveries" immediately and move to the best sites or, like the Dorchester Company, ascribe their failure to "ill choice of the place." [26] The New Plymouth merchants interpreted the Pilgrims' desire to move from Plymouth to a more strategic location as restlessness or envy, and told them curtly that it would be better for them to "fixe your eyes upon that which may be done ther, then languish in hopes after things els-wher." But the Pilgrims knew better than the merchants where the furs were. Their success as traders after the company dissolved was based on trading posts in Maine, Rhode Island, and Connecticut.[27]

To the merchants, operating on a delicate balance between investments and profits, accidents on the homeward voyages meant severe reverses. The capture by the French of the Pilgrims' first return cargo created a loss to the New Plymouth merchants exactly equivalent in value to that suffered by the Dorchester Company when its first load of fish "returned to a late and consequently a bad market in Spaine." The capture of the Pilgrims' *Little James* by a "Turks man of warr" in 1625 was the *coup de grâce* to the staggering New Plymouth Company.[28]

The dissolution of the companies started with the breaking off and selling out of a few of the merchants. This increased the burden on the remaining members, intensified the demand for returns, and ended by forcing the associates to disband and apportion profits and losses. Where possible they shifted the debt to the settlers. This they were able to do the more readily because of the poor bargaining position of the planters. Growing yields of fish and fur were accompanied by increasing debts to the men who supplied them with trading goods, clothes, and equipment. Exchanging things useless to themselves for goods they desperately needed, they were forced to sell cheaply and buy dearly. The English merchants covered their risks and made large profits by selling goods to the settlers at inflated prices. Faced with the competition of the well-supplied Dutch in Manhattan and the French in Canada, the settlers found the exchange value of their trading goods constantly diminishing. It was only after the men at Plymouth discovered the value of wampum to the Maine Indians that their trade balance rose significantly.[29]

4

With the breakdown of these organizations, control of New England's trade fell to a few leading colonists or to English adventurers of far different social and economic position from that of the men who headed the New Plymouth and Dorchester companies. Instead of conducting their operations from England, these adventurers gathered together partners, friends, and servants, outfitted a vessel or two, and came to America "on their perticuler," intending either to settle or to return home after a rich strike. These fly-by-night traders enjoyed great advantages over the merchants in England. Once their voyage was under way their costs were fixed. As temporary settlers, they lived at a bare subsistence level, and were free to explore and move about in search of proper sites. The main problem for them was to collect enough food and trading goods once their original provisions had given out or, if they planned more permanent plantations, to keep alive through the starving period when the first crops were growing. If by chance their ships were captured or wrecked, they did not have to abandon their hopes of success in trade. They could, like Walter Bagnall on Richmond Island, sell furs to fishermen or more affluent traders, and still accumulate fortunes like his, reputed to be £1,000, in a few years.[30]

These venturers who, with the Pilgrims and a few fishermen made the first substantial profits from the resources of New England, were almost to a man outcasts from the respectable world of the English middle class. The first to arrive on the scene, the Pilgrims' notorious enemy Thomas Weston, had probably been an interloper in the English cloth trade and was sought by the home authorities for arms smuggling. The most successful was John Oldham, a tempestuous, unscrupulous man, "a mad Jack in his mood," who was driven from Plymouth with "a bob upon the bumme" for his insistent refusal to respect the rights of the Separatists. Painstaking research has cleared Thomas Morton of the charge of murder, but he remains a quarrelsome, rootless individual who did, not hesitate to violate a royal proclamation and endanger the lives of the settlers by selling arms and liquor to the Indians. Edward Astley, at Castine, Maine, was described by Bradford as "a very profane yonge man; and he had for some time lived amonge the Indeans as a savage, and wente naked amongst them, and used their maners." He too was packed off for illicit sales to the natives. None of these men were in sympathy with the religious and social ideas of the Pilgrims and Puritans.[31]

As for the fishermen-traders in Maine, there is no reason to question their contemporary reputation of being wild, ungovernable, occasionally vicious men. One who visited their communities later wrote,

If a man of quality chance to come where they are roystering and gulling in *Wine* with a dear felicity, he must be sociable and *Roly-poly* with them, taking off their liberal cups as freely, or else be gone, which is best for him, for when *Wine* in their guts is at full Tide, they quarrel, fight and do one another mischief, which is the conclusion of their drunken compotations.[32]

These men, together with a few of the Pilgrims, were in immediate control of New England's commerce at the arrival of the Puritans in 1630. By that time the Pilgrims owned a share in a trading post at the mouth of the Penobscot River, another at the present site of Augusta on the Kennebec River, and a third at the head of Buzzard's Bay. At three points on the lower Piscataqua, agents of the Laconia Company were building villages they hoped would become the main export centers for furs on the continent. The interlopers were gathering pelts on some of the Maine islands, in Massachusetts Bay, and in the neighborhood of Quincy. The fishermen who had been attracted to the fur trade had set up a string of temporary shelters along the deeply indented shoreline between Penobscot and Casco bays. Finally, in the south, the Dutch maintained a monopoly of the Indian trade along the shores of Long Island Sound by building a trucking post on an island in Narragansett Bay and two others on the mainland of Rhode Island and Connecticut. With the failure of the Dorchester Company to develop the fisheries near Cape Ann, that industry remained concentrated in the waters of southern Maine, controlled by merchants of England's west country.[33]

By the end of the decade the yield in colonial products of these scattered posts and stages offered English merchants new inducements to invest in voyages to New England.[34] The years of failure and experimentation were coming to an end, and increasing numbers of English merchants, including some of those who had lost heavily during the twenties, hastened to stake out claims to the proven grounds. This movement, which resulted in the permanent colonization of southern Maine, coincided with the arrival of the Puritans. Among these newcomers were merchants different from any who had engaged in American trade before. They picked up the threads of commerce spun by the earliest traders and wove a fabric of their own design.

II

Establishment of the Puritan Merchants

INTO THE COMMERCIAL situation of New England in 1630
the great Puritan Migration brought the first of the permanent merchants. Though clearly distinguishable from the interlopers, servants
of English merchants, and Pilgrims who had preceded them in trade,
they were not men of uniform background or training. Some whose
origins lay in the lower levels of London's commercial populace were
experienced tradesmen who put their skills to good use in the New
World. Others, gentlemen and yeomen of rural England, found in
the New World inducements to enter business for the first time.

Despite such differences all of the first generation Puritan merchants agreed that religious considerations were highly relevant to
the conduct of trade, that commerce, being one of the many forms
of human intercourse, required control by moral laws. But some of
the newly arrived merchants, as they assumed power over the exchange of goods, felt the restrictive effect of these ideas when acted
upon by a determined ministry and magistracy. In their confused
reaction to ethical control as well as in the progress of their business
enterprises lay seeds of social change.

1

Of the 65,000 Englishmen who emigrated to America and the West
Indies between 1630 and 1640, approximately 20,000 came to New
England. They arrived in fleets of vessels and in individual trading and
fishing ships, as family groups, village groups, or individuals. Many
had been torn from their deepest social ties by economic distress.
Most of them, sympathetic to the cause of religious reform, feared
persecution and sought a haven where they intended to build a god-
lier community. Almost none of these refugees could organize the
necessary transportation and start settlements independently. But
help was offered them by commercial companies seeking settlers to

develop their American holdings. In the case of New England the main controlling organization was an outgrowth of those unsuccessful enterprises of the 1620's that had attempted to profit from the products shipped back to England by the settlers they had sent out.

The New England Company, formed in 1628 out of the wreckage of the Dorchester Company, was typical of many early seventeenth-century colonizing organizations in its mingling of religious and economic motives. Inspired by the same Reverend John White whose hopes for the pious fishing community on Cape Ann had been frustrated two years earlier, it announced its purpose to be "the propagation of the Gospel of Jesus Christ and the particular good of the several Adventurers." Of forty-one subscribers identified, at least twenty-five were merchants.[1] A few of these were prominent men in the world of English business: Matthew Cradock whose investments in the East India trade were increased by £2,000 in the very year of the founding of the New England Company; Richard Bushrod, thrice Member of Parliament from Dorchester; Simon Whetcome who had commercial bases in both London and Dorset.[2] Other members were connected with both gentry and *bourgeoisie:* Sir Richard Saltonstall, nephew of the lord mayor of London, justice of the peace and lord of a manor; Isaac Johnson, brother-in-law of the Earl of Lincoln and owner of substantial country estates; and John Humfrey, a London lawyer, son of one of the "Capital Burgesses" of Dorchester and future husband of another sister of the Earl of Lincoln.[3]

All the members of the company were interested in the movement to purify the Church of England; most of them had invested in other Puritan commercial ventures.[4] But, though they hoped and worked for the establishment of a Puritan refuge, being men of substance and influence in public affairs, they were themselves not easily torn from their English roots. In the New England Company they harmonized their desire to further both the true religion and their own fortunes. They looked to the New World not only for a haven but for profits, the more satisfying in that their extent would measure the success of a godly enterprise.

The company proceeded in the manner usual for such organizations. It took out a patent from the Council for New England covering the area between the Merrimac and Charles rivers and from sea to sea, and obtained stock subscriptions amounting to £2,940. With this capital it bought what remained of the Dorchester Company's equipment and by September 1628 sent over a shipload of settlers under the direction of John Endecott to start operations on the site of Salem.

Until the spring of 1629 this organization and these purposes satisfied the leaders of the company. But to protect their title to the Massachusetts area from conflicting claims, they sought and obtained in March of that year a royal charter granting them full powers of government over the settlers in the district. This document, which turned the New England Company into the incorporated Massachusetts Bay Company, opened new possibilities to the merchants and their Puritan friends.

While the governor, Matthew Cradock, sent Endecott warnings against interlopers and demands for quick returns,[5] a growing crisis in England was pressing into definite plans the notions of a group of harried Puritans. The year of the New England Company's existence had been a time of anxiety in the nation, marked by the forced collection of royal duties, the assassination of Buckingham, the king's favorite, and Parliamentary remonstrances. Two weeks before the issuance of the Massachusetts charter Parliament was dissolved and Charles I was free to violate religious sensibilities, a variety of property interests, and common sense in his attempt to raise funds and enforce conformity.

The panic that struck even the most stable Puritan circles coincided with a period of economic distress in certain regions and precipitated the resolve of a group of East Anglian gentlemen to leave England.[6] Some of their leaders — John Winthrop, Thomas Dudley, and Emmanuel Downing — were connected in one way or another with the same Earl of Lincoln whose brothers-in-law were members of the Bay Company.[7] Hoping to use the Puritan trading company to achieve their purposes, this interrelated, compact association of "persons of worth and qualitie" proposed on July 28, 1629, to advance the plantation by transporting themselves and their families to New England. But they would do so only if the company would "transferr the govnment of the plantacion to those that shall inhabite there, and not . . . continue the same in subordinacion to the Company heer, as now it is." Negotiations went on through the summer, and on August 29 the company agreed to the proposal, "soe [long] as it may bee done legally." [8]

By this vote the company effected its own elimination. Though they were sincerely interested in the establishment of a Puritan colony, the original investors, with a few exceptions, were not themselves prepared to emigrate. The trading company they had organized in hope of profits was dead, and they proceeded to inter its remains.

Aiming to get back at least a part of their first investment, the merchants worked out a scheme by which the existing joint-stock was in effect frozen, and its assets and debts taken over by ten undertakers, half to live in England and half in America. This new group, in exchange for 50 per cent of the beaver trade, the monopoly of the salt manufacture in the colony, the sole right to transport goods and immigrants, and the privilege of establishing a "magazine" of goods to sell to the settlers at fixed prices, agreed to "beare all charges . . . and to pay the [original] underwryters their principall by them brought, at the end of 7 years." The profit from these privileges promised the new undertakers sufficient rewards for the debts and risks they were assuming.[9]

This change in its economic organization was part of a more general transformation of the company. Through the year 1629 new names began to appear on the company's attendance list. The royal charter of March had included on the directing board of assistants William Pynchon, a well-to-do gentleman from Essex, who began to attend meetings in May. Clerics like Hugh Peter and John Davenport, gentlemen like John Winthrop and Thomas Dudley were added to the roster. The climax was the election of Winthrop to the governorship in October. Thereafter the leadership of the company was securely in the hands of men whose main occupation was not trade.[10]

The consequence of this change in the directing personnel of the Bay Company was momentous. These new leaders made the crossing to America themselves and as settlers assumed control of the new society. The first magistrates of the Bay Company, therefore, were men whose life experiences were those of an intensely religious minority within the lesser English gentry. Hammered to a fine edge by controversy and steeled in the fires of persecution, the piety of these Puritan leaders was keen and effective. Their lives were dedicated to the search for righteousness, for the knowledge of which they drew upon a body of thought worthy of their inspiration. In Calvinism they found doctrines that might be applied to every aspect of life. It is only in the light of certain of these tenets that the lives of the Puritan merchants can be understood.

2

The ethical keystone of the great edifice of Calvinism was the conviction that all men were totally responsible for their behavior. The heart of the question, as a sixteenth-century writer put it, is not the quantity of sin but the fact that God's majesty is offended at all; " . . . be the thing never so little, yet the breach of his Commandment deserveth death." [11]

To men for whom life was moral experience, no actions were more relevant to the overwhelming consideration of salvation than those touching the welfare of one's fellow men. For, however discouraging to those who found a righteous life a simpler matter when lived in solitude, the Puritan's obligation to live intensively as a social being was nothing less than God's will. Society was an organism functioning for the good of all its members. Each component sought its own welfare, yet contributed and was subordinated to the whole. In a world of sinful men seeking salvation, a compact society had the advantage of a readier discipline exerted by those in authority. This fact was of first importance, for men in positions of political power were, in their official capacities, limited agents of God. Those you have called to public office, Winthrop told a bumptious General Court, "have our authority from God, in way of an ordinance, such as hath the image of God eminently stamped upon it, the contempt and violation whereof hath been vindicated with examples of divine vengeance." [12] Leaders, once selected, were to whip the moral sluggards into line, for their own good, for the welfare of society, and for the glory of God.

The variety of men's occupations made it possible for each individual to find the work in which he could best acquit himself of his obligations. But it also meant that some men were more exposed to temptation than others. Those whose work bore broadly on the welfare of others were called upon to exert a scrupulousness in their transactions commensurate with the temptation to sin. Of all private occupations trade was morally the most dangerous.

The soul of the merchant was constantly exposed to sin by virtue of his control of goods necessary to other people. Since proof of the diligence he applied in his calling was in the profits he made

from precisely such exchanges, could a line be drawn between industry and avarice? The Puritans answered, as had Catholics for half
a millenium, that it could, and they designated this line the "just
price." [13]

They assumed that there existed an ideal standard of valuation applicable to every situation. An unjust figure was the result not so
much of the mechanical operation of an impersonal market as of some
individual's gluttony. A just charge was one willingly paid by a person
experienced in such matters and in need of the article but under no
undue compulsion to buy. The Reverend John Cotton laid out the
principles clearly: "A man may not sell above the current price, i.e.,
such a price as is usual in the time and place, and as another (who
knows the worth of the commodity) would give for it, if he had
occasion to use it. . ." A merchant's personal losses or misfortunes
ought never to be reflected in an increased valuation, "but where
there is a scarcity of the commodity," Cotton wrote, "there men
may raise their price; for now it is a hand of God upon the commodity,
and not the person." [14] As for the particular determination of the
price, in case private men cannot agree on a common estimate, "the
governor, with one or more of the councell" or perhaps "certaine
select men" will be able to make the matter clear. Convinced that
justice could be reached, the Puritans sought only the detailed figures
in concrete situations.[15]

Equally treacherous to the soul of the businessman and the good
of the public was the fact that the merchants came into control of
the available supply of money and charged interest on debts. One
who controlled supplies of cash or credit held a knife over a vital vein
in the social body. Such a power had for centuries required the
closest regulation, which it had duly received along with its rationalization in the literature on usury. But in the sixteenth century the
medieval excoriation of all interest-bearing loans had given way to
a qualified acceptance of interest within the limits of justice and official determination.[16] The New England Puritans took over the
continental Calvinist phrasing of this acceptance. The principle was
clear. "What rule must wee observe in lending?" asked Winthrop
rhetorically.

ANS: Thou must observe whether thy brother hath present or probable,
or possible meanes of repayeing thee, if ther be none of these, thou must
give him according to his necessity, rather then lend him as hee requires;

if he hath present meanes of repayeing thee, thou art to looke at him, not as an Act of mercy, but by way of Commerce, wherein thou arte to walke by the rule of Justice. . . If any of thy brethren be poore etc. thou shalt lend him sufficient that men might not shift off this duty by the apparent hazzard. . . From him that would borrow of thee turne not away.

QUEST: What rule must wee observe in forgiveing?

ANS: Whether thou didst lend by way of Commerce or in mercy, if he have noething to pay thee [thou] must forgive him (except in cause where thou hast a surety or a lawfull pleadge) Deut. 15. 2.[17]

John Cotton, flourishing *"Exo. 22. 25. Lev. 25. 35, 36,"* asserted quite simply: "Noe increase to be taken of a poore brother or neighbour for anything lent unto him." [18]

Though church and state in New England most readily impinged on the professional life of the merchant in regard to just price and usury, the assumption of justified control of economic life had a far wider applicability. If prices came under the aegis of authority so also did wages. Encouragement, even direct subsidization of economic activity, no less than restriction, flowed from the same obligation to manipulate material life for spiritual ends.[19]

Such precepts had a special appeal to a predominantly agricultural people whose emigration was at least in part due to economic distress. Many settlers had lost their stability in a rapidly changing world where "trades are carried soe deceiptfully and unrightusly as that is almost inpossible for a good upright man to maynteyne his charge and to live comfortably in his profession." [20] The Reverend John White, who had inspired the founding of two commercial companies, voiced a typical thought in writing to Winthrop,

I heare shopkeeping begins to growe into request amongst you. In former age all kinde of retailing wares (which I confess is necessary for mens more convenient supply) was but an appendixe to some handicraft and to that I should reduce it if I were to advise in the government. Superfluity of Shopkeepers Inholders etc. are great burthens to any place. We in this Towne where I live . . . are of my knowledg at Charge 1000*li* per annum in maintaining several familys in that Condition, which we might well spare for better employments wherein their labours might produce something for the common good which is not furthered by such as drawe only one from another and consequently live by the sweat of other mens brows, producing nothing themselves by their owne endevours.[21]

At a time when mercantilism in Europe made the needs of trade a reason of state, some of these ideas of the New England leaders were archaic. Yet they were able to survive and even to flourish because the governing Fathers, being, in John Hull's phrase, "no babes nor windyheaded men," understood the necessity to found their society on a solid economic base.[22] They merely insisted that the life of business be placed within a structure whose proportions had been drawn by the hand of God.

These ideas were put into use in the very first years of the Puritan settlements and helped shape the development of institutions and traditions from the start. Nowhere else did Calvinist doctrines of social ethics find such full application. In Geneva, Scotland, and the Netherlands theory had always to be qualified to some extent by pre-Calvinist practices. In New England, doctrine literally preceded practice.

3

The commerce to which these ideas first became applicable advanced along lines drawn both by the pre-Puritan traders and by the needs of the newly arrived settlers. In 1630 the most highly developed enterprise in New England was the exportation of furs by the Pilgrims. Three years earlier the Pilgrims' debt of £1,800 to the English merchants had been assumed by eight of the Plymouth colonists in exchange for a six-year monopoly of the colony's trade. Lacking capital and needing reliable contacts in England, they had drawn in four of the London merchants previously associated with them and appointed Isaac Allerton their agent.[23] In this arrangement economic privilege within the Plymouth Colony had become the reward for orthodoxy. The eight Pilgrim monopolists were the chosen of the choice, the leaders of the colony in every sense. Economic privilege became "the visible pearl of great price which alone could compensate the Elect of God for the toil and effort necessary to establish His Church in the New World." [24] Though these men controlled the government of the colony, they kept their political and economic powers separate. They had come to engross the fur trade by virtue of a grant by a government which felt that their monopoly would prove to be of public benefit. If habit and desire tended to blur the clarity of their obligations, a jealous citizenry restored it. Among four demands made by a grand jury in Plymouth early in 1639 was the desire "to be informed of the undertakers of the trade what wilbe allowed to the colony for the use of the said trade during the years past." [25]

The Plymouth traders started with the disadvantages of a poor location, complete lack of capital, and venal agents and partners in England. The geographical difficulty was overcome by establishing posts at spots strategic for the fur trade though hundreds of miles from Plymouth. Trucking houses in Maine on the sites of Castine and Augusta became receptacles for the furs moving down the Penobscot and Kennebec rivers. From their post at the head of Buzzard's Bay the Pilgrims sent boats into Narragansett Bay and along Long Island Sound. Greatly aided in their exchange position by the discovery that the Indians valued highly strings of certain shell beads called *wampumpeag*, or wampum, the Pilgrim undertakers extended their trade quickly into southeastern as well as northern New England. Following explorations led by the ubiquitous John Oldham, they established their last inland station at the end of the six-year period well up the Connecticut River at Windsor.[26]

During the lifetime of the undertaking and for about three years thereafter, the Plymouth fur trade flourished. Governor Winthrop of the relatively rich and populous colony to the north complained in 1634 of the Pilgrims' "having engrossed all the Cheif places of trade in N:E: viz: Kenebeck, Penobscott, Narigancet, and Conecticott. . ." [27] But after 1637 there was a precipitous decline. The 1638 fur shipment was smaller than that of any of the previous six years. By the end of the decade the trade had come to a complete standstill.[28] It was never revived and after 1640 Plymouth failed to produce a group of merchants engaged in an overseas export trade. The Pilgrim fur traders either settled into agricultural or political pursuits or, like Edward Winslow, moved to other places where their energies had freer play. The town became an economic satellite of Boston, and its businessmen thereafter retailed European goods imported by others to whom they returned the agricultural surpluses of the neighboring farms. The men through whose hands thousands of pounds of furs had passed in the first half of the decade ended their careers with very modest fortunes.[29]

The explanation of this sudden fall in the Plymouth fur trade lies in its purpose and its resulting organization. It was intended to be a means for the colony to acquit itself of the burden of debt to the English merchants. But new capital was needed to establish and maintain the trade by means of which the obligation was to be repaid, and it could only come from the same entrepreneurs who already held the colony in debt. The result was that the four English merchants and the unscrupulous Isaac Allerton used the Plymouth monopolists as a channel through which to draw a fortune in furs. By charging excessive rates for trading goods, assigning to the monopolists' debt the cost of their private ventures, and particularly by putting up with a woefully inaccurate bookkeeping system,[30] they dissipated the part of the profits that ought to have accrued to the Pilgrim merchants. In fact, they managed to keep the debt growing faster than the Pilgrims could increase their remittances in furs. When in 1647 the whole enterprise was scrutinized and compounded for the last time, it was discovered that the Pilgrims still owed £1,200 despite exports of beaver between 1631 and 1636 worth at least £10,000.[31]

The Pilgrims, as Bradford wrote, had been "hoodwinckte." [32] But if their naïveté and the venality of their English associates kept them from profiting from the trade it did not stop the flow of furs itself. The decline was the result, rather, of the Pilgrims' inability to maintain the distant posts by which they tapped the furs and to keep others from establishing themselves closer to the source of supply along the river routes. The costs of expansion in the trade increased steadily as the fur-bearing animals near the coast were eliminated. New posts had to be built farther inland, requiring transportation over longer distances and heavier equipment. At the same time competition by their wealthier neighbors reduced the exchange value of their trading goods, decreased the profit margin, and necessitated greater investments.

In such a situation the Pilgrims, once surpassed by more powerful traders, were incapable of retaliating or recuperating. As a consequence, their contacts with the peltry sources were destroyed in quick succession. In 1635, D'Aulnay, in behalf of the governor of French Acadia, seized their posts on the Penobscot, and the Pilgrims demonstrated the poverty of their resources in an *opéra-bouffe* attempt to recover it. In the same year settlers from Dorchester, Massachusetts, invaded the Pilgrim enclave at Windsor, Connecticut. Charges by Plymouth that the newcomers cast "a partiall, if not a covetous eye, upon that which is your neighbours, and not yours," were to no avail; the Pilgrims were forced to concede the location. The Kennebec region also proved to be too attractive to remain in their hands; in 1637 they accused the Bostonians of cutting in on their patented rights to the site of Augusta. The increasing competition, their resolve not to deal further with the London merchants on whom they depended for trading goods, and the attractions of a sellers' market in livestock and provisions persuaded the monopolists to drop the northern fur trade altogether. Finally, their insecure contacts in Narragansett Bay were easily disrupted by the first settlers in what became Rhode Island.[33]

As early as 1637 the fur monopoly, renewed annually after 1634, was becoming a burden to its owners. In 1639 Bradford and his partners stated flatly "that they will hold the trade no longer than November next." In 1640, since "the trade is not now followed by any man, and there may be some smale thinges some tymes had of the Indians in the plantacions within the goverment," the monopoly was eliminated and anyone was permitted to submit to the governor for approval the conditions under which he proposed to enter the trade.[34]

4

While the Pilgrims witnessed the decline of their fur trade, the Puritans in the Bay Colony, drawing on greater resources and more effective political support, moved swiftly ahead in exploiting the peltry supply of Massachusetts and Connecticut.

The undertakers of the Massachusetts Bay Company had been guaranteed 50 per cent of the fur trade as part of their exclusive privileges. But though this sub-company survived its seven years and seems to have paid its debts and even some dividends, it did not develop its monopoly.[35] For one thing, only two of the five emigrating undertakers were in New England one year after the arrival of the Puritan fleet,[36] and these men, Winthrop and Dudley, did not devote themselves to fur trading. The undertakers' franchise had been considered valuable because of the anticipated competition for pelts between the mouths of the Merrimac and Charles rivers. The quantity of beaver and other furs in this coastal region in 1629 was unknown, but expectations ran high. The most enterprising of the pre-Puritan traders, John Oldham, had been so optimistic that he had guaranteed the Massachusetts Bay Company, in return for the management of the company's trading stock, a profit of 300 per cent in three years, contenting himself with the "overplus of the gaines," an offer which the company, considering Oldham a man "altogeather unfitt for us to deale with," flatly refused.[37]

Such optimism for the fur trade in the Bay region had been ill-founded. The streams between the Merrimac and the Charles rivers were short and did not tap the richest beaver meadows. Nor did there exist a large Indian population near the coast to bring out the pelts from the interior. The wandering traders had collected most of the local furs, and by 1633 the lack of penetrating rivers and the low fertility of the beaver combined to make the Bay area almost valueless for the trade. Consequently, those hoping to profit from this valuable commodity were forced to build inland posts, and for this the finances and interest of the sub-company were inadequate. As a result, except for occasional shipments of skins by John Winthrop, Jr. who seems to have managed the company's business affairs in New England,[38] the undertaking as it affected the fur trade had only a legal existence.[39] The development of this commerce fell to a number of independent settlers whose business affairs were entirely free from the control of English merchants.

During the first three years of the Puritan settlements the centers of the fur trade clustered around Massachusetts Bay. The report of the colony treasurer for the years 1632–1633 shows the locations of those who paid taxes on the 622 pounds of beaver collected.[40]

		Pounds of Beaver Taxed
Roxbury		400
Pynchon	400	
Dorchester		97
Davis Wilton	2¾	
town constable	61¾	
Holman and Collecott	32½	
Charlestown		45
town constable	1	
John Woolridge	44	
Lynn (Saugus)		26½
Turner	26½	
Medford		22
Thomas Mayhew for Cradock	22	
Cambridge		16+
Goodman Webb	15	
town constable	1+	
Boston		15½
town constable	15½	
		————
		622+

These quantities were insignificant compared with the 10,000 pounds reputedly carried off yearly by the Dutch or the 3,738 pounds actually exported by the Pilgrims in 1634.[41] By this year it was clear that these cargoes, small as they were, marked the end of the supply in the vicinity of Massachusetts Bay. But an approach to new sources was at hand, based on the prevalent conception of New England geography.

It was commonly believed that the source of all the northern furs was a vast lake somewhere in northwest New England. From this "Lake of the Iroquois," as Champlain called it in 1612,[42] flowed all the great rivers of northern America that emptied into the Atlantic: the St. Lawrence, the Kennebec, the Piscataqua, the Merrimac, the Connecticut, the Hudson, the Delaware, and even the Potomac. In moving west of the Bay region, the Puritan merchants hoped to cut off all competitors by reaching this heart of the fur country. It was to accomplish this diversion of the Great Lake furs that the New England merchants in the 1630's moved their trading posts deeper into the interior.[43]

The Mystic River, closest to the Bay itself, was the first target. As early as 1629 Matthew Cradock, the leading backer of the Massachusetts Bay Company who never personally migrated to America, had established a private plantation near Medford on the Mystic River. His agents developed this independent estate rapidly, even to the point of laying out a deer park. Their main task was to ship home furs and other commodities as rapidly as possible, and despite wranglings among themselves and Cradock's rueful belief that he was ruining himself "by reposing trust in maney not worthey to bee trusted," they did manage to give Cradock some return on his large investment. But the Mystic like the Charles River trailed off insignificantly a few miles from the coast, disappointing those who had hoped that its broad mouth indicated a wide stream penetrating deep into the interior.[44]

The Merrimac River, on the northern border of the Massachusetts grant, was even more tempting. Licenses to collect furs along this stream were granted as early as August 1632 [45] and three years later Simon Willard led a dozen families through seventeen miles of wild land to plant the village which, in 1640, became known as Concord, Massachusetts. Not only was this settlement well located to cut off some of the inland furs before they reached the coastal towns, but in itself, with its "seven natural ponds, more than nine miles of river, and a large number of smaller streams," contained a veritable treasure in beavers.[46]

But the greatest efforts, reflecting the highest hopes, were directed toward the fertile river valley that divided western New England. Believing that the Connecticut River was another Hudson in its arterial flow of pelts, the Massachusetts fur traders scrambled after John Oldham and the Pilgrim Edward Winslow to set up trading houses on the banks of the broad stream. It was a veritable gold rush. In two years, 1633–1634, traders from Plymouth and Massachusetts Bay, together with a few competing Dutchmen from New Amsterdam, established trading centers on the sites of Windsor, Hartford, and Wethersfield. In 1635 William Pynchon, hardly the man to stand by idly while his fur supply was cut off, planted his own village farther north than the others, at Agawam, now Springfield, Massachusetts.[47]

The location of the last major settlement in Connecticut was also selected mainly with an eye for commercial possibilities. In 1637 the *Hector* brought to Massachusetts the Reverend John Davenport and a large number of his parishioners of St. Stephen's Church, Coleman Street, London. This group was distinguished both by its religious intensity and by the wealth of its leaders. Theophilus Eaton, his son-in-law Edward Hopkins, Richard Malbon, and David Yale were among the most important merchants to immigrate before 1660, and they intended to build not only a holy community, but a prosperous commercial center as well. A few months after their arrival they resolved to plant their village at the mouth of the Quinnipiac River in southern Connecticut, and in 1638 the settlers moved to the site of New Haven.[48] Its location was promising for trade. New Amsterdam offered a market for agricultural products, the Quinnipiac and neighboring rivers a source of furs. The spacious harbor would accommodate a large commercial fleet. The merchant leaders of New Haven prepared to make the most of their excellent situation and resources.[49]

Thus, by 1640 the Massachusetts fur traders had helped to spread the fringe of settlement from the coast west to the Connecticut, south along Long Island Sound, and north to the Merrimac. Rapidly increasing accumulations of pelts confirmed their belief that the New England rivers flowed east and southeast from a central lake district which they were well on the way to controlling. It was their moment of highest optimism. In idle times as they waited at the edge of the forests for Indian trappers to bring in their catch or whiled away long

evening hours in drafty, half-dark cabins, they might have dreamed of
life as colonial merchant princes, or conjured up visions of a triumphant return to the homes they had left in England. God's ways were
mysterious, but was it too much to hope that He would keep the
wealth of a continent from falling to Romish Frenchmen and the
grasping Dutch while His children starved in the midst of plenty?

5

If the fur traders considered their claim to divine support, they
could have taken comfort in the purity of their belief and in their
faithfulness to the true church. For they were almost to a man members and regular communicants of the first Puritan churches of New
England. Theophilus Eaton, called by Edward Johnson one of the
"faithfull servants of Christ," [50] saw eye to eye with the devout Reverend John Davenport and, along with Captain Nathaniel Turner,
who had moved from Lynn to Quinnipiac in search of furs, was a
founder of the first church in New Haven.[51] Edward Hopkins, cele-
brated for his piety in one of Johnson's atrocious poems,[52] was a model
of the Calvinist layman in his adopted town of Hartford. With hardly
an exception the Puritan fur merchants wherever they settled —
Pynchon in Roxbury and in Springfield, Willard in Concord, Thomas
Stanton and William Whiting in Hartford, and Collecott in Dorchester — were pillars of the first and most orthodox churches.[53]

The same men were even more prominent in civil affairs. Pynchon
was one of the eight first commissioners of the Connecticut Colony
and in 1641 by a grant of power from the Massachusetts General
Court became virtually the manorial lord of Springfield.[54] In 1640
Hopkins was elected governor of Connecticut.[55] Eaton was the leading figure in New Haven's civil life from its first days, as were Willard
and young Winthrop in their communities.[56]

This uniform degree of orthodoxy and political influence among
the first fur traders is an indication of the selective factors at work in
the formation of the group. From the start Massachusetts, like Plymouth, had maintained close control over the commerce by setting
prices for skins and taxing the income from them. Its implied monopoly was made effective in 1636 when it authorized the Standing
Council to farm out the fur trade "to such persons as they shall think
meete, for a tearme of three yeares," and at a yearly rent. Connecticut
granted similar exclusive privileges. As a consequence, close connec-

tions with the governments of the Puritan colonies, as distinguished from the towns, became an important requirement for entrance into the trade. Equally important as a limiting condition was the need for capital in amounts far above the capacity of most of the settlers. This became increasingly important as the hunt for furs carried the merchants farther and farther inland.[57]

In social origins, however, the fur merchants of the 1630's were not necessarily of the merchant class. Usually, in fact, they were of the gentry or had been prosperous yeomen. The sale of landholdings in England gave them a sizable sum of money to start with in America, and their connections with the leaders were such as to assure them entrance into the government-controlled fur trade.[58] No special qualities or skills were needed in this commerce other than shrewdness and energy.[59] Consider, for example, the background of the leading Puritan fur trader of the period.[60]

William Pynchon was the grandson of one of the new men who managed to find firm footing in the shifting sands of Elizabethan society and ended their careers closer to the universal goal of establishment in the landed gentry. Rising from yeoman to "gent.," the grandfather William increased his properties, married an heiress, and sent his son to Oxford. This young man, the emigrant's father, became a substantial country gentleman and ran the family estates at and near Springfield, Essex, which he passed on to the founder of Springfield, Massachusetts. William, the future settler, seems to have followed the pattern of most young squires, apparently had nothing to do with the world of commerce, and found in the Puritan movement spiritual satisfaction and a compelling cause. At the age of thirty-nine or forty he pledged himself to emigrate to New England, and in 1630, as a patentee of the Massachusetts Bay Company, left England for the crude settlement of Roxbury, Massachusetts. With the considerable capital raised from the sale of his land in England, and drawing on his privileges as a magistrate in the colony, he launched himself in the business of fur trading.[61] His success seems to have been immediate; in October 1632 he estimated that his collection of skins during the following year would total at least five hundred pounds.[62]

Pynchon was but one among many, and the early careers of some of the others differed in detail from his. Some were acquainted with trade before they arrived, some had started lower on the social scale — but neither mercantile nor agricultural experience was needed. Success in the fur trade required capital, connections, and an enterprising spirit.

Those whose activities were restricted to the fur trade were in a fortunate position in regard to ethical controls. The commerce in animal pelts had only a superficial connection with New England society as a whole. Neither a product of the settlers' labor nor a satisfaction of their needs, it required only that settlements follow and secure the posts set up at strategic points. The trade rose and fell according to pressures irrelevant to the daily existences of the settlers. In this traffic in luxury goods sellers were separated from buyers and users by 3,000 miles, and the moral injunctions against taking advantage of a neighbor's distress and violating the laws of justice in business dealings lost their urgency. The fur merchants were free to pursue their gain as they could.

6

Meanwhile other colonists were beginning to deal in commodities vital to the daily lives of the immigrants. During this decade, when resources were still undeveloped and population rose from a few hundred to twenty thousand, certain men learned to profit by supplying the settlers' needs. They imported and exchanged the necessities of life — food, clothes, and equipment — and to many they seemed to have an undue power concentrated in their hands. Consequently, unlike the fur merchants, they were obliged to seek their profit in the white hot glare of public scrutiny. They quickly discovered, if they did not already know, the special importance to them of the fact that "It is a tough work, a wonderful hard matter to be saved." [63]

Their enterprises, born of the needs of uprooted settlers, were nourished by the severe inflation of the settlement years. For all its planning, the Massachusetts Bay Company was unable to supply the settlers with sufficient provisions, nor could it adequately control the distribution of what food there was. [64] Skilled labor was in similar short supply. Wages shot up out of all proportion to rates in England, and from its first meeting in America the General Court was engaged in setting wage ceilings. [65] Likewise, manufactured goods quickly became unobtainable, and it was soon discovered how overwhelmingly important was a pound of nails, a yard of cloth, or a simple iron cauldron. Such things were absolute necessities to people whose lives had already been brought uncomfortably close to the primitive, and for these commodities they would pay almost any price.

The resulting inflation spiraled out of the control of the General Court. Corn prices, set rigidly to allow the universally sought grain to be used as currency,[66] became a grievance to those who had to accept it in payment for debts contracted when the spiral was lower. Local variations in supply within the Massachusetts jurisdiction led to differences in the fairness of prices set. Immigrants continued to throng into the Bay, widening the gap between supply and demand. In September 1635 the General Court, still insisting on the theory of universally equitable wage- and price-levels, despaired of its own regulations and repealed the law fixing the ceilings.[67] It attempted partial solutions of the price-level problem,[68] and finally deposited responsibility for the wage-level question in the laps of the towns.[69] In March 1638 the colony's legislators resorted to the ancient and honorable therapy of appointing a large committee of notable citizens to study the economic difficulties "and to bring into the next Generall Court their thoughts for the remediing of the same." [70]

It was in this economic situation that the first Puritan import merchants established themselves. The inflation intensified the effect of immigration, helping to destroy the European character of occupational and economic groups. Carpenters and masons discovered that in terms of Old World values they had acquired the income of their social superiors. Gentlemen whose style of life depended upon the maintenance of a staff of servants found themselves unable to feed and clothe their retainers, who themselves responded to the situation by fighting for release from service. Tradesmen, craftsmen, and servants became farmers. And men whom London business leaders would have considered rank upstarts entered trade, prospered, and called themselves merchants.

There was a single important requirement for one hoping to enter the import trade in New England: he must be able to gain control of a stock of commodities desired by the settlers. For a brief period ownership of goods was acquired by going directly to the side of the occasional ships that arrived with freight and negotiating with the captains or ship's merchants for a part of their cargo.[71] This method of acquiring goods, which gave the advantage to the settlers with the most ready cash, was unstable and proved to be transitory. It did not provide for resupplying the same men's stock; those who bought and sold the goods of one ship might fail to refill their stores from the next. Furthermore, competitive buying at the dock helped force prices up and gave those who bargained successfully with the ship captains the possibility of monopolizing certain needed supplies. The dangers of such a possibility were palpable, and the Puritan government soon asserted its right to control this aspect of the economy for the public welfare.[72]

In March 1635 it awarded to nine men representing nine towns around the Bay the exclusive right to board incoming ships, examine the goods, decide on the prices, and "acquainte their partners therewith." These men and their "partners . . . togeather, or the major parte of them" were given the right to buy the goods, which were to be stored "in some maggasen" near the ship and to sell them to the inhabitants of the several towns at 5 per cent profit "and not above." [73]

Such a restriction of access to incoming goods, however appealing it might have been to the Puritan magistrates, reflected more clearly the traditional English method of controlling trade by placing it exclusively in the hands of a responsible group whose rights and obligations were defined than it did the realities of life in New England. The exercise of such rights which might have formed the basis for a guild of merchants engaged in foreign trade required amounts of capital and an institutional complexity that did not exist in America. A law that demanded of other buyers that they stand by idly while nine fortunate individuals monopolized the middleman's profit could not be enforced. Moreover, the buying of goods sufficient to satisfy the needs of a whole town required ready money in amounts above that possessed by the nine assignees. And was it realistic to hope that supercargoes and sailors with goods to sell would limit sales to these men when others might pay more? Within four months of its enactment this law, which might have affected the society and economy of New England significantly, was repealed. The magistrates had to content themselves with licensing both wholesale and retail buyers and reserving for the government the first choice on any incoming cargoes.[74]

The group of importers which the Puritan magistrates failed to create by franchise grew independently. The key to its formation was credit, for it was by credit alone that the necessary goods were brought from Europe to America.

Lacking the means by which to judge the financial capacity and business acumen of strangers, potential English creditors could rely only on personal ties to men in New England. Blood relationships between English suppliers and New England merchants were an exceptionally useful bond. Thomas Lechford described the beginning of a typical family credit arrangement in praising the prospects of Henry Grey, "heretofore citizen and merchant of London," to the young man's future father-in-law. "His brother also a citizen of London hath promised to stock him with 100£ worth of commodities from time to time, if the Lord keepe open the way, and he is to have half the profit which may be of especial advantage." [75] John Cogan, said by Winthrop to have been Boston's first shopkeeper, was the brother of Humphrey Cogan, a merchant in Exeter, England.[76] Valentine Hill, a leading Boston merchant from the time of his arrival in 1636, drew bills of exchange on his brother John, "merchant at the Angell and Starre in Cheapside." [77] Joshua Hewes, brought up by his uncle, Joshua Foote, a member of the London Ironmongers' Company, began his business career shortly after his arrival in 1633 by selling cutlery and ironware, but branched out into general merchandise which he received in large shipments from his uncle. Foote himself became so interested in the trade that he sent over his son Caleb and used the cousins as factors in his own transactions.[78] The success of Henry Shrimpton, who called himself "a Brasyer" upon his arrival in Boston in 1639 and who left property worth £11,979 at his death twenty-seven years later, can be understood only in terms of the great advantage he had in drawing for credit upon his brother Edward, a London merchant. Like Joshua Foote, "Edw. Shrimpton & Companie" soon sent over goods on its own account and began to specialize in exports to New England.[79] The successful establishment in New England of the fortunes of the Hutchinson family of Lincolnshire was similarly related to the affluence of the elder William's brother Richard, a flourishing London ironmonger and perhaps also to that of another brother, John, woolen draper in their native town of Alford.[80]

If not related to their English creditors, the first New England importers must themselves have had previous experience in business and to have left behind friendships and reputations which they could draw upon in attempting to finance their new ventures. Robert Keayne had been a merchant tailor in Birchin Lane, London.[81] The career, like the life span, of Thomas Savage, a country boy who rose from apprentice to full membership in the Merchant Tailors' Company, was

almost identical with that of Keayne.[82] One of many of their neighbors who emigrated to America was Edward Tyng, a merchant of
St. Michael's Parish, who, with his brother William, became a prominent Boston trader.[83] William Alford had been a member of the London Skinners' Company.[84] John Cogswell,[85] and Anthony Stoddard,[86]
of Boston, John Evance,[87] Stephen Goodyear,[88] Thomas Gregson,[89]
Richard Malbon,[90] and of course Hopkins and the Eatons of New
Haven had all been involved in the business life of London before
their departure. Others, like William Vassal of Stepney, Middlesex,
Richard Bidgood of Romsey, Hampshire, and John Coggeshall of
Essex County had also started in trade while in England, though not
in the capital city.[91]

Outport or provincial contacts like those of Cogan, Vassal, Bidgood,
or Samuel Cole were exceptions. To a remarkable extent the first exchanges of goods were carried on between London and Boston. In
fact, the bulk of the traffic originated in a few streets of the English
capital. Most of the English exporters lived within a stone's throw of
the main artery of the medieval City: Cheapside, Cornhill, and Leadenhall streets. This district, radiating north and south through hundreds of twisting alleyways, contained a heavy concentration of
the important guilds and shops of the realm as well as residences of the
wealthiest merchants. Cheapside, the central marketplace of the ancient city, had within it not only the Sadlers' and Mercers' halls but
Goldsmiths Row, stretching for two blocks from Old Change to
Bread streets.[92] Linking Cheapside and Leadenhall was Cornhill Street,
packed with stalls and shops and inhabited, John Stowe wrote, "for
the most part with wealthie Drapers." [93]

The district as a whole was the scene of continuous agitation during
the 1630's. Its wealth attracted the particular attention of the royal tax
officials whose cavalier manner made compliance a humiliation as well
as an injury. Charles' attempt to facilitate tax collection by relocating
the dispersed goldsmiths in their ancient row created one of the series
of panics that measured the drift between monarch and London subjects.[94] New paths into the future were sought. A number of the
boldest or the most desperate of the City's tradesmen already affiliated
with the radical Puritan movement, joined the hundreds of uprooted
East Anglian cloth workers and husbandmen from all over England
in their exodus to the New World.

Once in America they sought to recreate the life they had known at home. Congregating in the towns around Boston Bay, in Salem, and in New Haven, they saw many of the same people with whom they had pushed through the crowds of Cheapside a few years earlier. From the first they called the main thoroughfare of Boston Cornhill, and along it and the intersecting King Street, which led to the wharf, many established their residences. The list of property owners on Cornhill between Milk and Dock streets during the first decade reads like the roster of expatriated tradesmen and shopkeepers of the old business district. Among them were the Tyngs, the Hutchinsons, Hill, Keayne, Parker, Sedgwick, Coggeshall, Edward Gibbons, and Thomas Buttolph. The mercantile community of New Haven was composed almost entirely of ex-inhabitants of Coleman Street, the extension of which, Old Jewry, led like the stem of an inverted T into the juncture of Cheapside and Cornhill.[95]

The settling together of friends and the use of old street names were fragments of the settlers' never-ending attempt to make the wilderness of America familiarly English. The transplanted tradesmen added another when, in 1638, they formed the Ancient and Honorable Artillery Company.[96] Behind it lay the memory of The Honourable Artillery Company of London, chartered by Henry VIII as the "Fraternitie or Guylde of St. George." In the course of a century this organization had changed from a well-trained band of London longbowmen to an elite officers' club which, by 1614, had a waiting list of "divers of the better sort of citizens of the best means and quality." [97] The recent Pequot War was ample reason for the establishment of an officers' training company, but it did not explain the similarity in occupations between the memberships of the two groups. No less than half of the twenty-four original members of the Boston Company — which was headed by Robert Keayne, an ex-member of both the Merchant Tailors' Company and the parent military group — were merchants.[98] The occupational concentration quickly increased; within two years the Artillery Company included almost every merchant in the Bay area. Richard Malbon, once a communicant of St. Stephen's, Coleman Street, headed still another artillery company in New Haven.[99]

In Europe few of these men would have been considered the social equals of the Artillery Company officers or of the heads of the guilds, and none of them could have vied in prestige and power with the City aldermen. They had been for the most part small tradesmen and shopkeepers. None of them had held municipal offices. Despite the fears and confusions of the thirties, the disruption and chaos of the forties, no merchant in the first rank of the English *bourgeoisie* came to New England in those years. No immigrant in this period could have approached in wealth a Peter Blundell of Tiverton, who left £40,000 to found a school, or stood equal in fortune, influence at court, and holdings in land to Sir William Cockayne, whose schemes almost wrecked the national economy.[100] The most important merchants to immigrate to New England during the decade were Theophilus Eaton, deputy governor of the Eastland Company and at one time a diplomatic envoy of James I, and Edward Hopkins, a "Turkey merchant in London, of good credit and esteem." [101]

But the immigrant tradesmen became men of consequence in New England. In the communities around the Bay, and in Salem and New Haven, they assumed command of local affairs. Of the twelve merchants who were charter members of the Boston Artillery Company, nine were elected representatives of their towns to the General Court and the other three, like almost all the rest, were repeatedly chosen selectmen.[102] An overwhelming majority of Boston town officials from the first town election of 1634 to 1640 had once been tradesmen in the Cornhill district of London and were now New England merchants. The Boston town meeting election results for August and September 1636 were typical: at least seven of the ten selectmen and all three representatives to the General Court were merchants.[103] Five of the seven men elected to manage the affairs of Dorchester at the end of the decade were merchants.[104] In Salem a slower commercial development and the residue of pre-Puritan settlers delayed the acquisition of leadership by the merchants for a decade, but even in the thirties John Holgrave, Edmund Batter, Thomas Gardener, and William Hathorne, all of whom were starting their careers in trade, served as selectmen.[105] Similar distinction was given the merchants of Cambridge.

Yet their direct political influence stopped short of the larger community. Despite their strategic economic position and their rapid assumption of authority in the port towns, they did not attain control of the colonies' governments. Though the towns could choose the merchants deputies to the Massachusetts General Court, they could not find the support in that body needed to elect them to the dominating Council of magistrates, or governor's assistants, as they were still called. Of twenty-two magistrates elected between 1630 and 1640, only Coddington and Vassal were merchants; the latter served for a single term in 1630 and Coddington left Massachusetts after the disputes of 1637. No merchant was elected governor, deputy governor, or secretary of the colony.[106] The destinies of Massachusetts and Connecticut still remained in the hands of the same group of Puritan gentlemen that had guided their founding.

7

In social origins the transplanted London tradesmen were unique among the settlers. Most of the colonists had known only life on the land, either as gentlemen, independent farmers, tenants, or laborers; consequently, both the magistrates and the majority of the population brought with them the attitudes and desires of rural Englishmen. To them land meant not so much wealth as security and stability, tradition and status. Shaken out of their familiar ways by economic and political disturbances, caught up in varying degrees by the cause of religious reform, most of the 20,000 Englishmen who migrated to America in the 1630's sought to recreate the village and farm life they had known. They accepted and probably welcomed the medieval social teaching of orthodox Puritanism if only for its inspiring support of the idea of the close-knit community that existed for the good of all its members and in which each man was his brother's keeper.[107]

For the merchants, bred in London and the bustling outports, these needs and ideas were less urgent. The great metropolis was a hothouse of new values and attitudes. In contrast to that of the average agriculturist, the life pattern of merchants who, like Thomas Savage and Robert Keayne, could boast of having received "no portion from my parents or friends to begin the world withal," and, after a career of constant striving, having emerged triumphant from financial losses "sufficient to have broken the backe of any one man in the Country"— such life patterns were characterized by geographical and social mobility.[108] To such men the authoritarianism of Winthrop's government, which suggested security and status to most of the settlers, tended to imply constriction and denial. Freed from the complexities and competition of the Old World cities and trained in some aspect of the production and distribution of goods, the merchants experienced a release of energies in America which frequently struck the

Puritan leaders as brashness and insubordination. Conflict between men who had risen through the struggles of city life and the leaders of the Puritan Commonwealth was implicit from the start.

Yet the right of the merchants to participate fully in the community life was not challenged. All of them were received into a church and made freemen of the corporation. The difficulty took the form of a series of clashes between the merchants and the public authorities. Some of these were trivial and easily handled by the usual processes of law.[109] Others led through subtle ways to serious trouble. In a society where theology and political theory were interwoven, thin lines of doctrine were often the threads upon which rested the justification for the use of power. Dissatisfaction with the magistracy stemming from different assumptions as to the right of self-expression, political and economic as well as religious, could be voiced in hair-splitting theological disputes. One such controversy threatened to sever the Boston merchants from the rest of the community.

The "Antinomian schism" of 1636–1637 which rocked the Bay Colony to its foundations turned on the relative importance of inner, direct religious experience and conformity to the Calvinist laws of behavior in the attainment of a Christian life. The magistracy steadfastly maintained that conformity to the letter of the law, careful performance of religious duties, was essential discipline and that it should be evident in one before he was to be admitted to church membership. To them the dissenters were dangerous mystics whose belief in the prior importance of spiritual illumination was not only a doctrinal heresy but also a threat to civil and ecclesiastical polity.

The merchants, with striking uniformity, backed the dissenters. The challenge centered in the person of Anne Hutchinson, whose husband, son, and brother-in-law were among the most prominent early merchants. Her party was composed predominantly of inhabitants of Boston, already the main seat of New England commerce.[110] Among her adherents considered dangerous enough to be disarmed by the General Court were William, Richard, and Edward Hutchinson, Edward Rainsford, Thomas Savage, Robert Harding, Richard Parker, Edward Bendall, and John Coggeshall. Most of these merchant heretics left Massachusetts for the exile of Rhode Island, either with the Hutchinsons to Portsmouth or with William Coddington to Newport. The "Antinomian schism" uprooted some of the most flourishing merchants of Boston and prepared the soil of Rhode Island for the growth of a commercial community.[111]

The divergence between the merchants and most of the rest of the Puritan population manifested itself more explicitly in public condemnations for malpractices in trade, particularly overcharging, usury, taking advantage of a neighbor's need. The public clamor that accompanied one such incident grew to such proportions as to indicate that an important source of discontent had been touched.

Robert Keayne was a typical self-made tradesman of London.[112] Starting as a butcher's son in Windsor he had risen through apprenticeship in London to prominence as a merchant tailor. Transplanted to New England in 1635, he was received into the church, made a freeman of the corporation, and immediately assumed a leading position in local affairs. He moved into a house and shop on the southwest corner of Cornhill and King streets in the heart of Boston, one lot distant from the First Church and facing the central market square. Drawing on the "two or 3000 lb in good estate" he had brought with him, he reëstablished contact with his London friends and commenced his career as a retailer of imported manufactures. For four years he rode the wave of the inflation, selling badly needed goods to the immigrants for whatever prices he could get. But in November 1639 he was struck down by both church and state. Keayne was charged in General Court with "taking above six-pence in the shilling profit; in some above eight-pence; and in some small things, above two for one." [113]

It had all started with a bag of nails he had sold at what he claimed was a perfectly reasonable price. Once this single charge had exposed the merchant to public censure, a variety of other accusations, such as overcharging for "great gold buttons," a bridle, and a skein of thread, were fired at him. Haled before the highest court he was made to face a barrage of denunciation. So agonizing were the resulting wounds that in drawing up his Last Will and Testament fourteen years later he referred again and again to the incident as if to ease the pain of that "deepe and sharpe censure that was layd upon me in the Country and carryed on with so much bitterness and indignation. . . contrary or beyond the quality and desert of the complaynts that came against me." The public ire was expressed not so much in the court's conviction of the merchant as in the fact that the fine was fixed at no less than £200. But even that was cheap considering the state of public feeling. Keayne later wrote that "if some could have had their wills they would have had the fyne mounted up to 1000lb yea 500lb was too little except some coporal punishment was added to it, such as my mans [sic] standing openly on a market, day with a Bridle in his mouth or at least about his necke, as I was credibly informed. Here was well guided zeale." [114]

So far only the civil sword had struck. The church then took up the matter. The elders studied "how farr I was guilty of all those claymors and rumors that then I lay under," and exposed his defense to a most "exquisite search." Though he escaped excommunication, a fact he later boasted of, he was given a severe admonition ". . . in the Name of the Church for selling his wares at excessive Rates, to the Dishonor of Gods name, the Offence of the Generall Cort, and the Publique scandall of the Cuntry." It took a "penetentiall acknowledgment" of his sin to regain full membership in the church. [115]

To Keayne the most painful part of this episode (and also of his more famous involvement three years later with Goody Sherman and her sow) [116] was not the fine or the admonition but the public insistence that he was a sinner.

. . . the newnes and straingnes of the thing, to be brought forth into an open Court as a publique malefactor, was both a shame and an amazement to me. It was the greife of my soule (and I desire it may ever so be in a greater measure) that any act of mine (though not justly but by misconstruction) should be an occasion of scandall to the Gospell and profession of the Lord Jesus, or that my selfe should be looked at as one that had brought any just dishonor to God (which I have endeavored long and according to my weake abilitie desired to prevent) though God hath beene pleased for causes best knowne to himselfe to deny me such a blessing, and if it had beene in my owne power I should rather have chosen to have perished in my cradle than to have lived to such a time. [117]

The merchant was as devout a Christian by his lights as his brother-in-law, the Reverend John Wilson. He had dedicated himself to the life of the spirit in the most befitting way. Not only had he been regular in his church attendance but he had kept notes on the sermons he had heard that he might refer to them later. He had studied the sacred books far into the night and left as the fruit of his labor "3 great writing bookes which are intended as an Exposition or Interpretation of the whole Bible . . . as also a 4th great writing booke which is an exposition on the Prophecy of Daniel, of the Revelations and the Prophecy of Hosea . . . all which Bookes are written with my owne hand . . . and worth all the paines and labour I have bestowed upon them, so that if I had 100lb layd me downe for them, to deprive me of them, till my sight or life should be taken of me I should not part from them." He had followed the Calvinist precepts of personal conduct. Never had he indulged in "an idle, lazie, or dronish life" or allowed himself "many spare houres to spend unprofitably away or to refresh myself with recreations." Naturally, he had prospered despite all the malice of his adversaries.[118]

Finding evidence in the social teachings of Calvinism for the rectitude of his life, he could impute only sinfulness to those who attempted to blacken his name. But his enemies also drew upon religious ideas for the justification of their attack. To them it seemed clear that by all the relevant Calvinist standards of justice in business, Keayne had sinned. In his scramble for profit he had trampled underfoot the notion of a just price. He had dealt with his debtors usuriously. He had put the increase of his own wealth above the common good. No amount of public benefaction could make up for such evil practices.

The original charge against the distraught merchant fell like a spark into an incendiary situation. The settlers, predisposed to believe middlemen parasites, found themselves utterly dependent on them for the most essential goods and equipment. Incapable of understanding or controlling the workings of the economy, they sought to attribute the cause of the soaring prices and the shortage of goods to human malevolence. Instances of merchants taking advantage of the situation [119] confirmed them in their belief that only the most rigorous discipline of the businessmen could save them from misery. In the same Calvinist social teachings that had justified his life to Keayne they had a grammar for the translation of economics into morality, and in the machinery of the Puritan church and state a means of effecting these ideas. From the same texts the Puritan magistrates and the merchants read different lessons. The former learned the overwhelming importance of the organic society which subordinated the individual to the general good. Keayne learned the righteousness of those individual qualities whose secondary but attractive virtue it was to aid in the fight for success in business. Keayne's advice to the "Reverend Eldrs of this Country" that they "be as easily perswaded to yeeld in civill and earthly respects and things as they expect to prevayl with any of us when they have a request to make of us" would have implied to Winthrop the severance of the moral sinews in the body of Puritan society.[120]

Keayne's Last Will and Testament expresses the dilemma of the first Puritan import merchants. Its 50,000 words were written under the compulsive need to gain final approval from a generation that seemed to confuse diligence with avarice. To be both a pious Puritan and a successful merchant meant to live under what would seem to have been insupportable pressures. It meant to extend to the life of business a religious enthusiasm which must be continuously dampened lest it singe the corners of another's life. It meant to accumulate as much wealth as one righteously could, only to dispose of it, like a steward, according to the principle *uti non frui*. It demanded against the natural desire to live spontaneously and heedlessly the total rationalization of life. Above all, it required an amount of self-discipline that only great faith could sustain.

8

Such were the men who, among the thousands of immigrants in the Puritan Migration, devoted themselves to trade. Their enterprises extended farther than to the exportation of furs and the importing of European goods. In this decade efforts were made to develop the fishing industry, to start home manufactures, to exploit the stands of timber, and to begin the building of ships. But by 1640 none of these ventures had grown past infancy, nor did they affect the character of the merchant group.

These activities were not carried on in isolation. While the port towns of Massachusetts, Connecticut, and Rhode Island were being settled, the enterprises of the west-country fishing merchants continued off the coast of Maine. In New Hampshire new English commercial companies pressed forward in their hunt for beaver skins. Both the Puritans and their neighbors to the north were expanding in all directions and collision between the two groups was inevitable. It took place during the following two decades, and, along with the English Civil War, an economic crisis, and a wide extension of Puritan commerce, helped shape the history of the New England merchants.

III

ᴄʜᴀᴘᴛᴇʀ ᴀﾑᴊᴜˢᴛᴍᴇɴᴛˢ Adjustments and Early Failures

IN ENGLAND during the two decades from the seating of the Long Parliament to the Restoration of the Stuart monarchy, 1640–1660, civil war and a political revolution snapped the organizing cords of public life. In Britain's overseas possessions these same years witnessed a large growth in population, industry and commerce, and social institutions. In New England the Puritan leaders reached the climax of their careers as they extended their control over New Hampshire and Maine and brought the settlements close to what they considered to be upright communities. "A spirit of industry and frugality prevailed," wrote Hutchinson a century later, "and those who lived in the next age speak of this as the *aurea ætas* in which religion and virtue flourished." [1]

The innovation that lasted longest, however, was not the rule of the Puritan oligarchy, which did not survive another generation, but the organization of economic life. Despite acts of navigation, large increases in population, and changes in both the quantity and types of supply and demand, the character of the economic system as it emerged in this period remained essentially the same until just before the American Revolution.

1

The economy of New England did not develop autonomously but was built upon the framework of British society. The growth of the merchant group was as much affected by the Civil War in England as it was by the continuance of the Puritan regime in New England.

By April 1640 the crisis in English affairs responsible for the Puritan exodus to America had reached its climax. Faced with a defiant Scotland which refused to stomach Laudian Episcopacy, reduced to financial impotence by the inability to collect more than a trickle

of tax money and gifts, Charles I summoned Parliament. Looked to
for obedience and grants of taxes, Commons paid Charles in denunciation and demands for redress. Dissolution followed immediately and the king, brought, his councillors said, to extreme necessity
by Parliament, groped about frantically for funds with which
to enforce his disastrous policy. City mobs and army mutinies precipitated a recall of Parliament, which, meeting in November,
assumed command of public affairs. This Long Parliament set out on
its famous twenty-year course of reformation. Welcoming petitions
of grievances from all, honoring the victims of "Popery," it proceeded to impeach Strafford and Laud, to pass the Triennial Act, to
propose the abolition of Episcopacy, and to eliminate the courts of
Star Chamber and High Commission.

Although the spirit of Puritanism was not the determinant in every
decision to leave England, it had been the main force behind the
movement as a whole. The pressure that had dislodged Englishmen
from their homes and sent them 3,000 miles to New England now
found a new release in supporting this defiant Parliament and, eventually, the Civil War. By the end of 1640 the migration that had flowed
steadily throughout the thirties stopped almost completely. Ship
arrivals became a rarity and the New England leaders' hopes for a
more populous commonwealth vanished as Parliament's first acts
toward "a general reformation both of church and state . . . caused
all men to stay in England in expectation of a new world." [2]

The ending of the Great Migration also destroyed the embryonic
economy of the Puritan Commonwealth. Based on the distribution
of imported manufactures, it had required payments to the English
exporters to assure continuation of shipments. Means of repayment
had not been found in fur, for the pelts, controlled by a small group
of licensed merchants, were insufficient to pay for the incoming
supplies. The imports had been bought with the cash or credit carried
to America by the immigrating heads of families, the liquidation of
whose small estates in England provided a surplus after transportation
costs had been paid with which to start life in the New World. Thus
Francis Kirby wrote of a "neer kinsman" who was preparing to
emigrate,

He hath brought with him all his estate, which he hath heer or can have
dureinge the life of his mother, my sister. He had almost 200*li.* when he
began to make his provision for this voyage. I suppose the greatest halfe

is expended in his transportation, and in such necessaries as will be spent by him and his family in the first use; the lesser halfe, I suppose he hath in mony, and vendible goods to provide him a cottage to dwell in, and a milshe cow for his childrens sustenance.[3]

Once spent, the cash resources of the family could not easily be recovered and most of the settlers, if they had occasion to buy or sell a year or so after immigration, most frequently did so by barter.

By May 1640, as this source of payment was ceasing to renew itself, friends in England warned the settlers that their credit with English merchants was collapsing:

It is a very greate greivanc and generall Complainte among all the Merchants and dealers to New England that they can have noe Returnes, and theire bills are very naught insomuch that if there be not some Course taken for beter payments of our Creditors our tradeing will utterly cease.[4]

During the next few months panic and depression in New England followed in quick succession. Those who had cattle for sale, concerned that "yf passengers Com not over with money, the prize of Cattell will fall spedily," filled the markets with their animals, thus increasing the very losses they sought to escape.[5] Agricultural production continued unchecked and produce glutted the coastal trading towns. "Merchants would sell no wares but for ready money, men could not pay their debts though they had enough, prices of lands and cattle fell soon to the one half and less, yea to a third, and after one fourth part." Grain finally ceased to have any monetary value and a cow worth £20 the year before could be bought for £4 or £5.[6]

The responsibility for relieving the situation fell to the leaders of the Puritan governments, and their actions showed clearly their belief in the reality of their power over the lives of the settlers and the distinctive cast of their minds. Like medieval churchmen they believed their duty in such situations was to protect the people as consumers, not as producers. To the chagrin of the merchants, they took steps to preserve the populace from the consequences of the money shortage and the rapacity of middlemen. They moved in two directions, toward relieving the indebted settlers of the fear of total impoverishment at the hands of creditors, and toward the establishment of a permanent, self-sufficient economy.[7]

Credit had made possible not only importations from England but also distribution of goods in New England. In the case of most settlers who found advances of goods necessary, credit could be obtained in exchange for mortgages on crops or on land. These debts were contracted in money values. When crop prices fell, many settlers were deprived of all means of repayment save their land, confiscation of which meant to them not only impoverishment but also reduction to the status of transient laborers. On October 7, 1640, the Massachusetts General Court attempted to solve the problem by a law stating that property seized for debts was to be assessed

at such prizes as the same shalbee valewed at by 3 understanding and indifferent men, to bee chosen, the one by the creditor, another by the debtor, and the third by the marshall; and the creditor is at liberty to take his choyce of what goods hee will; and if hee hath not sufficient goods to discharge it, then hee is to take his house or land as aforesaid.[8]

Behind this law lay the idea that the lack of money hid from view the true picture of New England's wealth. The settlers, the legislators believed, far from being impoverished, "have sufficient upon an equall [just] valewation to pay all, and live comfortably upon the rest." Three "understanding and indifferent men" strong enough in spirit to stand firm before passing financial storms could assign truer values to the debtors' property than creditors or merchants interested in cheap purchases.

On the same day the General Court found a means "for preventing of the like mischeife for time to come." In the future, it ruled, all debts, however contracted, would be paid in "corne, cattle, fish, or other commodities, at such rates as this Courte shall set downe from time to time, or . . . by apprizment of indifferent men." Four months later Connecticut passed a similar law which specified that payments be made in "merchantable Indean corne at three shilling, fower pence the bushel." [9]

Such legislation eased the debtors' burdens but did not eliminate them, and creditors moved rapidly to recover what they could of their outstanding debts. By 1642 the assiduity of the latter group again caught the attention of the General Court which, in a fit of annoyance, ruled that if it felt that a plaintiff had "no just cause of any such proceeding," it would not only assign court charges to him but "may further impose a fine upon him if the merit of the cause shall so require." In June the Court ruled that cases of debt were to be tried not where the action arose but only where either "the plaintiff or defendant dwelleth." A law of 1644 which in effect permitted a debtor to escape foreclosure by absenting himself from the jurisdiction of Massachusetts was followed by an extraordinary bill passed by the magistrates but defeated by the deputies which provided that the Commonwealth assume private debts "where is not sufficyent to pay such creditors as shall first sue, and by suite recover on the debtor." [10]

These laws rested squarely upon the premises of Puritan economic thought. The assumption that "indifferent" men could establish "an equall valewation" was a practical application of the idea of just price. The defense of debtors from foreclosure was a means of limiting the consequences of economic greed. To Winthrop, who grieved to see it "the common rule that most men walked by in all their commerce, to buy as cheap as they could, and to sell as dear," such laws were the least that a conscientious ruler could provide. They were but crude and weak gestures in accord with the decrees of the Highest Legislator. Man-made law could not, of course, match the justice and effectiveness of the providential stroke dealt a Mr. Taylor, who, guilty of over-charging for his quarts of milk, "being after at a sermon wherein oppression was complained of . . . fell distracted." [11]

2

Though such laws saved a number of settlers from destitution, they did not provide the needed clothes, household implements, and equipment. This could be done only by finding a local commodity valuable enough in England to serve as a new means of payment or by developing a self-sufficient economy based on the large-scale home production of essential goods.

Fortune, the Puritan leaders might well have thought, favored their prosperity, for in the skins of the fur-bearing animals they had an easily transportable commodity that was avidly sought in the European markets. If the New Haven merchants could draw the furs from southern New England and reach into Manhattan's hinterland, if Narragansett Bay gave access to rich beaver meadows which could be controlled by the Puritans, if New Hampshire proved to be the fur country it was reputed to be, if, above all, the Great Lake of the Iroquois could be reached and the peltry in its surrounding swamps drawn into the New England ports, the problem of returns could be solved and New England's import trade firmly based.

In attempting to reach the fabulous Lake, the Puritans were anticipated by the Laconia Company of London, chartered in 1629. Its patent from the Council for New England was awarded to a group of London merchants led by the indefatigable Sir Ferdinando Gorges, who refused to give up hope of profiting from his New England holdings, and Captain John Mason, like Gorgès a soldier, in spirit more akin to Walter Raleigh than to the contemporary merchant colonizers. Invested with title to "All those Lands and Countrys lying adjacent or bordering upon the great Lake or Lakes or Rivers," the Laconia Company in 1630 sent an expedition to the Piscataqua River to explore the passageways to the Lake and to send home what returns it could. It set up a well-supplied agency at the mouth of the Piscataqua and built trading posts on the sites of Portsmouth and South Berwick, New Hampshire. But within three years of the arrival of the agents in America the venture was declared a failure by the merchants, its servants paid off and dismissed, the property divided, and the company's activities reduced to backing occasional fishing expeditions.[12]

The collapse of the Laconia Company followed the pattern of the earlier commercial expeditions to New England. Continued support of the merchants was absolutely necessary for success, and their interest could be retained only by immediate and lucrative shipments from New England. Returns sufficient to satisfy the merchants were expected to come from the region of the Lake, not from the coastal fur supply from which, in fact, during the three years of the company's existence were drawn not more than five hundred pounds weight in pelts. Nor could secondary enterprises like fishing or viniculture justify further financial backing. The company's servants were caught in the characteristic dilemma of the pre-Puritan settlement companies. "If the colonists concentrated on exploration," a recent writer has stated, "then profitable returns might not be immediately forthcoming. If they attempted to satisfy the demand for immediate returns they could not carry on with the real purpose of the expedition." Walter Neale, in charge of the expedition, undoubtedly went as far into the interior as he could on the Piscataqua. But he found the river navigable only a short distance, and further exploration could be done only on horses, of which the settlers had none.[13]

Attributing the failure to lack of transportation and financial support, Mason, in assuming sole title to New Hampshire after the company's collapse, hoped that "if there were once discoverie of the lakes, that I should in some reasonable time, be reimbursed again." Until his death in 1635 he kept the embers of hope glowing by re-supplying the scattering settlers and having sawmills built along the river. The attempt to tap the source of North American furs through a New Hampshire river ended with the Laconia Company which left behind it in New England three clearings and a dozen English-men as evidence of its ambitions.[14]

Shortly thereafter, the licensed Puritan fur merchants, their num-ber and capital supplemented by several leading coastal importers new to the peltry trade, followed the Laconia Company in the search for the swampy El Dorado. The New Englanders were no more aware of the location of the Great Lake than the London merchants had been. By 1642, when a wandering Irishman, perhaps one of the Laconia Company employees, reported that he had seen from the summit of the White Mountains "the great Lake which Canada river comes out of," it was well known that the New Hampshire and Maine rivers, like the Merrimac and Connecticut, were difficult to navigate past the fall line. Another entrance, therefore, had to be found. Since the Hudson was controlled at its mouth by the Dutch, the merchants turned to the next broad inlet southward, the Delaware River. By 1644 its shores, already occupied at several points by the Dutch and Swedes, had been visited by expeditions from England in quest of the same lake. From their leaders came confident reports of the existence of "a great mediterranean sea" to be reached by a five-day journey up the Delaware. Similar information about the region probably reached Boston from the New Haven merchants who had experimented, as yet unsuccessfully, with the fur trade along the same river.[15]

Confident that the Delaware was a waterway to the heartland of furs, a group of Massachusetts merchants, "being desirous to discover the great lake," petitioned the General Court in 1644 for incorpora-tion as a "free company of adventurers." The petitioners, Valentine Hill, Robert Sedgwick, William Tyng, Francis Norton, Thomas Clarke, Joshua Hewes, and William Aspinwall, were Boston im-porters; none had previously been licensed to trade in pelts. Seeing in furs not only profits by direct sales to Europe but also the remit-tances necessary for financing future importations, they projected large plans. Their petition to the General Court included a request for a twenty-one-year monopoly of all the fur outlets they could establish in three years. Such a franchise meant the elimination of governmental control over a large part of the future trade which the Commonwealth considered its peculiar trust. It had no desire to grant away such power. But the merchants, presenting themselves as servants of the public in its need for supplies, were in a strong position. The conditions of fur trading were changing. Neither the government nor individuals could launch such expeditions as the merchants planned. Progress would come only through the joint efforts of men willing to assume the burden of investment and risks. In effect, the government now was asking favors, not bestowing them, and though "very unwilling to grant any monopoly . . . perceiving that without it they would not proceed, granted their desire." [16]

The plan of the company was to send a pinnace loaded with trading goods up the Delaware as far as it could go and then to have the party advance by small skiffs and canoes to the Lake. Chartered by the General Court in April 1644, the company quickly organized its expedition. Backed by £700 worth of equipment and supplies as well as official letters to the Dutch and Swedes, they sent out the pinnace in May and awaited results. In July the vessel returned with discouraging news. The explorers reported that no sooner had they received permission from the Swedes at the mouth of the Delaware to proceed to the Lake in exchange for their promise not to trade along the way than an agent from the Dutch at Fort Nassau, fifty or so miles above the Swedes, appeared with orders to block their passage altogether. Faced with the prospect of being bombarded from shore or captured by the Dutch, and fearful that the master of their pinnace, "a drunken sot," would betray them to their enemies if they had occasion to leave the larger vessel for canoes, the exploration crew returned to Boston "with loss of their voyage." [17]

Ill fortune pursued the company further. A trading expedition to the same region that winter, after collecting five hundred skins, was surprised by Indians who killed half the crew, plundered the cargo, and kidnapped the interpreter and a boy. The company was now totally ruined. A £200 legal judgment against the master of the first pinnace for "drunkeness and denial to proceed" was small recompense to the merchants for their losses and the wreckage of their hopes.[18]

There remained one approach as yet untried to which another group of Puritans turned. In October 1645 a number of merchants

from the towns north of Boston — Richard Saltonstall, Simon Bradstreet, Samuel Symonds, William Hubbard, and William Paine of
Ipswich, Richard Dummer of Newbury, and William Hathorne of
Salem — hoping to discover the "great lakes, and other lakes that lye
up in the countrye," and to build trading posts at unoccupied places
along the rivers and coast, petitioned for a monopoly charter similar to
that granted the Boston merchants the previous year. That they were
no longer thinking in terms of river navigation but rather expected to
send their servants cross-country is indicated by their request to be
empowered to use "a caravan, to be advanced any way up in the
country as farr as wee shall thinke meete." The group was chartered
as requested but nothing came of its plans. If it ever sent out its exploring caravan no record of the trip has survived. There is no reason
to believe that the expedition ever left Ipswich. This was the last attempt by the Puritans to seize the source of the furs. The Great Lake
of the Iroquois with its "hideous swamps" and invaluable beaver
meadows had eluded the New England merchants.[19]

3

But if the heart they sought was hidden, the great artery of the
Connecticut River and the myriad capillaries of winding streams and
brooks lay exposed. While the coastal merchants were paying dearly
to learn the futility of attempting to reach the Lake, the original fur
traders, located strategically along the waterways, were developing
the real, though limited and temporary, possibilities of the commerce.

From the first year of his settlement in Springfield the growing piles
of beaver, moose, and otter skins in his warehouses gave evidence to
William Pynchon of his shrewdness in choosing to remove to this
wilderness spot. His town stood just above the highest navigable point
on the Connecticut River and from it he could intercept the river
traffic before it reached Windsor and Hartford. Licensed to control
all legal trade in the region, he sent out agents to make contact with
the local Indians. Branch posts on the streams tributary to the Connecticut spread his reach from Northampton to Windsor, including
important posts at Hadley and Westfield.[20]

There are no records of William Pynchon's income from furs before he returned to England in 1652. But it must have been considerably larger than that of his son John who between 1652 and 1657 sent
off 13,802 pounds of beaver skins worth no less than eight shillings a

pound, or in all, £5,520 16s. Included in the same shipments were hundreds of other skins — otter, muskrat, moose, and mink. For the years 1658–1674 John's incomplete records show shipments of 6,480 beaver skins worth probably £3,714 8s., as well as over 2,000 pelts of other animals. The most profitable year recorded of the Pynchons' fur trade was 1654, but by that time the peak of the commerce was past. After Pynchon's agents had amassed the furs within reach of the friendly local Indians they could continue only by extending their contacts to the tribes within the influence of the Dutch at Fort Orange. These individual traders could not compete with the agents of the powerful Dutch West India Company, and the decline indicated by a comparison of the figures for 1652–1657 and 1658–1674 deepened during and after King Philip's War.[21]

By the end of the century the once profitable business that had accounted for the founding of Springfield and a cluster of other western Massachusetts towns was gone. It had never become an integral part of the economy of the region. Operating, so to speak, over the heads of the settlers, it affected their lives only indirectly as remittances for goods they needed or as local currency. By the time the fur trade of the valley towns had diminished to a trickle, barter had become characteristic of large transactions as it long had been of small. Local merchants, lacking any commodity worth shipping to England, imported goods only from the New England ports, from Manhattan, and occasionally from the West Indies — places where their agricultural produce found a market.

The fur trade in the Connecticut Valley disappeared but the families that had lived by it did not. The economic and social basis of their lives changed as they accustomed themselves in various ways to the disappearance of their prime remittance. The Pynchons, descendants of William's son John, and their associates, the Parsons and Wiltons of Northampton, the Westcarrs of Hadley, and the Coopers of Springfield, multiplied and flourished in their frontier hamlets, but no longer as merchants. William Pynchon had never considered his vocation simply that of a trader. In England he had been a landed gentleman with large holdings in the Essex countryside, and he succeeded in transferring that status to the clearing on the Connecticut River. As chief magistrate, main landowner, and employer of almost every settler in Springfield, he could rightly have considered his role that of a manorial lord. His day books and journals, extant from 1645, show him during the best years of the fur trade deeply involved in supplying goods and equipment to the neighboring farmers as well as in buying and marketing their crops. To the tenants who paid him in produce or labor he sold manufactured goods and equipment. His trading posts became branch retail stores and there he collected the local crops for transshipment to the coast for sale. John, inheriting his father's legal and economic position, invested widely in land and as the fur trade declined emerged as a landed potentate of the upper Connecticut Valley.[22]

William Whiting of Hartford, who had shared with Thomas Stanton the first Connecticut fur trade monopoly, died in 1647 leaving an estate worth £2,854. The inventory of his property shows Whiting to have died at the midpoint of the transition from merchant to agriculturist. Stanton moved to the border region between Rhode Island and Connecticut where, in 1650, he was granted control of the fur trade along the Pawcatuck River. John Tinker of Windsor moved first to Boston, then to the trading post towns of Lancaster and Groton, Massachusetts, and finally to New London where he ended his days as a liquor distiller and retailer. Governor Hopkins returned to England in 1652 when it was clear that the Connecticut Valley would not develop as a commercial center. Trade had become an auxiliary to landowning and agriculture. Thenceforth "merchants" along the Connecticut River derived their main income and way of life from the land they cultivated. For them trade was not overseas commerce but the accumulation and wholesale disposition of their own and neighbors' farm goods to other New England merchants.[23]

While the merchants in the west were draining the furs from the upper Connecticut Valley the traders on the east coast were extending their scope back from the small semicircle around Massachusetts Bay to a new frontier circumference formed by the Nashua and Blackstone rivers. Passing over the outermost settlements to establish posts closer to untouched streams and ponds, they collected the furs of east central Massachusetts.

Simon Willard, in settling the town of Concord, Massachusetts, in the midst of virgin beaver meadows, had made the first important overland break westward out of the trucking area of the Bay. He did not stop there. Before a decade had passed he was familiar with the Indians along the Merrimac River, and by 1648 was welcome enough to the natives as far north as Concord, New Hampshire, to negotiate between them and the proselytizing Reverend John Eliot.[24] Concord, Massachusetts, was soon superseded as a trading center. Lancaster, on the Nashua River, and Chelmsford, at the southernmost bend of the Merrimac, were settled within a decade. Willard himself moved to Chelmsford, where he secured his monopoly of the Merrimac trade against the strong desire of the settlers who sought in the local peltry a means of procuring badly needed goods. In 1659 Willard and his associates tightened their control of the eastern fur trade by buying the trading rights of Lancaster and Groton. Thereafter, their only competitors, trucking at Marlborough, Sudbury, Concord, and Cambridge, were insignificant.[25]

The rewards from the trade in the east matched those of Pynchon in the west. In 1658 Willard and his associates along the Merrimac paid a higher tax for their furs than did Pynchon, whose unusually small catch for that year was worth approximately £530 in the London market. If, as is likely, Willard's trade throughout the decade of the fifties was only slightly less than Pynchon's, its average yearly gross value was no less than £800. The volume of business of the minor traders was in direct proportion to their distance from the coast. In 1658 Tinker at Lancaster and Groton was taxed on a catch worth £64. In the same assessment both Brooks and his partners at Concord and Stone in Marlborough listed £40 worth of furs; both Stedman in Cambridge and Parmenter in Sudbury £16 worth.[26]

The eastern fur trade like that of the west was quickly exploited and exhausted. Its drop in volume after 1660 was sharp; by 1675 it was entirely gone. Lacking deep inlets into fresher fur country, the eastern traders had to depend on the local supply of fur-bearing animals. When the beavers, which are neither highly reproductive nor migratory, were cleaned out of the area they simply became extinct in that locality. After King Philip's War the fur trade had no place in the economy of Massachusetts.[27]

The fortunes of the eastern fur traders declined rapidly. At the end of his life Willard had almost nothing to show for his years of effort in exploiting the eastern furs. His final inventory consisted of £82 7s., Indian debts worth £300, and 1,521 acres of land, most of it undeveloped. Against these credits had to be placed his own debts amounting to £296. Thus, besides his land, most of which had been given to him by the Commonwealth for his many public services, Willard died propertyless.[28] The other eastern traders were no more fortunate.

Those of Willard's old associates like Brooks, Wheeler, and Hench-
man, who were leaders in their communities at the end of their careers,
had been so at the start and added little more to their property than
was given to them as proprietary shares in common land or as rewards
for public services.

Such was the brief flowering and quick withering of the fur trade
in the two districts of its richest growth, the upper Connecticut Valley
and northeastern Massachusetts. But greater hopes had been held and
more concerted plans made for other regions. The London merchants,
who with John Davenport organized the migration from Coleman
Street to Boston, moved on to the harbor at the mouth of the Quinnipiac River mainly because it was considered to be a strategic location
for trade.[29] They hoped to make New Haven a great port center for
the commerce flowing between America and Europe and among the
coastal towns. Located in the middle of the unoccupied stretch of
coast between Saybrook and Manhattan, the harbor, they believed,
would surely develop into the funnel for goods moving south from
central New England and north from the southern and middle
colonies.

It soon became evident that this faith was misplaced. The narrow
Quinnipiac River ran its short course through land barren of fur-
bearing animals. Control of distant posts, therefore, became obligatory. With the Dutch firmly in control of the Hudson River trade the
New Havenites turned to the Delaware. Here too the Dutch, now
supported by the Swedes, refused to tolerate encroachments on their
Delaware preserve and drove off New Haven's settlers. For fifteen
years the New Haven merchants used every device and influence they
could command to gain control of the Delaware, but without success.
When, in 1655, the Dutch replied to New Haven's last, desperate attempt to settle a group in the region by a sudden conquest of the
whole valley, the New Havenites gave up all hope of sharing in
the Delaware fur trade.[30]

Cut off on the west and south by the Dutch and on the north by the
more powerful Connecticut towns, New Haven found itself confined
to a small and relatively infertile coastal enclave. Efforts to make it
yield large sources of exchange were futile. But enough furs and local
produce were accumulated to permit one costly shipload to be sent to
England by which, it was hoped, transatlantic commerce might be
started. But "The Great Shippe" did not reach England and was never

seen after its departure from the Quinnipiac. The loss which wiped out at a stroke goods worth an estimated £5,000 would in any case have been a major misfortune; under the circumstances it was a fatal disaster to the economy of the town and to its merchants' hopes for a prosperous future. Commercial relations with England were never established and, instead of becoming the trading center for New York and the middle colonies, New Haven was itself absorbed into Manhattan's commercial orbit. The leading merchants, their capital rapidly consumed, scattered, some moving to more prosperous colonies, some back to England. By the Restoration, New Haven had become "little else than a colony of discouraged farmers." [31]

Elsewhere in New England the fur trade proved to be less profitable and had even less effect on the lives of the merchants and the development of the permanent economy. In 1632 two prominent merchants of Plymouth, England, set up a large fishing station and trading post on Richmond Island opposite the mouth of the Spurwink River in Maine. From here their agent, John Winter, sent to English and south European markets large quantities of fish, fish oils, clapboards, and pipestaves, but the merchants' hopes for a good yield of furs were never realized. In 1634 Winter wrote back that,

The tradinge heare aboutes with the Indians is not worth any thinge, for heare is no Indians lives nearer unto us then 40 or 50 myles, except a few about the River of Salko. For the planters heare aboutes, yf they will have any bever, must go 40 or 50 myles Into the Country with their packes on their backes, and put away most of their goods within a small matter as good Cheepe as they pay for yt, [so] that yt is hardly worth their labour.

The petty traders and stranded fishermen ruined what little commerce with the Indians there was, for "their be so many traders that one spoyleth the other. They put away their goods at so low Rates to the Indians that they gett but litle by yt." The trade of Thomas Purchase on the Androscoggin River and of a few isolated settlers on the Kennebec who managed to command a bit of New England's original fur supply was short-lived.[32]

Similarly ineffective in determining the development of the commercial group was the fur trade in the Narragansett Country. Of the original settlers at Providence and other points at the head of Narragansett Bay, Roger Williams, whose extraordinary career as a divine has obscured the fact that he was the son of "a self-made London shopkeeper" and had once been an apprentice in the Merchant Tailors' Company, was the first resident Englishman to collect the furs of the region. It was probably in the summer of 1636 that Williams built his trading post at Wickford Harbor on the western edge of Narragansett Bay. For the next fifteen years, despite his profound involvement both here and in England in theological and political controversies and his endless activity as leader of Providence Plantations, Williams managed to keep the post operating. He used a large canoe, a shallop, and a pinnace to broaden his contacts with the natives and to maintain communication between the post and Providence. After 1645 he found it necessary to employ John Wilcox as resident manager and partner in the trade.[33]

Competition quickly appeared. In 1637 one Richard Smith, then of Taunton in the Plymouth Colony, set up a rival post near Williams' where, in 1648, after a perambulating career in Rhode Island, Long Island, and Manhattan, he located permanently. The Arnolds of Pawtuxet entered the scene with the illicit but highly effective bargaining advantage of liquor and firearms. Despite this competition and the continued presence of Dutch traders along the coast of Long Island Sound, Williams' business was profitable. His post had been well placed to intercept the trade moving south by well-known Indian trails, and even as late as 1651 when the trade was clearly on the decline Williams was netting £100 annually from furs. In that year, however, pressed for funds to finance a necessary trip to England, he sold out his interest at Wickford to Smith. Wilcox was quickly eliminated and the fur trade of the Narragansett Country, such as it was, became mainly the property of the Richard Smiths, father and son.[34]

The peltry supply of Rhode Island, like that of other parts of New England, thought to be very plentiful in 1640, was collected rapidly in the forties, declined in the fifties, and was practically defunct by 1660. The Smiths made the most of the brief flourishing of the Narragansett fur trade and, alone among the merchant families of Rhode Island, founded their dealings in cattle and agricultural produce on this early form of enterprise. The transference from the fur trade to general commerce and from trucking-post owner to landed proprietor was completed in the lifetime of the second Richard Smith, who died in 1692 possessed of a large landed estate, eight Negro slaves, and £1,159 worth of plate, buildings, cattle, and miscellaneous personal property. Other Rhode Islanders besides the Smiths, Williams, and the Arnolds undoubtedly dealt in furs of the Narragansett region at one time or another, but did not owe their prosperity to this commodity. After the Dutch and the Pilgrims had skimmed the cream of the trade in the early period, only the few traders operating from posts on the western shore of the Bay were in a position to found fortunes on the trade. Of these, only the Smiths succeeded.[35]

With the indigenous supply of pelts rapidly consumed, further advances in the New England fur trade could be made only by breaking out of the confines of the region. Canadian furs were inaccessible by virtue of both distance and the firm grasp of the French. Hope for the merchants lay only in bridging the Dutch moat — the Hudson River. In 1659, the attempt of a new company of merchants to settle a colony between Springfield and Fort Orange was frustrated by Stuyvesant's stubborn opposition; and in 1672 a final effort to tap the western furs from the Hudson, now in the hands of the English, met equally firm resistance from the Duke of York's governor, Lovelace. In neither case was a single beaver skin added to the merchants' stocks. In 1675 the outbreak of King Philip's War put a definite close to all efforts to reach the western furs. The only success in attracting furs from outside New England was that of Edward Gibbons, a Boston merchant of vast enterprise, whose complicated dealings at one point gave him control of the commerce of Nova Scotia. But his power over the trade of this disputed province, resting as it did on a momentary balance of interests among highly placed individuals in Europe and America, was easily overthrown and had no permanent consequences.[36]

4

With the disappearance of furs from New England went not only hopes for great fortunes but also an important form of remittance to English creditors. The elimination of the fur-bearing animals, following the disappearance of money, threatened to keep from New England the goods considered necessary for a decent manner of living. Fur and coin had become interchangeable and merchants were forced to seek substitutes for beaver as they had for coin itself.

As early as 1645 merchants like Edward Gibbons were groping for means to make up for the lack of this second currency. To a creditor's creditor Gibbons wrote,

... being ingaged some moneys to Mr Fogg: he standing ingaged to yorselfe: who is very desirous to make you returnes: Now Bever being out of my hands: and hard for him to procure at this time, therefore I thought meete to tender you a sixteenth part of the good shipp called the tryall of Boston with what belongs to hers. . .

Such transactions were makeshifts, however, and merchants like William Tyng whose "bonds are to be paid in Beaver at money price" were fortunate if they were permitted to acquit their debts, as Tyng hoped to, in fish or in "good woollen and linnen cloth and stuffs." For the most part the merchants had neither ships, stores of cloth, nor indulgent creditors.[37]

One solution to the problem entailed what seemed in the first years of settlement to be insuperable difficulties but was in complete harmony with the most fundamental motivations of the Puritan leaders. A sense of destiny weighed heavily on them. They viewed their great adventure as a holy procession into the future, a deliverance from the corruptions of the Old World. Trade, any sort of overseas commerce, for all its advantages, was not only replete with moral dangers but also drew the new commonwealths back into close relations with the homeland. Debts to English merchants represented to them a mortgage on their hopes for a free life in the New World. If the harsh demands of economic reality could have been silenced by decree of the Puritan magistrates, New England's economy would have been as independent as its churches and government.

Independence in economic terms meant the creation in New England of native manufactures which could supply the goods hitherto obtainable only in Europe. The settlers needed a great variety of English manufactures, almost all of which were made exclusively of iron or cloth. Cargoes unloaded on the Boston wharves were comprised mainly of iron pots, pans, weapons, and farming and building equipment, side by side with bolts of cloth and piles of stockings, coats, and blankets.[38] If these commodities could be produced in New England, lesser needs such as pottery, leather goods, gunpowder, and salt would present no serious problem. It was the large-scale production of iron and cloth that independence demanded.

The hope that these basic goods would some day be provided by native industries had been present in the minds of the emigrating Puritan leaders as far back as the first days of the Bay Company. While still in England they had ordered their advance agents to be on the watch for mines of all sorts, and as soon as they had organized their government they held out encouragement for those willing to start manufactures.[39] Yet as long as immigration continued and they were able to supply their needs easily they went no further. The end of the Great Migration with the resulting economic crisis impelled them into action in this direction as in so many others. After 1640, at the same time as they advanced the fur traffic in an effort to right their trade balance, they took the first important steps toward eliminating their commercial dependence on England.

In June 1641, when the economic future of New England looked most hopeless, the General Court started a serious drive to develop the region's native resources. It offered to those who discovered or developed mines control of all the minerals they found in common or private lands as well as the right to purchase land directly from the Indians.[40] These were valuable privileges and by the end of the year samples were brought forward to prove the value of several deposits, particularly those in the swampy soil of Saugus and Braintree. How many men prospected and how many, besides Thomas Dexter and Robert Bridges of Lynn, came on encouraging finds of ore is not recorded.[41] What is certain is that the leadership of such enterprises was taken by that most versatile and talented man of affairs, John Winthrop, Jr.

This learned Puritan merchant and colonizer left for England late in 1641 probably with samples of ore from Braintree and with the intent of finding English capitalists interested in backing an ironworks in New England. No man was better equipped for such a mission. He knew New England and its problems thoroughly; in the science of metallurgy he was at least a well-informed layman; and he was acquainted with men in high places in England. That he was also a good salesman is attested by the results. When he returned to America two years later he had with him a managerial commission from a newly formed iron company, a shipload of expert miners, foundrymen, and laborers, and £1,000 in cash. The group he represented, informally organized as early as 1642 as The Company of Undertakers for the Iron Works in New England, was headed at the start by a number of wealthy merchants sympathetic to the Puritan cause, several of whom were related to New England settlers.[42] As the enterprise grew and larger and larger advances were demanded of the stockholders, the lesser among them, who had supported the venture mainly out of a sense of obligation to their friends and to the Puritan movement, withdrew and control of what became an enterprise capitalized at no less than £15,000 was taken by a group of powerful businessmen among whom were Lionel Copley, one of the leading iron manufacturers of England, and John Becx, a London merchant of Dutch extraction, the owner of blast furnaces and forges in Gloucestershire, who headed the company during its most active years.[43]

Upon his return from England, Winthrop threw himself into the complicated task of organizing the ironworks. He spent the end of 1643 and early 1644 surveying all the possible sites for the works and finally recommended to the undertakers a plot on the outskirts of Braintree from which some of the first promising ores had been taken. Here, Winthrop argued, could be found not only the necessary "Ironston" but also timber for charcoal and "workmen of all sorts." Either his recommendation or Boston's offer of 3,000 acres to the company if it built near the town's Braintree lands was convincing, for it was in Braintree that the first furnace was built.[44]

Winthrop's next duty was the difficult one of negotiating with the General Court for a charter of incorporation that would satisfy both the Puritan magistrates and the London undertakers. He soon discovered that on certain crucial points the interests of the two groups were almost irreconcilable. In his first petition to the Court he asked only for the elementary needs of the company: the right to search for and to dispose of ores, to make certain necessary uses of private property with suitable recompense to the owners, freedom from taxation, ownership of needed waste lands, and the "priveleges of a plantacion" at the appropriate stage in the development of the works. These requests caused no trouble and Massachusetts was prepared to grant them. However, before doing so the Court made it clear that it favored the works only insofar as it served the vital needs of the settlers for an independent supply of iron products. The unclaimed wasteland that the company selected was not to be used merely for the production of crude iron to be exported and refined overseas. The magistrates insisted that within ten years the undertakers set up on their sites "an iron furnace forge in each of the places, and not a blomery [furnace] onely." In November 1644 the General Court clarified its position by giving the company in return for wide privileges three years "for the perfecting of their worke and furnishing of the country with all sorts of barr iron." Free land, tax exemption, church privileges, freedom from militia duty — all this would be given the company and its employees, provided that the adventurers shall with all expedition prosecute the work to good perfection, aswell the finery and forge as the furnace, which is already set up, that so the country may be furnished with [all] sorts of barr yron for their use, under the rate of 20*l* per tunne.

And if the works were to be located "remote from church or congregation . . . the undertakers wilbe pleased to provide some good meanes whereby their fami[lies] may be instructed in the knowledg of God." To these concessions the Court added in the final charter of October 1645 a twenty-one-year monopoly of all ironmaking within its jurisdiction. But in return it made doubly sure that the company was legally prevented from using such generosity to profit without serving the public need. It gave the adventurers the right to export only such quantities of their products as were over and above what "the inhabitants shall have neede, and use of, for their service, to be bought and paid for by the said inhabitants." [45]

Such clauses proved to be no more than temporary blocks to the irresistible tendency of the situation. The heart of the matter was that ownership of the works was in the hands of absentee businessmen who would judge the wisdom of their investments by the profits they earned and not by the contribution they made to the welfare of the community. If the works were to serve the Puritans' purpose the undertakers would eventually have to be bought out, and not by the Commonwealth itself, there being "no stock in the treasury," as the elder Winthrop observed. Individual settlers would have to be led to invest in the company, and the Court made every effort to keep the way open for them to do so. The New Englanders wrote into the charter a provision that any inhabitant was to have the right to invest in the company equally with the undertakers "not lesse, in one mans name, then fifty pounds with allowance to the adventurers for the stock of one thousand pounds by them already disbursed." They also sent a proclamation to the towns informing them of the project and urging all inhabitants "of sufficient ability . . . to come in to share in the worke." At least £1,500 was needed "to finish the forge, etc., which wilbe accepted in mony, beaver, wheate, coales, or any such commodities as will satisfy the workmen . . ." The cause was worthy and the need was great but the financial capacity of the settlers was small. A few prominent merchants rose to the occasion, but they did not nearly supply the "one halfe at the least" of the total capital of the company as the magistrates hoped they would. The undertaking

as it was launched was an investment by English capitalists in an undeveloped colonial economy.[46]

The first experiences of the company in the production of iron
proved that Winthrop, for all his knowledge and experience, had used
poor judgment in recommending the site at Braintree. The land there
was mainly privately owned and the Boston grant was far from the
actual works. The company had no desire whatever to start buying up
land at inflated prices and repudiated an unauthorized purchase Winthrop made. Moreover, neither water, workmen, nor timber proved
to be plentiful and the transference of the main plant was clearly in
order. It was at Saugus, at a spot appropriately called Hammersmith,
near extensive bog iron deposits, that the main furnace and refinery
were built and it was there that the first large quantities of iron were
produced. Bars and sows of crude iron, cast iron wares like the famous
Lynn pot, and wrought iron products came in increasing numbers
from the company's expanding plants. By 1648 they were producing
a ton of iron a day.[47]

Unquestionably the company was serving its purpose in providing
a local supply of ironware. But if the General Court was satisfied, the
English investors were not. For them the company was providing
only endless trouble and expense. Setting up a complete iron manu-
factory in the New England woods was proving to be far more expensive than they had anticipated. Timber near Saugus may have been
plentiful, but labor was not; skilled ironworkers were nonexistent in
Massachusetts and almost unobtainable in England.[48] Every piece of
equipment had to be transported 3,000 miles and the company was
at the mercy of the local merchants for all supplies for their laborers.
Losses, not profits, were rising with production and the undertakers,
mystified and troubled, searched for the root of the difficulty as they
dunned the stockholders for larger advances to maintain and expand
the works.[49] Part of the trouble, they undoubtedly reasoned, was the
result of sheer bumbling in handling the company's affairs, and the ire
of the undertakers fell in 1645 as it did again in 1650 on the head of
their American agent. That Winthrop's attention was focused on the
welfare of the Puritan community and not on the ledgers of John
Becx and Company was clearly one cause, the adventurers probably
thought, of their extraordinary costs. When his unauthorized land
purchase was followed by unexpected bills drawn on the company,
the undertakers gave in to their suspicions of Winthrop's loyalty and

replaced him as resident manager with an experienced and highly recommended individual named Richard Leader.[50]

It was under Leader's guidance that the final terms of the charter were agreed upon, and the undertakers might well have realized how little their losses could in fairness be attributed to Winthrop's agency when they received copies of that document. In May 1645 they wrote a stinging letter to the General Court which struck the magistrates as in "stile more sharpe" and "conclucions more preemptory then rationall." Becx and his friends found the clause in the charter which prohibited exports of iron until the needs of the inhabitants were satisfied repugnant to their interests, for there was almost no currency in New England. Purchases could only be made in agricultural produce or cattle, and what were the adventurers supposed to do with such commodities? Surely, the adventurers argued, they deserved the right to export as they chose and to demand cash for the iron they sold in New England. Their huge investment would make possible cheap iron for the inhabitants; it was pitiful reward for them to be paid in barnyard fowl and crops. And what damage would be done if they exported the whole product of the works? New England would still be greatly profited by the wages earned at the furnaces and forges and by the large purchases of provisions the company was obliged to make.[51]

To these arguments the Court replied by acknowledging the public service the company was performing, especially in regard to the cheapness of the iron. But no matter how cheap it was, the settlers could not be asked to buy only for cash: "as wee use to say, if a man live where an oxe is worth but 12d, yett it is never the cheaper to him who cannot gett 12d to buy one, so if your iron may not be had heere without ready mony, what advantage will yt be to us, if wee have no mony to purchase it?" It was a simple question of the trade balance, the Court informed them. "So long as our ingate exceeds our outgate" we will have little if any money, and "if wee must want iron so often as our mony failes, yow may easily judge if it were not better for us to procure it from other places (by our corne and pipestaves, etc.) then to depend on the coming in of mony." If the company were to export all its iron, what justifiable purpose would the whole enterprise serve? True, there would remain to the inhabitants wages and a special market for agricultural produce, but this "will hardly recompence the wood and timber which, being in the harte of the tounes, would have binn of some worth to us." From this position the Court would not retreat. In a supplementary agreement of November 1646 it allowed a number of modifications of the existing terms; but, though it went so far as to relieve the company of the necessity of providing church facilities for the workers, it did not alter the main provisions of the charter.[52]

After 1645 the production facilities of the works expanded rapidly under Leader's guidance. To the original furnace at Braintree was now added at Hammersmith the equipment of a complete iron industry: blast furnace, refinery, a slitting and trimming mill, storage barns and warehouses, and even a private wharf and vessel. Its products were varied to suit the local market. To the standard cast wares like pots were added products like salt pans, a "greate furnace for boyleing sope," anvils, and scale weights. By 1650 when a complete inventory was taken the warehouses at Hammersmith contained 106 tons of pig, sow, and scrap iron, and over seven and a half tons of cast iron pots. The real property of the company at this location was worth £2,770; that at Braintree £292 13s. 2d. The company's total assets in New England were £4,302 13s. 2d.[53]

Yet, for all of this, "the Company," Leader informed Winthrop, "are very much discontented." They still were seeking some return on their money, and their property in New England so far represented only funds expended. They decided that if they could not get credits out of New England at least they would accept no debits and they limited their agent's right to draw bills of exchange on them. But operating expenses had to be met; unpaid workers could not be put off. Leader found it increasingly necessary to run up bills on the local merchants and by 1650 had debts to the laborers and provision dealers amounting to £1,865 15s. 11d. Far from honoring these obligations and Leader's efforts in their behalf, the undertakers, out of coin and patience, grew querulous and, thinking the worst of their agent, dispatched one of their number to examine his conduct of the enterprise. This investigator, a "grave man of good fashion" named Dawes, accomplished nothing except the complete alienation of Leader who resolved "they shall provide them an other Agent, except a more cleere Understanding cann be maintained betwext us." Harmony could no more be maintained between this agent and the London capitalists than it had been in the case of Winthrop, and in 1650 Leader was dismissed from the company's employ.[54]

In replacing Leader, the undertakers hired not one but two agents who were to share the directing of the business and so act as checks on each other. First, and for the sole job of managing the producing plants, they employed John Gifford, whose considerable experience in iron production had been gained in the works of the Forest of Dean. The business end of the industry now received the separate attention of a factor, one William Awbrey, who, residing in Boston, was to perform the duties of head accountant and sales manager. His contract specified that he was to receive all goods sent by the undertakers from England and all products of the works, which he was to "vend and sell at the best Markett in the best maner and to the utmost benefitt that he may or can." Later instructions made clear that, since the success of the works now depended upon the New England and, more broadly, the American market, Awbrey was to pay particular attention to local needs. He was to note especially the demand for nails and rod iron and not overlook the boom market of Barbados for the sale of such items. Profits might be transmitted in nails or negotiated further in trade.[55]

Buoyed to high expectation by this arrangement as well as by the welcome addition to the labor force of a large number of Scots captured in the battles of Dunbar and Worcester,[56] the undertakers might justifiably have relaxed in contemplation of their profits. But to have done so would have been to place a reliance upon human nature and a scheme of divided authority that took no account of the effect of unaccustomed power. Given complete control over an enterprise that was large even by European standards, seeing on all sides business opportunities that did not exist in the relatively cramped economy of England, Gifford looked this way and that until he no longer perceived the difference between the company's affairs and his own.

He started his managerial career with an ambitious development project in the course of which he purchased more land and brought the company's farm under cultivation. This move was expensive and the undertakers might well have challenged Gifford's judgment on this point had there not been much more worrisome innovations to engage their attention. Not only were Gifford's outlays for provisions remarkably high but his charges on the company included the wages of an unauthorized clerk, a horse and saddle for himself, the repair of his dwelling house, and the astonishing "prodigalyty," as Becx put it, of "a pue for him and his wife in the meeting house." Unjustified as these expenses were they could at least be checked in the accounts. Only later did the undertakers discover that Gifford had been shipping iron privately to Manhattan, Delaware, and Barbados, and that he had not the least notion of a careful accounting and inventory system.[57]

Such things could not be concealed for long, however, and by 1652 it was becoming clear to the owners that their affairs were in worse shape than ever. They demanded a full accounting from Awbrey but were informed that this eminent clerk had been smitten by a severe "malloncolly" and could render no accounts for the time being. Bitterly disappointed in the results of their organizational scheme and impatient for exact information on the state of their enterprise, they fired long and threatening letters at Gifford, interviewed an employee he had discharged, and finally in desperation devised a new group to manage the unreliable managers. They appointed four New England merchants, three of whom were stockholders in the company, to be commissioners to oversee the whole business and to call into account both Gifford and Awbrey. Further, they ordered all refining and finishing to be done at the Braintree plant which they now placed in control of the clerk Gifford had fired, leaving the latter in charge only of pig iron production and under the authority of the four New Englanders.[58]

But it was too late. Despite the fact that stocks of iron were slowly accumulating at Hammersmith, debts to local merchants and laborers were still rising. Bills held by individual merchants totaled hundreds of pounds each. The solvency of the company was threatened and the nervous creditors, their faith in ultimate payment weakened, looked to England for reassurance. But the undertakers, adamantly refusing to sink more money in the ironworks until it began to repay their earlier investments, declined to honor even at a large discount the bills drawn on them. When, in 1652, a number of protested bills returned to New England, word circulated among the Boston merchants that the company's credit was worthless. The creditors panicked, demanded immediate payment, and, amid a blizzard of legal documents signifying bankruptcy, the company collapsed.[59]

Thereafter, "instead of drawing out bars of iron for the country's use, there was hammered out nothing but contention and lawsuits." [60] The resulting litigation, which occupied the New England courts for at least two decades, involved not only the principal figures in the company but dozens of lesser merchants and workmen as well. Everyone descended on the courts at once. The creditors sued for their money; the company sued Gifford for breach of contract and damages; Gifford filed a countersuit; one of the more vulnerable commissioners was sued as liable for the company's debts; [61] and most of the cases were appealed. Eventually, the works themselves were handed over to the major creditors, all Massachusetts merchants, who installed their own manager and tried to continue production. Gifford spent some time in a New England jail but contrived to get back to England where he convinced the undertakers of his honesty and of the treachery of the New Englanders and their courts of law. His story was the more credible as most of the court decisions had gone against the adventurers. No one in New England seemed worthy of trust. The leading commissioner, Henry Webb, a large stockholder in the company, turned out to be one of its largest creditors as well, and while still the legal representative of the company joined in filing suit against it. All the commissioners were suspected of disloyalty and were replaced by Josiah Winslow and the venerable Robert Keayne, who in turn were succeeded in 1657 by none other than the reinstated John Gifford. The undertakers, convinced of "Corruption in that Countrye," planned appeals to the highest courts of England. In 1661 they petitioned the Council for Foreign Plantations for a hearing of their case, claiming that their property in New England had been seized for false debts. No action was taken, however, and the company had to be content with transferring some of its assets to land and sawmills in New Hampshire. Eventually most of the real property of the company was gathered into the hands of one of the creditors, William Paine.[62]

This Boston merchant, together with his son John and a number of other resident merchants, reorganized the company and tried to continue supplying the settlers with iron. But although Paine and his associates produced over three hundred tons of bar iron between 1658 and 1663 they found it impossible to keep their organization out of debt. John Paine was obliged to mortgage the works in 1664 and lost possession of it by foreclosure in 1676. By this time the works were abandoned and in a state of complete disrepair. Two years later the neighboring inhabitants petitioned the General Court that the company's dam be torn down so that the fish in the Saugus River might return to their former spawning grounds.[63]

So ended the most important attempt in the seventeenth century to make New England's economy independent by building native manufactures. But this was not the only attempt. Young Winthrop, foreseeing in 1655 the ultimate fate of the Saugus ironworks, realized that yet another effort would have to be made, this time by local merchants, to assure the necessary supplies of iron goods. Finding a promising ore field between New Haven and Branford, Connecticut, he approached the discouraged merchants of the New Haven colony for financial support. A few of them, and particularly Stephen Good-year, aware that their trade and hope of breaking out of the confines of New Haven were dwindling, saw the potential benefits of internal developments such as Winthrop proposed, and, aided by generous grants from the colony and town, set up a furnace on the site of East Haven.[64] But their enthusiasm evaporated as the costs and difficulties became known. Unable to continue the works alone, they leased them to William Paine and Thomas Clarke of Boston, who hoped to process the crude iron of the New Haven furnace in the Hammersmith refinery. Though in 1663 Reverend John Davenport of New Haven could report with pride that the furnace had produced five sows of iron, the problems of making the new works profitable were insuperable. With production failing to justify either further investments or the necessary damage to the fertile fields in which the works stood, the enterprise followed Hammersmith into limbo.[65]

Other attempts to utilize the scattered deposits of bog iron in New England for manufactures were made at Taunton, Concord, Rowley, and Pawtucket. Small quantities of iron were produced at each of these furnaces but production was not sustained, and all of them lapsed into inactivity.[66]

5

The same years that saw laws passed in support of fur trade and ironworks witnessed also legislation aimed at fostering a native cloth industry. Hopes for a widespread production of homespun cloths had been high from the time the first settlers of New England had discovered excellent pastures for sheep and a plentiful growth of wild hemp. Sheep had accompanied the first Puritan settlers to America and by 1640 numerous flocks were grazing on both special reserves such as Prudence Island in Narragansett Bay and on small private fields. But in the emergency of 1640 the magistrates turned first to the encouragement of fabrics that could be grown in one or two seasons rather than to the necessarily slow increase of the wool-bearing animals. In May 1640 the Massachusetts General Court sent out an inquiry to all towns within its jurisdiction for information concerning the available resources for spinning and weaving, specifying particularly flax and cotton wool from which the popular fustians, dimities, and hollands could be made. In 1641 the Massachusetts legislature instructed the Weld-Peter mission to England "to seek out some way, by procuring cotton from the West Indies . . . for our present supply of clothing. . ." In the same year the Court passed a law "for the incuragment of the manifacture," offering a bounty of three pence on every shilling worth of linen, woolen, and cotton cloth spun and woven by the settlers. Connecticut ordered every family to plant hemp or flax "that we myght in tyme have supply of lynnen cloath amongst ourselves," and announced that Governor Hopkins was sending out a ship to establish "a trade of Cotten wooll" and that the towns would be obliged to buy the wool he procured in quantities proportionate to their ratings on the last tax list.[67]

These laws were well heeded, so well in fact that Massachusetts was compelled to rescind its bounty within a year "because too burthensome" and Connecticut had to legislate against the hoarding of hemp seed. It took Hopkins eighteen months to fulfill his promise, but when he did so it was with a shipment of £400 worth of cotton. Massachusetts meanwhile had ordered the collection of wild hemp and "that the honest and profitable custome of England may be practiced amongst us" required all servants and children to put to use all their spare time, especially in the mornings and evenings, "so as all hands may be implied for the working of hemp and Flaxe, and other needful things for clothing." [68]

With such encouragement the work progressed, especially in the town of Rowley which had been settled by a group of Yorkshire cloth workers, men who hardly needed the suggestion of the Court to resume their old trade. By 1643 John Pearson built on the Rowley mill river the first fulling, or cloth processing, mill in the English colonies; but as yet there was only the smallest beginning of an industry that, it was hoped, some day would furnish cloth to twenty or thirty thousand people.[69]

Ultimately it was the spinning and weaving of woolen cloth that would measure the success of the textile industry, for cotton and linen fabrics would not suffice for the settlers during chilly autumns and long, bitter winters. In 1645 the General Court, observing the suffering occasioned by "the want of wollen cloaths and stuffs" as well as the supposed dangers of cottons, ordered the towns to do what they could to increase the sheep flocks and to take orders from potential sheep buyers for an eventual large importation from Europe.[70] In 1648 it instructed the towns to permit sheep raisers to graze their flocks on the village commons and to fine all molesters of the valuable animals. Five years later, when there were probably 3,000 sheep in Massachusetts, the Court passed regulations for the washing and "right ordering of wools" and in 1654 exposed one of the hindrances to wool manufacture when it prohibited the exportation of sheep and lambs. But even if there had been enough wool there certainly were not enough cloth workers, and two years later Massachusetts passed an extraordinary law which reflected as much the failure to establish the desired industry as it did a remarkable faith in social legislation. It ordered that all idle hands, especially "weomen, girles, and boyes," spin threads "to theire skills and abillitie", and that the selectmen of every town assess each family "at one or more spinners" and that everyone designated a spinner "spinn, for thirty weekes every yeare, three pounds per weeke of lining, cotton, or woollen . . . under the pœnaltie of twelve pence for every pound short." [71]

There is no way of measuring the results of this law which so typically exaggerated the efficiency of state power in frontier communities, but by the time of its passage it was apparent to all that New England would not in the foreseeable future develop a textile industry sufficient for its needs. To John Hull it seemed a commonplace that "the sum of the returns of the country" should be sent to England because as yet New England obtained its "clothing (most of it) from thence." [72] In Rowley itself the chief magistrate had written to friends in England about the lack of clothing and reported that the inhabitants of that local cloth manufacturing center were considering "(upon prayer) what way to take for some way of Trading out of Englande." [73] By 1660, although the inhabitants of the remoter villages

had no choice but to use only the cloth they could weave for themselves, most of the better fabrics worn by New Englanders was being
imported from England. An idea of the proportion of native and foreign textiles in use is suggested by the fact that during the nine years
between 1673 and 1682 the most productive weaver in Rowley, which
at that time contained not more than forty families, processed at Pearson's mill considerably less cloth than one Boston merchant imported
in one shipload in 1650.[74] In the two decades before 1660 spinning
and weaving became not the full time or even the regular part time
activity of well trained workers but rather the occasional occupation
of a population of farmers and petty artisans who bought almost all
their textiles from the port town importers or from middlemen. Despite
the sufficiency of raw materials for clothmaking, the settlers, Edward
Johnson wrote, "deem it better for their profit to put away their cattel
and corn for cloathing, then to set upon making of cloth." [75]

No more successful were the attempts to create indigenous manufactures of other needed commodities. Young Winthrop was ingenious
and omnicompetent but by his best efforts he could not develop a
successful saltmaking establishment or graphite mine.[76] Nor did glass-
making flourish in this early period of New England history.[77] The
future of industrial developments in the region was presaged only by
the relative success of the distillery Emmanuel Downing built in
Salem, and his pride in writing to Winthrop that "the water I mak is
desired more and rather then the best spirits they bring from London"
was entirely justified.[78]

IV

The Legacy of the First Generation

WHATEVER its danger to the purity of men's souls or to the independence of the Puritan Commonwealths, overseas trade alone could furnish the settlers with the materials needed for maintaining reasonably comfortable lives. Yet the governments which sent envoys to England to seek financial help, legislated in defense of harassed debtors, encouraged fur trading, and subsidized manufactures could do little to further the development of commerce. This was left to the individual enterprise of the transplanted London tradesmen who had imported and distributed goods from England during the first decade. Though these men participated in the expansion of the fur trade and in the attempts to start manufactures, their main efforts after 1640 went toward creating a type of commerce capable of continuing the flow of goods from England. They assumed that since, once the furs were gone, the natural goods of New England largely duplicated the produce of England, exchanges were to be made in places outside of England and profits translated into credits in England. Finding the markets and actually launching the trade was a difficult matter, however, attended by disappointments and losses. But within twenty years this form of commerce had been established and had become the dynamic economic force in New England. Such it remained for a century and a half.

The men who came to control New England's foreign trade became large figures in the affairs of the port towns; their influence extended into frontier villages and over wide stretches of uncleared land in the interior. Trade, in making material and real the value of men's labors in fields and on the sea, created dependences and networks of relationships which, though long-lasting and important to the whole community, had no preordained place in the Puritan scheme of things. They would have to be shaped to occupy a modest and respectable position. But the merchants who represented this new economic force had become, by virtue of the very services they performed for the public, parts of the separate, intractable world of Atlantic commerce. The Puritan magistrates found themselves dealing with men whose vitally necessary enterprises seemed at times to threaten the integrity of the established order but which could not be controlled without being made less useful. As time went on the problem of whether and how such control was to be exercised became overshadowed in importance by the increasing difficulty of containing the merchants at all within the structure of Puritan society.

1

The vision of New England as the center of a great fishing industry had been an attraction to Englishmen at least from the time of John Smith's American sojourn. Occasional forays into New England waters had verified Smith's claims that this southern region had two fishing seasons instead of one as in Newfoundland and that the fishing grounds were not only fertile but also, being close inland, easily workable. Despite the failure of the Dorchester Company and the withdrawal of the New England Company's settlers from Cape Ann to Salem, the idea of a profitable New England fishery operated by English entrepreneurs persisted and was caught up by the undertakers of the Massachusetts Bay Company. Like all their business plans, this hope was realized, if at all, in only a few isolated expeditions to New England backed by individual adventurers like Francis Kirby and Emmanuel Downing. The Puritan leaders themselves were anxious to start an independent fishery, but during the first decade they were occupied with a multitude of tasks and could do little to further such a project except legislate and appoint investigating committees.[1]

There were among the colonists, however, men experienced in fishing and willing to continue their old trade. Some equipment was ordered from England to aid them and shore lots well located for fishing were assigned to them.[2] Hugh Peter, that ambitious, worldly cleric whose fascination with the things of Caesar was to cost him his head, made a serious attempt to start the native fishery. But his intent "to set up a magazine of all provisions and other necessaries for fishing, that men might have things at hand, and for reasonable prices," was not fulfilled — frustrated, perhaps, by that characteristic desire of the Founders to centralize the control of business enterprise. The same idea was put forward in 1640 by Matthew Cradock to whom it seemed that "a Magazine for Fish" was the "onely way by Gods assistance" that New England would be able to make the necessary returns to England. Though none of these organizing plans materialized, individual fishermen among the settlers did begin to resume their trade and their catch did help feed the colonists during the first, trying years.[3]

A large part of the fish consumed by New Englanders before 1640, however, was obtained not from the local fishermen but from the west-country and foreign fishing vessels that occasionally came into New England waters. Though the west-country fishing in the Gulf of Maine had fallen off in the 1630's, there were still yearly voyages to the Isles of Shoals and to the islands and shores of northern New England. Trelawny's settlement on Richmond Island survived by becoming almost exclusively a fishing station, and innumerable inlets along the coast of Maine were now the homes of isolated groups of fishermen. By the end of the decade the reputation of the local fishing grounds was reviving to the point of attracting new ventures by Bristol fishing merchants. But these fishing activities were independent of the Puritans and, until 1640, were conducted as an adjunct to the profitable west-country business of supplying fish from the Grand Banks of Newfoundland to the tables of Catholic Europe. Though the scattered fishing settlements did make available to the Puritans a supplementary food supply, they contributed nothing to the Puritans' attempt to utilize New England's fish in creating a new balance of trade.[4]

This situation was entirely changed during the early years of the fifth decade. The normal commerce of England was interrupted by the upheavals of the Civil War. Sailors, fishermen, and ships were impressed for naval service. Ports were besieged and Bristol changed hands twice between 1642 and 1644. Though the royal forces held Devon and Cornwall, most of the west-country ports stood by Parliament and a number of them were the objects of damaging attention from the royalists. Even in ports untouched by war, business diminished rapidly as the effect of disrupted communications in the hinterlands was felt. The fighting extended to the sea, and vessels from the opposing sides pursued each other into distant ports where they attempted to seize or sequester the enemy. Under such conditions the English fishery in North America declined as the annual fleets to Newfoundland thinned out, and the relatively few vessels accustomed to visiting New England seemed to be disappearing altogether.[5]

If the shock of civil war broke the thin ties of the west country to the New England fishery, its indirect effect on New England was, in part, to rouse the settlers to a greater effort in fishing. In response to the settlers' need for food and the merchants' desire for exchangeable commodities, experienced fishermen and farmers along the coast seeking winter employment [6] went out in increasing numbers to test the wealth of the sea. Starting with the barest equipment, they began to work the local grounds diligently. Nantasket, Marblehead, the Isles of Shoals, Hog Island, and Monhegan Island soon became exclusively fishing communities populated by permanently settled New Englanders.[7] As such, they were far from being model Puritan societies. Not a single inhabitant of Marblehead in 1644 could claim the freedom of the Commonwealth and by 1647 a court order ruled "that noe wimin shall live upon the Ille of Showles." But the industry flourished. Winthrop reported that in 1641 no less than 300,000 cod were caught and six years later £4,000 worth of fish was brought into Marblehead alone.[8]

Ultimately, the success of the fishery depended as much on the ability of the merchants to organize and dispose of the yearly hauls as it did on the size of the catch, and during these same years the merchants entered the business in a large way. Besides buying the cargoes from the fishermen and equipping and supplying their voyages, they sent exploratory expeditions to such distant places as Sable Island off Nova Scotia and, in 1645, to Newfoundland. But as yet they were only serving a local market. They lacked the capital and business contacts to link the New England fishery to foreign markets.[9]

Their needs dovetailed with the desires of certain London merchants who, in this decade of change and confusion, were furthering their ambition to share in the control of the North American fishery. There was no question of their competing with the west countrymen in the Newfoundland fishing industry itself, for the westerners had the advantage of a century's experience, a sufficient labor force, and complete equipment. What the Londoners sought was a share in the valuable carrying trade between the American fishing centers and the markets of Europe and the Wine Islands (Madeira, the Azores, and the Canaries) — a trade hitherto monopolized by west-country, Dutch, Flemish, and French shipmasters. Though they were able to write into the Navigation Act of 1651 clauses that extended to the fisheries the ban against foreign vessels trading in colonial products, they could not easily dislodge the established carriers from the profitable Newfoundland routes. The infant fishery of New England fitted into their plans smoothly. It offered the Londoners a rich and uncontested supply of American fish without involving them in the difficulties and risks of the fishing industry itself. Not only were there native fishermen at work in New England but the local merchants were becoming experienced in organizing the annual hauls and preparing them for wholesale disposal abroad. And the Londoners had precisely what the New England merchants lacked: capital, shipping, and established markets.[10]

Men separated by three thousand miles of ocean, however, do not enter into business combinations automatically no matter how well their needs complement each other. Overseas commerce in the seventeenth century was capricious. Arrangements were interminably delayed by the accidents of sailing. Demand fluctuated incalculably as unforeseen crop failures created markets which the arrival of a few ships eliminated overnight. Reliable factors and correspondents were therefore of paramount importance, for frequently the success of large enterprises rested on their judgment. The London merchants might have understood the possibilities of the New England fisheries but they would not have ventured there without knowledge of the region's businessmen and its economic condition. There were in London, however, other merchants of established reputation who were already in touch with the New England businessmen. These men — City relatives and friends of the immigrant tradesmen — brought the two groups together. With their help certain New England importers were able to negotiate with groups of London merchants seeking shiploads of fish prepared for sale in southern markets. The result was a series of contracts between the two groups of men that accounts for one of the important early forms of the New England fish trade.

These agreements between the London and New England merchants varied greatly but had certain characteristics in common. The over-all enterprise was planned and launched in London; the Londoners kept the ownership of the goods throughout the voyage; the New Englanders acted as suppliers to the home country entrepreneurs. An example is the bond, dated February 20, 1646, by which Robert Houghton "of St. Olaves in Southwark merchant" pledged to George Gifford and Benjamin Whetcomb, London merchants, that Robert Sedgwick of Charlestown, Massachusetts, would load on their ship *Mary* 1,500 quintals of fish within twenty days of its arrival in Massachusetts. The merchants' plan was to make up an outwardbound cargo of manufactures to be sold in New England, pick up the fish as arranged in London, and dispose of them in Spain or the Wine Islands. The profits of the voyage would be returned to England either in bills of exchange or in semi-tropical products to be sold in England.[11]

The significance of this contract lies not only in its business arrangements but also in the importance of the individuals involved and in the relationships among them. Gifford and Whetcomb, together or in other *ad hoc* partnerships, became steady buyers of New England fish. Houghton, though himself a "brewer," was both son and brother of London fishmongers who may well have made the first contacts with the London buyers. Not only was Houghton a sympathetic friend of the New England settlers and probably a member of a Puritan church, but he was also Sedgwick's brother-in-law. He was thus in an excellent position to negotiate between the London fishmongers and the New England wholesalers and did so throughout the period.[12] Sedgwick, whose organizing ability was to gain him an important role on the stage of European affairs, had previously been an importer of manufactures. Now, often in partnership with Valentine Hill, another Puritan tradesman new to the fishing business, he became one of the leading New England fish dealers.[13]

Another, more complete, example of such an arrangement may be seen in this statement, signed in August 1650 at the Isles of Shoals:

Shipped by the grace of God in good order and well conditioned by mee Wm Davis of Boston in and uppon the good shipp called the George Bonaventure . . . now rideing at anchor at Marblehead and by Gods grace bound for Bilboa, to say, three hundd seventy six Kint of dry and merchantable New Engl. cod fish. and nine kint of refuse fish and is by the order and for the Acco of Mr Samuel Wilson of London mercht, being marked and numbred as in the Margent. and are to be d[elivere]d in the like good order and well conditioned at the aforesaid port of Bilboa (the danger of the seas only excepted) unto Mr Joseph Throckmorton or to his Assignes, he or they paying freight for the sd goods with primage and average accustomed.

The *George Bonaventure* had arrived in July loaded with cloth which was sold for the accounts of the owners, John Leverett, Edward Shrimpton, and Thomas Bell and Company of London.[14]

Documents such as these attest to the important role played by the London merchants in developing the New England fishery. The extent of the Londoners' involvement in this commerce cannot be estimated as no statistics remain, but the fact is indisputable that this type of trade served to introduce the New Englanders to the southern markets and supplied them with contacts and shipping during the first, critical years in the growth of New England's commerce.[15]

This triangular trade of the Londoners, the most important form of business organization in the early New England fishery, was not inflexible. Variations were present from the start. Occasionally, the contracting partnership would include merchants in the Wine Islands or in Spain as well as in England. Frequently the master of the London ship would be a partner in the company and he would contract for the fish when his vessel arrived in New England. The arrangements could become quite complicated when each of the members of a large partnership was involved at the same time in other fishing contracts with the same suppliers and when most of the shipments went on the same vessel. In such cases bills of exchange circulated quickly among the Boston merchants as the agents and principals settled accounts. These bills were the credits the New Englanders sought; with them they could pay for the goods sent from England or invest in property.[16]

Different as such combinations were, they had in common the confinement of the New Englanders to a relatively small part of the total flow of trade, and the profits that accrued to them as middlemen were less than they might expect if they could control the whole cycle. They sought continuously to enter larger and larger portions of the trade circuit and within certain bounds they were increasingly successful. Their expanded trade took two forms. First, by joining with other New England merchants they were able to finance independent voyages with fish to the southern ports, returning with wine and other semitropical products. And they became partners with the London merchants or with the agents in the southern ports for the total trip, entering their fish as capital and profiting proportionately to their investment.[17]

Though such arrangements were increasingly common throughout the period, the merchants did not reach their ultimate goal of controlling the total circuit themselves. The critical line in the polygon of trade was the outward voyage from England in which the all-important manufactures were brought to the colonial ports. The cargoes carried on this leg of the voyage almost always remained the property of English merchants until sold in New England.[18] It was only as minor shareholders that the colonials were able to claim some part of the profits from the outward passage. But they were able to gain full control of the secondary circuits between New England

and the southern ports, relying on a further exchange of goods to secure the profits from this trade. By the Restoration the New Englanders not only were in complete command of their own fishery but
also had a fleet of locally owned and operated vessels plying steadily
between their home ports and the southeastern Atlantic markets.[19]

By this time a number of New Englanders were clearly leaders in
the fish business. It is impossible to know precisely what personal qualities led to success in this field, but certain limiting factors were at
work in distinguishing this portion of their careers as merchants.
Men like Robert Sedgwick, Valentine Hill, Henry Shrimpton, Bryan
Pendleton, and Thomas Broughton, who succeeded in the business,
usually started with some capital, a reputation as sound traders, and,
without exception, close ties — usually kinship relations — with merchants in England. Without some capital with which to equip the
fishermen, advance sums for catches when they became available, and
buy up the necessary fishing stages, boats, lines, and nets needed to
expand their business, they could not have commanded the fish they
were called upon to supply; without good connections in London
they would have found it difficult to make arrangements with the
London fish dealers or the merchants in the southern ports; and without a good name they would not have received the contracts.[20]

These individuals, though clearly the earliest leaders in the trade,
did not comprise the whole group. The industry was growing quickly;
arrangements were for short periods, usually for single voyages; at
every level in the still informally organized business there were opportunities for new men to rise. It was relatively simple for a successful
fisherman to become an occasional wholesaler by buying up his
friends' catches or by joining with them for the purpose of contracting with the English shipmasters.[21] In this way fishermen like the Cutts
brothers of the Isles of Shoals rose from obscure seamen to fish dealers
and eventually, by expanding their enterprises with other commodities
into other markets, became wealthy merchants and landowners.[22] The
fishery became an important source for the recruitment of the merchant group.

2

Thus, in the second and third decades of the Puritan settlement and
as an adjunct to the external commerce of the British Isles, the fishing
trade of New England started its rise to prominence. But this is merely

to introduce the subject of the importance of the fishery to New England. For in these years the industry became a cornerstone of the region's economy. While large sales of fish were being made to the London merchants, the fishery was beginning to nourish a more general commerce which eventually bound New England tightly and inextricably into the economy of the Atlantic world.

The fish trade and contact with the English trading centers served not only to supply the Puritans with an indirect form of returns but also to acquaint them with other needs of the islanders and Spaniards which they were capable of supplying. Fish was but one form of food; agricultural produce was equally desired. And on islands that lived by the wine trade, barrel staves, hoops, and all manner of timber products found excellent markets. All this, as well as fish, New England could supply, and as the fish trade progressed so too did the beginnings of the commerce in provisions and lumber.

The first known exchange of such goods for the wine of Spain and the eastern Atlantic islands was undertaken not by the Puritans but by one of their predecessors in the New World, that stubbornly independent Anglican of Noddles Island in Massachusetts Bay, Samuel Maverick. In 1641, when the Puritan fishing merchants were first being contacted by the Londoners, he was engaged in a triangular trade by which he paid for purchases in Bristol by sending whale oil to Anthony Swymmer, his agent in that west-country port, and clapboards to one William Lewis in Málaga on the Mediterranean coast of Spain, who remitted to Swymmer credits for Maverick's account in the form of Spanish money and fruit.[23] In the following year the New Haven merchants launched one of their very few successful ventures by sending a vessel to the Canaries, and at about the same time an Englishman from Portuguese Madeira arrived in Massachusetts Bay, trading wine and sugar for pipestaves and provisions. In the next year two New England seamen contracted with an English business agent in Fayal, one of the Azores, to deliver fish, oil, pipestaves, and hoops.[24]

This year, 1643, seems to mark the real birth of New England's independent commerce, for no less than five New England vessels cleared port for the ocean routes. Thomas Coytmore exchanged pipestaves and fish for wine and sugar at Fayal. The locally built *Trial* made a successful trip to the Spanish ports of Bilbao and Málaga while the *Increase* of Cambridge traded in Madeira. Within another twelve months four more New England vessels visited the Canary Islands where Edward Gibbons already was involved in complicated dealings with the local merchants. And it was in that year that the first triangular slave voyage in New England history was made by one of the vessels trading in the Canaries, for she returned via Barbados where she bought tobacco "in exchange for Africoes, which she carried from the Isle of Maio." This voyage introduced New England to the trade in Negroes; but more important was the fact that its success stressed to the merchants the rich possibilities of commerce with the West Indies.[25]

During the years when the permanent economy of New England was beginning to take shape, the islands of the Caribbean, settled just a few years earlier, sprang into the forefront of European commerce. By 1640, when the New England merchants began to look abroad, a string of European colonies in the Caribbean Sea had been added to the original Spanish settlements in Cuba, Hispaniola, and Puerto Rico. "After 1625," writes a leading historian of the West Indies, "swarms of English and French colonists poured like flies upon the rotting carcase of Spain's empire in the Caribbean, and within ten years the West Indian scene was changed forever." The Lesser Antilles became a battleground of the expanding European empires. The island of St. Christopher in the Leewards was jointly possessed by the French and English; Barbados, Nevis, Antigua, and Montserrat were indisputably English; Guadeloupe and Martinique were French; and Curaçao, St. Eustatius, and Tobago were in the hands of the Dutch.[26]

The colonization of the American mainland had been part of the same movement of European expansion that led to the peopling of the West Indies, and New England grew up, as it were, in the company of these island dependencies. The Pilgrims at one point had considered settling on the Caribbean coast of South America and one of Winthrop's sons had spent two years just previous to the Puritan migration in Barbados, an island, he wrote to his father, "setled for a plantatyon for to-backow." [27] After 1630 information about the West Indies came increasingly to the New England merchants. Dutch seamen were already in control of a large part of the carrying trade of the islands and in the thirties their vessels occasionally stopped off in New England ports. Ships from the West Indies visited New England frequently in the years immediately preceding the slave voyage of 1644 (if such it may be called), and in 1645 George Downing, after a five-month stay in the West Indies, wrote a full report on the islands to his cousin John Winthrop, Jr. In his letter he spoke of Barbados as "a flourishing Iland" and added that he understood the inhabitants there to have "bought this year no lesse than a thousand Negroes; and the more they buie, the better able they are to buye, for in a yeare and halfe they will earne (with gods blessing) as much as they cost." [28]

From such sources as well as from letters from England the New Englanders learned of the needs of the West Indian settlers. The full picture of the Caribbean markets emerged only slowly, but it was quickly understood that the West Indians lacked the same commodities the New Englanders were already sending to the Wine Islands and Spain. And in return the New Englanders could obtain not only bills on English merchants but tobacco and the cotton they hoped to use in textile manufacture. Their high opinion of the slave trade gained from the earlier voyage was confirmed.

After 1644 the New England merchants turned their attention increasingly to the Caribbean. In 1645 some Bostonians sent a vessel to Africa which picked up wines at Madeira and sold its human cargo at Barbados. Several other direct contacts with that island were made in the same year, and a group of merchants sent a £400 letter of credit to an agent in Bermuda as the first step in opening trade relations with that island.[29] Toward the end of the fifth decade it became known in New England that sugar was becoming a major product of Barbados. As early as 1647 Winthrop had it on good authority that men in Barbados "are so intent upon planting sugar that they had rather buy foode at very deare rates than produce it by labour, soe infinite is the profitt of sugar workes after once accomplished." The accuracy of such reports was soon tested, and before the decade was out this commodity had taken a preëminent place in the cargoes to New England. No sooner had the West Indians set up their first sugar mills than the need for horses to work them and to transport the crops from the plantations to the docks became felt, and New England added another item to its list of exports. In 1648 the *Welcome* of Boston was preparing to transport eighty horses, and in the following year William Withington of Rhode Island hired a Boston vessel of forty tons to take cattle on the first leg of a voyage "from Road Island . . . unto Barbados and Ginney; and backe to Barbados Anttego and Boston her port of discharge." [30]

Meanwhile, contacts were multiplying in the east no less rapidly than in the west. Teneriffe in the Canaries was added as a permanent pivot of trade. The traffic in pipestaves to Spain, Portugal, and their dependencies was considered so valuable that the Massachusetts General Court ordered "all townes where pipe staves use to be shiped" to appoint two men to be "veiwers" charged with seeing that no faulty staves were sent abroad.[31]

In this first decade of effort by the merchants almost none of the goods which eventually figured in New England's trade were overlooked. Contracts were drawn up for shipping mast trees to England; shipbuilding rose to meet the growing need of the merchants for their own transportation and the steady demand for vessels by Englishmen and foreigners; and a growing fleet was dispatched to the tobacco plantations of Virginia and Maryland. By 1660 the outline of New England's permanent economy, formed in the forties and hardened in the fifties, was unmistakably clear. From that time until the American Revolution, though its magnitude and its place in the total life of the community increased, its main characteristics did not change.[32]

The commercial system built by the first generation of New England merchants was part of a newly created economic world. In the first half of the seventeenth century, particularly from 1620–1650, the leading mercantile nations of Europe flung their commercial frontiers westward to the American continent and made of the whole Atlantic basin a single great trading area. The character of each country's involvement in the crisscrossing web of transoceanic traffic was determined by the resources it controlled and its place in European affairs. The shape of England's Atlantic commerce was a polygon formed by lines drawn between port towns in the British Isles, Newfoundland, the American mainland, the West Indies, the Wine Islands, and the continent of Europe. Outward from the larger ports in the British Isles flowed shipping, manufactures, and investments in colonial property, the enhanced value of which returned as colonial products to be sold at home or abroad.

The New England merchants became important agents in maintaining the efficiency of this mechanism. They entered the flow of England's Atlantic commerce in an effort to pay for their purchases and to profit by advancing the exchange of European goods for colonial products. In no way was their commerce independent. Though the efficiency of the system permitted some of the New Englanders to limit their operations to a small area, a breakdown in any major part of the mechanism affected their trade immediately. Severance of the link to England would destroy the whole commercial system of New England.

3

Yet this intricate commercial mechanism with its many interrelated parts was not an impersonal machine existing above men's heads, outside their lives, to which they attached themselves for purposes of trade. The New England merchants of the mid-seventeenth century had witnessed the creation of this network of trade; they knew that human relationships were the bonds that kept its parts together.

The same principle was at work in the selection of agents, factors, and correspondents in the importing trade as operated in the fishery. Being both all important and extremely fragile and unreliable, commercial ties were best secured by the cement of kinship or long friendship. To a large extent the arrangements for the importation of goods that had existed in the thirties continued throughout the lifetime of the founding Puritan generation. Brothers, sons, and "in-laws" continued as agents of their English relatives. The old correspondences between the Shrimptons, the Footes and Joshua Hewes, the Hills, and the Cogans continued, but to them now were added new contacts among others entering the trade. Keayne's son Benjamin established himself as a merchant in Birchin Lane, London, and became his father's London agent. Thomas Fowle did business not only with his brother in London but with his brother-in-law Vincent Potter in Barnstable. Young John Hull built up his many-sided business with the help of his uncle, Thomas Parris, a haberdasher, and his "Coz Edw" Hull at the "Hatt-in-Hand" within Aldegate, London.[33]

No longer was it necessary for the New England importers to face only east in their dealings; they also had to cultivate correspondences throughout the Atlantic world. To some extent they did so with the aid of relatives and old friends or the relatives of friends who had joined the movement to colonize the island dependencies;[34] but they were also obliged to make fresh acquaintances among the merchants and planters in those areas. Two methods were most commonly used. Since most of the trade to the south was conducted in small vessels with small cargoes, a merchant would send his shipmaster to the markets he had selected with instructions to use his own discretion in selecting men to deal with.[35] Over a period of time some of these transient contacts became firm commercial bonds which formed the framework of a lifetime of trade. But, for those who had capital to start with and some knowledge of the distant markets, the best method was to send a letter of credit to someone of good reputation and in this way to found an agency that could be relied on for advice on new opportunities or dangers to avoid.[36]

The weaving of a network of correspondences was greatly facilitated by the migrations within the colonial area throughout the period. A number of New Englanders like William Vassal and Richard Vines transplanted themselves to the West Indies and became factors for their merchant friends in the Puritan colonies. Similarly, merchants were involved in the movement of people among and out of the West Indies and some of them became residents of the northern colonies.[37] Thus John Parris, a relative of Hull, moved to Boston where he engaged in large operations in an attempt to stock his Barbados plantation with slaves; his ultimate success as a planter was no doubt partly the result of his transactions in Massachusetts.[38] Men who moved south to the Caribbean like Vines or north to Boston like Parris carried with them friendships and a knowledge of affairs in their old home towns that were used in broadening the foreign connections of the New England merchants.

As a result, New Englanders contributed to the extension of a number of English family trading groups which in this period were spreading out over the Atlantic world. Younger sons seeking their fortunes were entering trade in the West Indies with the support of London relatives themselves anxious to profit from the importation of colonial goods. Often these families had kinsmen on the American mainland who joined in the growing enterprise. Thus the Winthrop family, starting with representatives in England and Massachusetts, ended with personal ties to Rhode Island, New London and Hartford, Connecticut; and, when young Samuel Winthrop moved from Teneriffe to Barbados and eventually to Antigua, to the West Indies as well.[39] The most complete family commercial system of which we have knowledge is that of the Hutchinsons; it is an almost ideal type of this sort of arrangement.

The Hutchinson family trading unit, which may be reconstructed from Peleg Sanford's *Letter Book*, was based upon the continuous flow of manufactures exported from London by the affluent Richard Hutchinson to his brothers Samuel and Edward and his nephews Elisha and Eliakim.[40] These four Bostonians, together with Thomas Savage who had married Richard's sister, retailed the goods in the Bay area and, through middlemen, sold also to the inland settlers. They conducted a large trade with the West Indies, sending provisions and cattle in exchange for cotton and sugar which they sold for credit on London. The West Indian trade of the Boston Hutchinsons was largely handled for them by Peleg Sanford of Portsmouth, Rhode Island, whose mother was another sister of Richard and who was, hence, cousin and nephew of the Boston merchants of the family.

Peleg, who had started his career as a commercial agent in Barbados, was in charge of the cattle farms in Rhode Island owned by the Bostonians; he exported their horses and provisions direct to Barbados where they were sold by his brothers, the Barbadian merchants William and Elisha Sanford. Peleg was entirely dependent on his Massachusetts relatives for his supply of manufactures, having to write to them not only for large cargoes of goods but also for halters for the horses and even for a frying pan. His own orbit of trade, reaching mainly to Boston and Barbados, also included Taunton and Bridgewater, Massachusetts, and Middletown and Hartford, Connecticut, for whose merchants he acted as middleman in the West Indies exchange.

Peleg and his Boston and Barbadian relatives operated in a constantly shifting series of combinations, as partners, as agents, or merely as customers to each other. What remained constant besides their locations and the direction of the trade flow was the ownership by the Bostonians of the imports, once they arrived in Massachusetts, and Peleg's agency for disposing of their cattle and sheep to the Caribbean markets. Peleg was an independent merchant in his dealings with the inland wholesalers and buyers and occasionally even in his West Indian trade, but not as an importer from England. In 1668 he did try to eliminate the Boston Hutchinsons as middlemen by establishing a direct trade connection with William Pate of London, an acquaintance from his days in Barbados, but the result was disastrous. Pate was unreliable, it seems, and, since the correspondence started by Pate's advancing a cargo of goods to the Rhode Islander, Peleg had no way of controlling him except to break off the connection. Horrified at the prices Pate asked and the poor quality of the goods he sent, he threatened to sever the association as soon as he had examined the first load of goods. By the end of the year the affair was ended and Peleg wrote to his brother William that he had been "much abused of my former Correspondent, therefore desiere yo to give me advice whome I may make Bould wth on tht accott . . ." [41] There is no indication that he was ever able to conduct a direct and independent trade with the home country.

The Hutchinsons with their Rhode Island and West Indian relations formed a self-conscious family group which considered it unfortunate but not unnatural that Edward Hutchinson should go to jail, as he did in 1667, as a consequence of his support of his nephew Peleg in a lawsuit. Their commerce illustrates not only the importance of kinship ties as a basis for commercial relations but also the consistency with which the New Englanders dealt with other Britishers whenever they could. For, though the New Englanders traded with the Dutch and French when their ships came to the New England ports or when they themselves went on peddling voyages to Canada or the West Indies, the overwhelming bulk of their commerce was conducted with other Englishmen. The reason for this was not that they paid the least attention to the navigation acts already in force or had moral objections to trading with foreigners, even with enemies of England,[42] but that business relations with foreigners were much more difficult to establish and maintain than they were with other Britishers. In Spain, where Britons had been trading for a century, the merchants almost invariably dealt with Englishmen resident in the port towns. The same was true in the Spanish and Portuguese dependencies in the eastern Atlantic. And in the American trade, what reliance could be placed on the bonds of Frenchmen to the north who desired nothing more than the collapse of the British settlements in the New World?

The employment of Dutch carriers by New Englanders[43] decreased less as a result of the effect of the Navigation Act of 1651 than as a consequence of the rise of shipbuilding in New England and the increasing interest of the merchants in freightage. The French West Indies were as yet not well enough developed nor the economic situation in the Caribbean tight enough to lead New Englanders to run the risks of attempting to start correspondences with unknown foreigners there. In long distance transactions they preferred to deal with their relatives and friends in the British Islands who, if necessary, could be brought to law in the British courts more easily than French merchants could. Their dealings in the French West Indies during this period were usually limited to face-to-face transactions carried on by shipmasters extemporizing cargoes.

The connection with England, in fact, continued to be the umbilical cord of their commerce. The failures of manufactures in New England meant that the colonists were utterly dependent on supplies from England, dependent, that is to say, upon the good will of a small group of London merchants. For the colonials could not compete with the English entrepreneurs in the home country markets and were obliged to purchase the goods they desired not from the producers in England but from the London exporters. Of the 204 "Cocquetts and Certificates of goods imported and exported" that were registered by William Aspinwall between 1645 and 1651, only eight were sent on the account of New Englanders.[44]

The importance of this primary tie to England was felt by the merchants at every turn. Every transaction between the merchants had an indirect relationship to men in the home country. Bills of exchange were only as good as the drawee's reliability and the drawer's credit in England. Good connections with English merchants were of the highest value to a merchant's business, and John Hull's trips to the home country were significant in the solicitude they suggest for his reputation on the London Exchange.[45]

4

Thus, despite their physical removal from the home country, and despite their advances into continental American trade routes, into the West Indies, and into Spanish markets, the New England merchants from the start conducted their trade mainly within the confines of the British commercial system. Nor was their involvement with England limited to economic matters. Politics and trade were as intimately connected in the New World as they were in the Old. The New England merchants could not escape entanglement in the tumultuous politics of Cromwellian Britain.

The victory of the Parliamentary forces over the royalists in the first phase of the Civil War was felt by the New England Puritans to be a triumph of the principles that guided their lives. But it also meant, by virtue of the overseas interests of the merchants, that the Puritan government was quickly forced to define its relationship with the new government of the home country. The issue was precipitated in 1644 by the seizure of a Bristol vessel before Charlestown in Boston Bay by a Captain Stagg, commissioned by the Earl of Warwick to prey on royalist shipping. The agents of the Bristol merchants, together with some traders from that town who happened to be in Boston, protested against the seizure and "began to gather company and raise a tumult." [46] When the confusion subsided the Massachusetts leaders began serious consideration of the problems presented by the seizure. The heart of the question was whether Parliament had the right to impose its power on Massachusetts which considered itself independent by virtue of its royal charter. Everyone consulted on the question wanted New England to maintain its independence. But there were at least three different opinions on the best way to achieve this end.

To the most orthodox Puritans, fiercely determined to keep New England a sanctuary for the true religion, all relations with outsiders were dangerous and none more so than the subordination to Parliament implied by accepting the legality of Stagg's commission. They maintained "that our's is perfecta respublica . . . subject . . . to no other power but among ourselves," and they were willing to accept isolation in preference to such dangerous involvements. The majority of the leaders, however, recognized the advantages that flowed from Parliament's favor and also the grim fact that if Parliament forsook them "we could have no protection or countenance from any, but should lie open as a prey to all men." Insisting that the charter freed them from appeals to England "in cases of juridicature, yet not in point of state," they advocated the compromise of opposing the Parliamentary commission in principle but allowing Stagg "to enjoy his prize." The merchants, however, sought neither isolation nor the partial independence derived from the support of Parliament. They advocated an active free-trade policy without concessions to any nation or party.[47]

The view that prevailed satisfied all but the extreme isolationists. The General Court sent a petition to Parliament in which it paid respect to the parent body's authority by announcing that Stagg would be allowed to keep his prize but protested strongly against such commissions as great discouragements to trade. It pointed out that such depredations severely deterred certain English merchants from continuing to send necessary supplies to New England. It concluded with the plea "that no such attempt may be made hereafter upon any shipps in our harbors," and that Parliament encourage English merchants to ship goods to the New England ports.[48]

The same compromise aligning New England with Parliament in principle but refusing to impose that body's wishes upon the local merchants was written into a law passed shortly after the Stagg incident. Acknowledging the legality of Parliament's reign, the General

Court declared that agitation in behalf of the king was an offense "of an high nature against this common wealth," but added,

that this shall not be extended against any marchant, strangers, and shipmen that come hither meerly for matter of trade and marchandize, albeit they should come from any of those parts that are in the hands of the king, and such as adhere to them against the Parliament, carriing themselves here quietly, and free from raising or nurishing any faction, mutiny, or sedition amongst us, as aforesaid.

Large as this concession was to the interests of the merchants, it merely extended to those in conflict with Parliament the privilege of trade in Massachusetts. The ultimate desire of the merchants was to open the Massachusetts ports to all, no matter what their relation to Parliament or England was. They proposed such a law but the magistrates, fearing the reprisals of Parliament, refused to accept it despite the fact that it was approved by the deputies. In 1645 a revised free trade bill, containing the main provisions of the earlier one, finally passed into law, only "few of the magistrates," according to Winthrop, "being then in the Court." [49]

Though the merchants' desire to harvest all the benefits and none of the disadvantages of Parliament's rule could be written into law, in fact it could not be satisfied indefinitely. The confusions in England and the weakness of Parliament's power outside the British Isles permitted New England to enjoy full freedom to trade throughout most of the period, but when actual war among the imperial powers broke out Massachusetts was forced to ban trade with the Dutch and French. And in 1651, despite the protests of the influential merchants, the General Court was obliged to obey Parliament in outlawing traffic with the stubborn royalist colonies of Barbados, Antigua, Bermuda, and Virginia — though not without expressing horror at finding itself treated by Parliament as if "wrapped up in one bundle with all the other colonies," and vehemently rejecting Parliament's claim to the right of appointing colonial governors. [50]

If England's colonial policies violated the interests of the New England merchants in this way it greatly favored them in others. In 1644 Parliament exempted all the trade of New England from the payment of the English import and export duties. Cromwell's expedition of 1655 which captured Jamaica was largely provisioned from New England; its naval purchasing agents became the largest single buyers of New England produce during the campaign. War threatened England's supply of naval stores from the Baltic and, fearful of being denied these essentials of sea warfare and transportation, the English government placed enormous orders for New England tar, timber, and turpentine. The merchants could not satisfy demands of such size, but they realized that the Navy Board in London was potentially their best customer and they did what they could to keep contacts alive for future transactions.[51] This was simplified by the fact that a number of their group had returned to England and some of them had risen to positions of power in Cromwell's government. Not only did Robert Sedgwick, the Charlestown merchant, become a Major General in charge of part of the Jamaican expedition, but Edward Hopkins, the London "Turkey merchant" who had moved from Massachusetts to Connecticut, returned to England in 1652 where he became Member of Parliament, Commissioner of the Navy, "Warden of the Fleet, and Keeper of the Palace of Westminster." Henry Vane, Hugh Peter, and a number of Winthrop connections occupied high positions in the English government, and Nehemiah Bourne, the New England shipwright and ship captain, after having been made "Rear Admiral of the Fleet of the Commonwealth of England and Captain of the St. Andrew" for his part in a sea battle with the Dutch, became one of the first Commissioners of Trade. The Charlestown shipwright Francis Willoughby, like Hopkins and Bourne, served the Commonwealth as Commissioner of the Navy. Most important of all, Richard Hutchinson, brother-in-law of the notorious Anne, and father, brother, and uncle of New England merchants, acquired great wealth as a London merchant and rose through the Navy Board to the treasurership of the Navy, one of the best posts in the entire British government for influencing the award of contracts for naval stores and provisions.[52]

5

Enmeshed in the politics of Cromwellian England, New England's trade was already a formative influence on the development of colonial society. It determined the character of urbanization in New England, shaped the growth of the merchant group and its relations with other parts of the community, and led the merchants, for the most part Puritans themselves, to challenge the Puritan leaders on important points of policy.

As trade rose and the European shipmasters sought a familiar New

England harbor where reliable merchants would be waiting to provide ship stores and cargoes, Boston, with its excellent harbor, access to the Massachusetts government, and flourishing agricultural markets, became the major terminus of traffic originating in Europe. To it were drawn the produce not only of the surrounding towns but also of New Hampshire, Rhode Island, and Connecticut as well. With the exception of Salem and Charlestown, the other promising mercantile centers slipped back toward ruralism. Plymouth, which had been the first trading center east of Manhattan, was described in 1660 as "a poor small Towne now, The People being removed into Farmes in the Country." The commercial promise of Newport faded within a decade of its settlement by the exiled Bostonians, not to be revived until the end of the century. And New Haven, whose optimistic merchant leaders had laid out "stately and costly houses," was "not so glorious as once it was" with its "Merchants either dead or come away, the rest gotten to their Farmes." Nothing had come of the grand schemes of Ferdinando Gorges; Maine continued to be a sparsely settled district of fishermen and trappers. The inhabitants in the string of settlements along the Piscataqua lived by farming and the lumbering made lucrative by the enterprises of the merchants. The whole hinterland from the Merrimac River to New London had become the producing area for the marts around Boston Bay. Food, worked timber, and cattle were carried from the inland towns to the port city where they could be exchanged for manufactured goods. The islands of Narragansett Bay had proved to be excellent grazing lands for cattle. The towns along Long Island Sound and the Connecticut River, though not within the immediate sphere of Boston, contributed to the stocks of produce and cattle sought by the merchants.[53]

This is not to say that these essentially rural districts had no trade except to Boston and Manhattan. On the contrary, there were men in the Connecticut River towns and along the Sound and Narragansett Bay who managed a considerable exchange of goods; but their dealings were different from those of the Bostonians. They dealt in a secondary orbit of trade, sending a small but steady flow of local produce to the southern colonies or occasionally to the West Indies. They had fallen completely out of contact with the European sources of manufactures. The Connecticut River grandees were, like the younger Pynchon, primarily landed squires and only secondarily merchants. The few men in the coastal towns of Connecticut or Rhode

Island who, like Edmund Leach and Walter Newbury, did devote themselves primarily to trade operated within a commercial sphere subordinate to that of the Bostonians and the Dutchmen.[54]

The towns differed in appearance and size according to their position in the orbits of trade. First, there were the secondary market centers, usually but not always inland. These communities, among which were now included Hartford, New Haven, and Plymouth, were the collection points for the agricultural surplus of the neighboring farming hamlets. There were among their leading inhabitants men who trafficked in these commodities, furnishing "the Sea Townes with Provisions as Corne and Flesh, and also they Furnish the Merchants with such goods to be exported." But these men were not full-time merchants; they derived their status in the community from the traditional values of rural Englishmen.[55]

The "Sea Townes" which were supplied by the inland market centers, were distinguished by some sort of external commerce, varying from that of Strawberry Bank (Portsmouth, New Hampshire) which supplied the neighboring ports with timber and provisions, to Milford, Connecticut, which had "gotten into some way of Tradeing to Newfoundland, Barbados, Virginia." [56] In these towns there were men who devoted themselves entirely to trade, but their interests did not dominate the affairs of their towns.

In three towns, however — the three towns in continuous commercial contact with Europe — the merchants imposed themselves on the lives of their fellow-townsmen with unique force. In Charlestown, Salem, and especially Boston, they exercised a decisive influence in public affairs. The satisfaction of the physical needs of their commerce transformed the appearance of the towns. Their expanding businesses required wharves and storehouses, shops and market places; the preparation and disposition of their cargoes called for laborers, handicraftsmen, and highways into the interior; the equitable conduct of trade called for official regulation of markets, weights and measures, the care and protection of the harbors, and easily accessible courts of law. Offering to the settlers not only the manufactures of Europe but also wealth and contact with the greater world left behind, they were not refused. Their mark was left most clearly on that commercial hub, the "Metrapolis" of New England, Boston.[57]

In thirty years the makeshift hamlet on the peninsula in Massachusetts Bay had grown into a thriving commercial community of 3,000 souls which could muster "fouer full companys of Foote and a Troope of horse." [58] Along the beach of the deep cove formed by the fingers of Fort Hill and the Mill Field, the merchants had built a string of wharves and warehouses near which stood their houses, elegant and impressive by the standards of the majority of the settlers.[59] The town was "full of good shopps well furnished with all kind of Merchandize and many Artificers, and Trad's men of all sorts." [60] Boston gave one visitor the impression of an English port city. The houses, he later wrote,

. . . are for the most part raised on the Seabanks and wharfed out with great industry and cost, many of them standing upon piles, close together on each side the streets as in *London*, and furnished with many fair shops, their materials are Brick, Stone, Lime, handsomely contrived, with three meeting Houses or Churches . . . Their streets are many and large, paved with pebble stone, and the South-side adorned with Gardens and Orchards. The Town is rich and very populous, much frequented by strangers, here is the dwelling of their Governour. On the North-west and North-east two constant Fairs are kept for daily Traffick thereunto. On the South there is a small but pleasant Common where the Gallants a little before Sunset walk with their *Marmalet*-Madams, as we do in *Morefields*, etc. till the nine a clock Bell rings them home to their respective habitations, when presently the Constables walk their rounds to see good orders kept, and to take up loose people.[61]

It was a merchants' town, and the General Court, in creating an inferior tribunal in Boston in 1651 to deal with the litigation arising from "the great concourse of people and increase of trade there," was justified in appointing seven merchants to be the new judges.[62]

The true center of the business life of Boston and, indeed, of the whole of New England, was the townhouse, the imposing edifice made possible by the legacy of Robert Keayne. This two-storied structure lay at the main intersection of the town, in the center of the market and meetinghouse square. Keayne's desire that the townhouse combine a shelter "for the country people that come with theire provisions . . . to sitt dry in and warme both in cold raine and durty weather" with a "convenient room or too for the Courts to meete in" and a "roome for a Library and a gallery or some other handsome roome for the Elders to meete in and conferr together," as well as an armory for the Artillery Company — all built on pillars so that "the open roome between the pillars may serve for Merchants, Mr of Shipps and Strangers as well as the towne . . . to meete in" — had been fully realized. Under the chambers of the court and library the merchants congregated daily. From this townhouse exchange radiated a large part of the commercial cords that laced New England to the other coastal ports, to the West Indies, the Wine Islands, Spain, and especially to England. Since, by 1660, almost all importations from England were handled by Boston merchants, their meeting place in the townhouse exchange was economically closer to the "New England walke" on the London exchange than it was to some of the market places of the surrounding towns. It was the exact pivot point of the primary orbit of Atlantic trade in New England.[63]

6

As obvious to contemporaries as was the impact of the Boston merchants on the physical development of the towns was the extent of their power over the lives of their neighbors. To the farmers and fishermen, forced to supply their constant needs with the fruit of irregular production, the merchants dictated prices and the terms of credit. The limited money supply of New England flowed into their hands. By 1650 good bills of exchange on England could be found only in the Boston Bay towns and in Salem.[64]

Complaints of the greed and injustice of the Boston merchants came from the fishermen of the north as from the farmers and cattle raisers of the south. The heir of Ferdinando Gorges asked the royal commission visiting New England in 1664 to consider ways of founding a port city in Maine as a "Means to relieve the Inhabitants from the great Inconveniency they are at by being forced to carry their Goods to the Bay of Boston and there also to buy at Second or Third Hand all such Goods of [those] Parts as are necessary for them . . ."[65] One observer of the New England scene described the lack of shopkeepers in Maine as the result of the practices of the "damnable rich" Massachusetts merchants who supplied all things needed,

. . . keeping here and there fair Magazines stored with *English* goods, but they set excessive prices on them, if they do not gain *Cent per Cent*, they cry out that they are losers, hence *English* shooes are sold for Eight and Nine shillings a pair, worsted stockins of Three shillings six pence a pair, for Seven and Eight shillings a pair, Douglass that is sold in *England* for one or two and twenty pence an ell, for four shillings a yard, Serges of two shillings or three shillings a yard, for Six and Seven shillings a yard, and so all sorts of Commodities both for planters and fishermen, as Cables, Cordage, Anchors, Lines, Hooks, Nets, Canvas for sails, etc.

The labor of the fishermen, the same writer stated, yielded them nothing,

for the Merchant to increase his gains by putting off his Commodity in the midst of their voyages, and at the end thereof comes in with a walking Tavern, a Bark laden with the Legitimate bloud of the rich grape . . . coming ashore he gives them a Taster or two, which so charms them, that for no perswasions that their imployers can use will they go out to Sea, although fair and seasonable weather, for two or three days, nay sometimes a whole week. . . When the day of payment comes, they may justly complain of their costly sin of drunkenness, for their shares will do no more than pay the reckoning; if they save a Kental or two to buy shooes and stockins, shirts and wastcoasts with, 'tis well, other-wayes they must enter into the Merchants books for such things as they stand in need off, becoming thereby the Merchants slaves, and when it riseth to a big sum are constrained to mortgage their plantation . . . and stock of Cattle, turning them out of house and home, poor Creatures, to look out for a new habitation in some remote place where they begin the world again.[66]

Similarly, in 1658 the General Court of Rhode Island wrote to its London agent complaining of the treatment the Rhode Islanders were receiving from the Puritans. Since "ourselves are not in a capacity to send out shipping of ourselves, which is in a great measure occasioned by their oppressinge of us," they wrote,

wee cannot have any thinge from them for the suply of our necessities, but in efect they make the prices, both of our comodities, and their own also, because wee have not English coyne, but only that which passeth amonge these barbarians, and such comodities as are raised by the labour of our hands, as corne, cattell, tobbacco, and the like, to make payment in, which they will have at their own rate, or else not deale with us. Whereby (though they gaine extraordinarily by us), yett for the safeguard of their own religion may seem to neglect themselves in that respect; for what will men doe for their God.[67]

The extent of the economic power of the merchants cannot be explained merely as a result of their control of goods and money. It was also the consequence of three peculiar conditions of their business enterprises: specialization was impossible; expansion required an increasing control over certain natural resources; and real property was the most secure, if not the only secure, form of investment.

Specialization in trade is possible only when a freely flowing medium of exchange or a banking system makes it possible for a merchant to realize the profit of his sales without entering into a further exchange of goods. In New England during this period, as, in fact, throughout most of the following century, the balance of trade and the supply of coin or paper was such that currency flowed out as fast as it entered, and no amount of legislation by mercantilist-minded colonials could reverse the process. Despite the establishment of the Massachusetts mint and the passage of laws against the exportation of coin, New England suffered from so chronic a deficiency of currency that as early as 1663 Winthrop, Jr. was led to propose to the Royal Society a scheme for a "banke without mony." [68] Payments to merchants for their goods were, for the most part, made in kind, and thus the larger a merchant's sales the greater the variety of goods he accumulated. The merchants sold manufactures, for example, not for coin or good paper but for crops, animals, fish, and percentages of ships or of current voyages. A man had only to enter trade in one commodity to become immediately involved in the exchange of several more.

The necessary variety of commodities dealt in by a merchant helps to explain the fact that shopkeeping did not become a separate occupation as the Boston merchants rose in wealth and power. All the leading merchants in the town, no matter what their economic or social position, maintained shops — general stores — where they sold imported goods and the produce of the New England farms in small quantities. The shops were valuable to the merchants not only because retail sales to the growing Boston population were lucrative but also because these retail stores provided a necessary outlet for the odd lots of goods left over from wholesale exchanges.

To be a merchant in Boston in 1660 meant to be engaged, wholesale and retail, in the exchange of a great variety of goods, to be ready to accept payment in all sorts of unexpected commodities and currencies, always to be seeking new markets in which to sell new kinds of goods and new kinds of goods to satisfy new markets. Versatility was one of the keys to success; to specialize was to decline. The merchants reached deeper and deeper into the inland regions of New England seeking control of the resources they needed for the expansion of their trade, especially timber, rough for masts and spars, or worked into planks, pipestaves, and barrels. If horses and sheep were valuable, why not raise them oneself instead of relying on a number of small farmers for a supply? With freight charges a considerable burden to a merchant, would it not be better for him to build his own vessels and add carriage and the vessel itself as salable commodities?

The merchants felt the necessity of expansion, and in the twenty years after the crisis of 1640 they spread their influence more and more widely. Two Hutchinsons bought control of the nineteen sawmills on the Great Works River in New Hampshire in order to assure themselves a continuous flow of lumber products. John Hull, the merchant mint-master of Boston, bought timber land and sawmills in New Hampshire, together with the Broughtons who had started out as fish wholesalers; he also raised cattle on his land in Rhode Island. A glance at the first fifty pages of the *Aspinwall Notarial Records* shows that during the single year 1645–1646 Valentine Hill dealt in fish, wheat, peas, pork, corn, cattle, ships, pipestaves, clapboards, tobacco, indigo, and sugar. Joshua Hewes, the ironmonger's nephew, started as a retailer of manufactures and ended his career as a dealer also in lumber products, tobacco, and sugar. And Edward Gibbons' multifarious enterprises included exchanges in every conceivable type of colonial commodity, from Nova Scotia furs, Spanish wines, and New England provisions, to lumber, ships, and cattle. The merchants in the port town developed the New Hampshire lumber industry, opened the Narragansett area of Rhode Island to cattle grazing, established and maintained the shipbuilding industry, and provided the markets for provisions that led to the quick cultivation of large and increasing numbers of farms.[69]

There were, of course, stresses placed on certain commodities by individual merchants, but these resulted not from a desire to specialize but from the accidents of demands placed on them by their correspondents and the resources they happened to command. But one commodity absorbed the intense interest of every merchant without exception — land. In an economy lacking both coin and a reliable and unfluctuating system of paper property, real estate was the best form of investment. The surviving records tend to exaggerate the importance of dealings in land because every land transaction was legally registered to assure clear title while every commodity exchange was not. Nevertheless, it is an unmistakable fact that the merchants were extraordinarily involved in the buying and selling of land. The balance of land transactions in the total recorded business life of Valentine Hill and the Boston Hutchinsons is so high as to suggest that they were primarily real estate agents, not merchants at all. What explains their endless trafficking in land is the satisfaction it gave to certain powerful desires which they could fulfill in no other way.

The first generation of New England overseas merchants were

London tradesmen in origin, and they conceived of the rewards of a life of trade in terms characteristic of their class. For centuries the goal of the London businessmen had been to prosper in trade, marry into a family of higher social standing, provide themselves with landed estates, and begin the process of transferring their family from the status of tradesmen or merchants to that of gentlemen.[70] The great social magnet was a secure place among the landed county families where alone might be enjoyed "the unbought grace of life." The New England merchants sought the same goal. Some of them remained in New England only long enough to make their fortunes and then returned to the home country where they bought into the land. Those who remained in the New World sought to recreate the process under different circumstances. Most of the merchants were engaged throughout their active lives in accumulating contiguous pieces of land which they eventually consolidated into large estates. They were aided in this by the grants of land made to them by the government in recognition of their services either as investors in the original Massachusetts Bay Company or as public benefactors. They bought from the natives, foreclosed on unfortunate debtors, and accepted land willingly as payment for debts. When enough property had been bought or granted to them they staked out their estates, built a house and out-buildings, and, like Robert Keayne at Rumney Marsh, Francis Champernowne at Greenland, New Hampshire, and Kittery, Maine, and Anthony Stoddard in Roxbury started the process of transforming themselves into New England country gentlemen.[71]

Landed property was a particularly valuable form of wealth for the merchants also because commerce was not transferable as such from father to son. The heart of a merchant's business lay in his reputation and the number and quality of his correspondents. The only business property he could claim besides a wharf, a shop, and parts of ships, was the stock of goods on hand and shares in current voyages. The merchants sought solid investments for their profits, investments that could be transferred to their children. This they found in real property — land and buildings.

Such land as could conveniently satisfy a merchant's social ambitions or prove of use to his children was, of course, within the periphery of settlement. But increasingly through the period the merchants invested in land that could not serve these purposes — blocks of unsurveyed wilderness land in New Hampshire, Maine, and western Massachusetts.[72] Such places they did not expect to visit, let alone inhabit. These purchases were the beginnings in New England of a consuming interest in land speculation. Most of these distant possessions, unseen and uncultivated, were acquired for the eventual value of their timber, their possible beaver supply, or for their potential increase in price as settlements multiplied and land became scarcer. But though the merchants were absentee land owners they were not absentee town proprietors. The General Court maintained a clear distinction between these personal grants and the physical endowments of new townships. The latter were the economic bases of the multiplying Puritan societies and the magistrates were not inclined to confuse them with the just rewards of merchants.[73]

Seeing in real property a means of social fulfillment, a form of transferable property, and a promising object of speculation, the New England merchants bought and sold, bequeathed and inherited, mortgaged and released land in a bewildering maze of transactions. By 1660 they were so involved in the ownership of land that the least disturbance of values or titles would bring them instantly forward in defense of their rights.

The effectiveness of such a defense would depend largely upon their access to political power, the institutional forms of which were solidifying during the same years that saw the growth of the commercial structure. Most influential in town affairs in the ports of Boston, Charlestown, and Salem, the merchants joined to form a separate political interest only in the Masachusetts legislature.[74] Even here, however, they were not dominant. Though the representatives of the three largest ports were consistently merchants and though certain other delegates were inclined to support them on many issues, the preponderance in the House of Deputies was held by men from rural, inland towns whose sympathies were frequently antagonistic to the merchants. And throughout the period the upper chamber, the Council of magistrates, despite the fact that occasional members like Gibbons were merchants of dubious enthusiasm for Puritanism, remained faithful to the aims of the Founders who knew the value of trade but who believed it served the community best when subordinated to the goals of religion. As a result the Massachusetts merchants were able to swing the General Court to policies that favored them as a separate faction only when these policies harmonized with the desires of the bulk of the legislators or when they bore no relation to them at all.[75]

Thus in 1643 the General Court lifted the 8 per cent ceiling on interest rates in the case of bills of exchange, which, relating mainly to transfers of commercial credits, satisfied the merchants without directly affecting other groups. It was only when economic conditions improved that the laws passed in the early forties to protect consumers against creditors and sellers were repealed. By 1646 it was no longer considered necessary to permit contracts in money to be paid in kind, and in 1650 the law permitting debtors to avoid payment and evade the usual consequences of attachment and confiscation of their property was repealed. But, when in 1651 it was decided by the majority of the deputies that the tax burden was unequally distributed owing to the easier assessment of visible property, "the estates of marchants, in the hands of neibours, straungers, or theire factors [being] not so obvious to view," the best efforts of the merchants and their sympathizers could not block the passage of a law assessing "all marchants, shopkeepers, and factors . . . by the rule of our common estemation . . . havinge regard to theire stocke and estate, be it presented to view or not . . ." [76]

Such laws were not efforts to penalize the merchants but merely to right what appeared to be a bad balance of interests. The importance of commerce to the Commonwealth was, in fact, well recognized by the members of the Court, and in the fifties they moved to support the merchants, though always in ways that promised little if any conflict with other groups. In 1650 a committee of six was appointed to "peruse and duly consider of the booke intituled Lex Mercatoria [Gerard Malynes' *Lex Mercatoria*], and make retourne of what they conceave therein may be necessarily, usefully, and beneficially improoved, for the dividing of maritime affaires in this jurisdiccion." Two years later the Court, following the precedent of the English Parliament, set up a board of trade to which all men might "come to discover theire greivances, and to advise of meanes for remedie, as also to propose their severall ingenuous waies for the promoting of trade." Apparently the committee did little if anything, and in 1655 the General Court, determined "to use our utmost endeavors for the procuring of suitable supplies," appointed separate committees for each of the four counties "to consider of some such way as whereby both merchandizing may be encouraged and the hands also of the husbandman may not wax weary in his imployment . . ." [77]

7

Economically all-powerful, politically influential but circumscribed, the merchants — willingly or not — were prime movers in a gradual, subtle, but fundamental transformation of New England society. Their involvement in the world of Atlantic commerce committed them to interests and attitudes incompatible with life in the Bible Commonwealths. Most of them did not seek the destruction of the Puritan society; but they could not evade the fact that in many ways commercial success grew in inverse proportion to the social strength of Puritanism.

The continued spiritual health of the Puritan community required both isolation from the contamination of Old World sin and the un-questioned authority of the Puritan magistracy. Evil was cancerous, spreading uncontrollably once it took root in sensitive flesh. If good men ruled the Bible Commonwealths the disease could only originate abroad. By performing their indispensable economic function the merchants robbed the Commonwealths of their cherished isolation. If the health of Puritanism required isolation and the most rigorous selection of newcomers, the well-being of trade demanded the free movement of people and goods and a rising population. Should strangers come freely to New England shores? Should the sailors and merchants of all nations traffic in the Massachusetts ports? On these points Puritanism and commerce flatly disagreed. "But now behold the admirable Acts of Christ," fluted Edward Johnson in surveying the success of the Puritan settlement:

the hideous Thickets in this place were such, that Wolfes and Beares nurst up their young . . . in those very places where the streets are full of Girles and Boys sporting up and downe, with a continued concourse of people. Good store of Shipping is here yearly built . . . also store of Victuall both for their owne and Forreiners-ships, who resort hither for that end: this Town is the very Mart of the Land, French, Portugalls and Dutch come hither for Traffique.

But in a different mood, contemplating the dangers that would confront the settlers, the same rhapsodist wrote,

. . . and whereas he [God] hath purposely pickt out this People for a patterne of purity and soundnesse of Doctrine, as well as Discipline, that all such may finde a refuge among you, and let not any Merchants, In-keepers, Taverners and men of Trade in hope of gaine, fling open the gates so wide, as that by letting in all sorts you mar the worke of Christ intended.[78]

The same attitude appeared in the legislation of the Bay Colony. Trade was welcomed by the Massachusetts leaders, but the General Court stood firm against the thronging strangers who followed in its wake. In 1645 Emmanuel Downing, Nehemiah Bourne, Robert Sedg-wick, and Thomas Fowle led a group that protested against a law limiting the residence of unaccredited strangers in Massachusetts to three weeks and also against the banishment of Anabaptists. Many of the Court, wrote Winthrop, agreed with the merchants in their desire to revise these laws, but the church elders lectured them so powerfully on the dangers of leniency that the Court ruled "that the laws mentioned should not be altered at all, nor explained." [79]

The laws stood but the problem persisted and in fact grew with the increase of trade. In 1650 the Court felt obliged to require that every stranger over sixteen years of age present himself upon arrival to two magistrates who would pass immediately on his fitness to remain, and in the following year this regulation was given the force of law. In 1652 the Court demanded a written oath of fidelity to the Massachusetts government of all whose loyalty was suspected and particularly "of all straungers who, after two moneths, have theire aboade here." How many individuals like David Selleck, a well-known shipmaster and merchant who was fined for allowing some Irishmen to come ashore in Massachusetts, felt the effect of these laws cannot be estimated, but the spate of legislation reflected the magnitude of the problem which tended to separate the interests of commerce and of Puritanism.[80]

The question of strangers was part of the more general and fundamental problem of the toleration of dissent in a Bible Commonwealth. The orthodox view, which had triumphed in the Antinomian controversy of 1637, was that toleration was an unmitigated evil, a sinful welcome to Satan's clamorous hordes. But it had become clear that this precept, made effective in law, was as harmful to trade as it was beneficial to the perpetuation of orthodoxy. Persecution, a growing number of merchants discovered, was simply bad for trade; it "makes us stinke every wheare," as the business-minded George Downing wrote to Winthrop, Jr.[81] Not only did it lessen the appeal of New

England to immigrants, but it also blackened the reputation of New Englanders in English trading circles.[82] At each point of controversy merchants appeared in defense of a softer, more latitudinarian policy.

The Remonstrance and Petition to the General Court of 1646 attacked the very basis of Puritan society by demanding the broadening of church membership and of the civil franchise.[83] The seriousness of its consideration by the magistrates reflected both the importance of its originators and the widespread sympathy it found among the settlers, particularly those of the younger generation. It was largely the work of the enterprising Dr. Robert Child who, though a medical man by profession, was a metallurgist by avocation and one of the leading spirits in exploiting the resources of New England. He had invested in the Saugus ironworks and young Winthrop's graphite mine, had attempted to set up a vineyard as a beginning of a wine industry, and had joined in supporting the fruitless search for the Great Lake. Yet he, like all but one of the signers, was outside the membership of the New England churches.[84] Of the other six signers, three — Thomas Fowle, Samuel Maverick, and David Yale — were Boston merchants and a fourth, John Dand, though apparently not engaged in trade in New England, had been a grocer in London. Their petition, expressing the increasing dissatisfaction with the civil and ecclesiastical limitations of Puritan orthodoxy, was rejected by the General Court after it had justified its position in a powerful counterblast. The remonstrants were lectured on their sins and fined severely, Child receiving the stiff penalty of £200. After enduring a number of indignities, Fowle who had been one of the most active merchants in Boston, the imaginative and energetic Child, and the affluent David Yale returned permanently to England. Orthodoxy had triumphed again, but its victory had been costly.[85]

In a series of less sensational disputes the merchants also found themselves in conflict with New England Puritanism. William Vassal, a merchant from Stepney, Middlesex, who had been one of the first magistrates of the Bay Colony, received similar treatment by the Commonwealth when he petitioned for greater tolerance in civil and ecclesiastic affairs and he too eventually returned to England to restore his fortunes as a West Indian merchant and planter. Conformity proved to be too confining even to that typical first generation Puritan merchant, William Pynchon, whose return to the home country in

1652 was stimulated by the public burning of his treatise *The Meritorious Price of Our Redemption*, which was written in the form of
a dialogue between a tradesman seeking enlightenment and a minister.
The Salem merchants William Hathorne and Henry Bartholomew
were among those who came to Pynchon's defense in the Court. Anthony Stoddard, the Boston merchant, was jailed for insolence to the
governor. Stoddard and Edward Hutchinson objected to the way the
church treated the thorny problem of the admission of members'
children, the latter requesting dismissal from the church over the issue.
In 1651, when the General Court endorsed the Confession of Faith
and Discipline written by the Synod of 1646 as the official statement
of orthodoxy, among the fourteen deputies who dissented were the
merchants William Hathorne, Henry Bartholomew, Thomas Clarke,
John Leverett, Jeremiah Houtchin, and William Tyng. The
same men objected to the General Court's fining of the Malden
church for its toleration of the "errors and unsaffe expressions" of
its pastor Mr. Mathews.[86]

If certain of the merchants stood in opposition to the institutions of
Puritan orthodoxy, none of them did so as anarchists. Their dissent
turned on points of dogma and of civil and ecclesiastical policy, but
as men of property they joined ranks with the most enthusiastic Puritans against the fanatical Quakers during the first phase of their persecution. Like the church elders, the merchants saw in the Quakers'
"superadded presumptuous and incorrigible contempt of aucthoritie"
the destructive "Spirit of Muncer [Münster], or John of Leyden
revived . . ." Though the treatment accorded Quakers by the Salem
merchant Edmund Batter was extraordinary in its brutality, a large
number of merchants joined in a petition to the General Court for
more severe laws against them.[87]

In general, however, the merchants for a wide variety of personal
reasons, all reflecting their discomfort in the constrictions of orthodoxy, sided with the dissenters in the attacks, small and large, directed
at the reigning magistracy. To be sure, there were men like John Hull
who managed to maintain the delicate balance between the total acceptance of social Puritanism and an active participation in commerce,
but they were a small minority of the whole merchant group. By the
1650's the merchants had become so clearly identified with the principle of toleration that the devout Edward Johnson attributed a series

of ship disasters to the "hand of the Lord" being against them. The merchants, he wrote,

. . . being so taken up with the income of a large profit, that they would willingly have had the Commonwealth tolerate divers kinds of sinful opinions to intice men to come and sit down with us, that their purses might be filled with coyn, the civil Government with contention, and the Churches of our Lord Christ with errors. . .[88]

Nor did the future promise a greater harmony between the merchants and the orthodox magistracy. By the mid-1650's the character of the rising generation was discernible and to the entrenched oligarchy it seemed pitifully weak. The children of the Founders, however well-intentioned they might have been, knew nothing of the fire that had steeled the hearts of their fathers. They seemed to their elders frivolous, given to excess in dress and manners, lacking in the necessary fierceness of belief.[89] The General Court voiced a common thought of the older colonists when in 1659 it included among the reasons for proclaiming a day of humiliation "the great security and sensuallity under our present injoyments" and "the sad face on the rising generation." [90] Among the merchants the spiritual distance between the two generations stretched widest. Young Winthrop evinced a spirit far different from the one that in 1633 had enjoined him to "feare nothinge more than securitie, and carnall confidence" when, twenty-two years later, he wrote to his brother Fitz-John,

I perceive by your letter that you were much possessed with the feare of Death, you must be [care]full that Sathan doth not delude you, it is good to be alwaies mindfull and prepared for death, but take heede of distrusting, perplexed thoughts about it, for that will encrease the sicknesse.[91]

The writer, merchant and scientist as well as public leader, was a far different man than his father had been, and the difference between them typifies the gap between the first two generations of Puritan merchants.

John Winthrop the elder is severe, dignified, stern, introspective, medieval; John Winthrop the younger is eager, outgoing, genial, responsive, modern. The younger man was broad-minded, but never sounded the depth of religious experience as his father had done; the elder had seen much of life, but only from the angle of a puritan magistrate.[92]

It is Winthrop, not John Hull, who typifies the second generation of native merchants.

The character of the merchant group was changing not only as a result of the differences between the first and second generations but also because by mid-century the group was being recruited in part from a different portion of English society. The growing economic promise of New England was beginning to attract men intent on careers in trade who were not only strangers to New England orthodoxy, but to Puritanism itself. They were adventurous Englishmen seeking their fortunes and they brought with them the spirit of a new age.

Within the single decade during which the first generation mercantile leaders were dying off — Keayne died in 1656, Cogan in 1658, Hill in 1661, Shrimpton in 1666, Allerton in 1659, Gibbons in 1654, William Tyng in 1652, Webb in 1660 — the new men began to appear. The first to make his presence felt was Thomas Breedon, who, in 1648, entered the records of New England as a supercargo on the *Thomas Bonaventure* of London, bound from Málaga to Boston. By 1652 he had settled in the New England port, bought property there, and started his tempestuous career as a New England merchant.[93] From the start it was clear that he was alien corn. His interests were entirely commercial, and he had little sympathy with Puritanism. His personality reflected a strange light from every facet. Even his dress was foreign:

He appeared in Boston [a contemporary wrote] in a strange habit with a 4 Cornerd Cap instead of a hat, and his Breeches hung with Ribbons from the Wast downw[ard] a gr[ea]t depth, one row over another like shingles on a house: The Boyes when he came made an outcry, from one end of the streete to the other calling him a Devill, which was so greate, that people woundering came out of there houses to see whatt the matter was.[94]

Leagued with a group of English merchants, Breedon was after big game in the commercial hunt and lost little time in joining with other New Englanders of similar interests and abilities. In 1658 he became the Boston agent, banker, and supplier of Colonel Thomas Temple ("Honest Tom Temple," as he claimed Charles I on the scaffold had referred to him) who by careful manipulation had managed to gain control of Nova Scotia with all its trade. Temple, another newcomer, an aristocrat and royalist, was extremely well connected with certain individuals in the ruling circles of England. As a relative of Lord Say and Sele he had access to the inner clique of merchants and government officials whose influence grew so rapidly under the Commonwealth and Protectorate.[95]

Temple and Breedon shared a broader view of British commerce and affairs in general than had been possible for the first Puritan merchants or even for their sons. Their eyes were constantly focused on England to which they hoped to return and whose interests they considered second only to their own. Breedon, like another important new arrival of the fifties, Richard Wharton, was an economic imperialist, "interested in business as a source of private wealth, of public prosperity, and of natural expansion." [96] Breedon and especially Wharton, who became one of the biggest operators in New England commerce and real estate, were the complete antitheses of that troubled Puritan, Robert Keayne. The devout shopkeeper of Birchin Lane was a gnarled and petty figure next to the ebullient Wharton whose interest in trade and land speculation, we are told by his biographer,

... was dependent on more than the material success he hoped they would bring. He enjoyed 'playing the game,' as his buoyant and enthusiastic letters testify. His imagination, power of organization, courage in taking risks, ability to inspire confidence in prospective investors, driving force, tireless energy, optimism, are all characteristic of the successful captain of industry.[97]

Wharton and Breedon were Restoration Englishmen — royalists, Anglicans, and commercial imperialists — who went to New England as John Parris had gone to Barbados, as fortune seekers in the almost untouched area of colonial commerce. To them the attitudes and institutions of Puritanism were annoying archaisms. In the years after 1660 such men proved to be effective catalysts of changes that favored their interests.

V

Introduction to Empire

THE EVENTS of 1660 were an important turning point in the history of the New England merchants. The lives of the merchants of the founding generation had been shaped by the impress of New England's geography and economics upon the desires and abilities of Puritan tradesmen; the careers of their successors were formed largely by the social and political institutions of Restoration England. To some colonial merchants the power that emanated from the home country was restrictive; but those who gained access to that power discovered in it opportunities for advancement and profit. For those so favored, England and its monarchy became magnetic; identification with it meant not only unique economic and political opportunities but social distinction as well. Increasingly, the merchants tended to arrange themselves along the lines of this preëminent influence.

At the same time the social groupings and institutions of the Founders were crumbling. The mere passage of years, attended by a "declension" of religious fervor, splintered the ecclesiastical unity within the Bible Commonwealths and weakened the position of the church. Continuously through the decades the voices of the guardians of the Puritan virtues were heard, shrill and anxious, pleading with the sons and grandsons of the Founders to remember the rock whence they were hewn. But stronger forces were at work, and the faithful witnessed a continuing alienation from ancient ideals and social forms.

1

The restoration of the Stuarts transformed the context of New England society. In the government of Charles II, the direction of colonial affairs became the privilege of royal officers rather than Parliamentary committees; these administrators — Privy Councillors, Lords of Trade, and consultants on colonial business — were neither religious enthusiasts nor advocates of *laissez faire*. Royalists like

Clarendon or converted Commonwealth men like George Downing and Anthony Ashley Cooper, they intended to consolidate the new empire and to regulate its affairs for the home country's good. Economically, this meant unifying the empire as a producing unit and directing the commercial organization which had grown up during the past half-century. In seeking these ends, political leaders drew upon a number of traditional ideas which, elaborated and supplemented by contemporary thinkers, became a body of mercantilist theory.

Though there were many disagreements among the theorists who attempted to lay out the details of this policy of economic nationalism, there was no doubt about the need to subordinate the interests of the colonies to the good of the nation. The terms of this subordination were written into law and brought home to the colonists in the Navigation Acts of 1660, 1662, and 1663. Those measures made clear to the New England merchants that the Atlantic trading system which they had helped to build was to be reshaped to fit political and dynastic needs. The parts of the structure containing English territories and English merchants were to be a unit, the success of which was to be measured by its ability to gather wealth at the expense of rival states. To this end the importation of colonial goods into England or the colonies was restricted to English or plantation-built vessels, owned by Englishmen and manned by crews predominantly English. Valuable colonial products which might otherwise have to be imported from other nations were to be sent only to England or to other British colonies. The self-sufficiency of the imperial unit was to be maintained by limiting the colonists' purchases to goods imported from the home country or from other English colonies. If these principles could be put into effect and the sale of British products abroad increased, the wealth of England could not fail to grow at the expense of the Dutch, French, and Spanish.

Just as these acts defined a new economic context for the colonial merchants, so the religious settlement of the Restoration contributed greatly to a new social orientation. In the first years of Charles' reign the century-long struggle between rival groups with conflicting ideas of doctrine, liturgy, ritual, and ecclesiastical policy came to a close. The conclusion rested upon the principles of establishment and toleration. Anglicanism, its clergy freed from fanatics and purifiers, became the unquestioned orthodoxy. The Church of England received all buildings, lands, and tithes within the gift of the crown. Its rivals, though nominally tolerated, were placed under heavy disabilities, ranging from exclusion from the universities to the loss of the franchise in corporate towns. Dissent was recognized but its adherents were excluded from positions of power. Those who sought status and the satisfactions of public influence must live within the confines of the Church.

From this settlement stems that profound distinction in English society between conformity and dissent, church and chapel. The decision "that the *Ecclesia Anglicana* was of another spirit than Geneva" meant that nonconformity became the sole expression of Puritanism.[1] It meant also that nonconformity was to center in the lower classes of society, that New England's Bible Commonwealths would seem to England's rulers not outposts of spiritual enlightenment and social and religious reform but distant, troublesome dependencies, hotbeds of the nonconformist fanaticism that had convulsed England for two decades.

These alterations in English public life at first seemed remote to most Americans. Within a single generation, however, the new meaning of empire altered the development of colonial society. It particularly affected those concerned with overseas commerce. Before two decades had passed it imposed itself forcefully on the daily lives of the New England merchants, affecting all their activities — political, economic, and social.

2

When it became evident that the New England leaders were suspect in Whitehall, a number of disaffected New Englanders who had long nursed grievances against the Puritan regime trooped to the council tables seeking revenge. Among them were merchants hoping to find in England levers of influence by which to arrange circumstances in New England to fit their desires. They were the first to take advantage of the fact that political affiliation with people in official London society, especially with those in circles close to the king, could be the key to commercial success in New England.

Foremost was Samuel Maverick, the ancient settler of Boston, still smarting from the indignities conferred on him by the Puritans. Between 1660 and 1663, appearing before the Council for Foreign Plantations, conferring with the Lord Privy Seal, and writing to

Clarendon frequently and at length, he managed to keep up a steady drumbeat of charges against the New England Puritans. The Massachusetts magistrates, he argued, fancied themselves independent of England, kept most of the population in subjection to their will by limiting the franchise to church members ("noe Church member noe freeman, Noe freeman no voate"), deprived them of liberties due all Englishmen, and had no regard whatever for the interests of the home country. They were, surely, tyrants and traitors. Yet it would take little effort to set things right. At least "3 quarter parts of the inhabitants in the whole Country are loyall subjects to his Majeste in theire harts," and, at the first sign of royal authority, would throw off the Puritan yoke and bring New England with its wealth in land and trade as well as its military power safely into the hands of the king. And in case the rulers were stubborn and refused to hand over the reins of government, "debarringe them from trade a few monethes, will force them to it." [2]

Maverick's purpose was not merely to revenge himself on his enemies but to advance England's fortunes and with them his own by influencing policies then being worked out to reduce the power of the Dutch at sea and in the colonies. He urged the appointment of a royal commission to investigate the situation in the northern American colonies, to put an end to the evils being committed daily in New England, and to arrange for the conquest of New Amsterdam. Hoping to have a share "(as a servant) in that worke," he mustered what support he could to have himself appointed a member of the commission. [3]

At the same time other New England merchants attempted to satisfy their ambitions in more specific ways. Chief among them were Thomas Temple and Thomas Breedon, seeking renewed control of Nova Scotia. Temple had been in possession of the lieutenant governorship and the trade monopoly of Nova Scotia since 1656, but his grip on that province was insecure. He had obtained his franchise through the influence of powerful relatives with whom he shared the trade, and he had taken Breedon into association in order to finance the commercial development of the region. [4] The change of government in England and the invalidation of previous grants was the signal for anyone with the slightest claim to the region to descend on the king and Plantation Board with demands for the proprietorship. Temple, the Kirks — who had been in actual possession as far back as 1628 and had lost out in 1632 when Charles I returned Nova Scotia to France — Thomas Elliott, a groom of the bedchamber, whose only claim seems to have been Clarendon's support, and Breedon himself were the most prominent contenders.[5] In October 1660 Elliott, to the great dismay of Temple and the Kirks, was assigned the governorship. Breedon, although ostensibly representing Temple's interest, took instant advantage of the fact that Elliott's concern was simply to obtain a sinecure and bought out his rights for £600 a year. Then, no doubt with Elliott's help, he managed to obtain the governorship of the territory for himself. At the news of this transaction Temple shipped immediately for London and with the help of his influential relatives managed to get his grant back again, though now burdened with a new tax of £600 a year.[6]

By the end of 1662 Nova Scotia was once again in the hands of Thomas Temple. But in the course of dealing with the councils and personages of the English government Breedon had greatly enhanced his position. Called before the Council for Foreign Plantations early in 1661 to testify on the condition of New England, he had delivered a broadside attack on the Bay Colony. Though it ill became him, he confessed, to say that people to whom His Majesty had granted a general pardon "had so much as a stinking breath," yet it was well known that in Massachusetts "the distinction of freemen and non freemen, members and non members, is as famous as Cavaliers and Roundheads was in England, and will shortly become as odious. . ." He ran through the charges Maverick was making familiar, adding new evidence. That the Puritans were utterly disloyal he had seen not only in their refusal to acknowledge the crown in their legal proceedings but also in their willful hiding of the two regicides who had escaped to New England. When, Breedon declared, he had demanded that the governor arrest them as criminals and traitors, he had been grossly abused, the marshal general "grinning in my face, 'Speake against Whally and Goffe if you dare, if you dare, if you dare.'" New England was far too valuable, he assured the Lords, to be allowed to slip away so easily or to be plucked by illicit French and Dutch traders. A rigorous system of bonding all shipmasters sailing to New England or perhaps a complete embargo might be worth investigating as a temporary measure until the colonies were brought under control.[7]

Breedon's performance was impressive. In its final report the Board recommended the employment of Breedon, "who hath a good estate and interest" in the colonies and who "seems to be a person prudent and fit for such a service" in case Massachusetts did not subject itself to the crown. Breedon returned to Boston newly endowed with influence in London, an outspoken enemy of the Puritans.[8]

Breedon's success in London, though not complete, had been considerable — certainly greater than that of "Colonel" John Scott of Long Island, a rascally adventurer of remarkable ingenuity, at that point representing the Atherton Company of New England. Scott's maneuverings in Whitehall had as their object control of the flat and fertile Narragansett Country that stretched from the western shore of Narragansett Bay to the eastern border of Connecticut. This valuable land had come to the attention of the New England merchants in the previous decade and the Rhode Island Assembly had confirmed a number of Indian gifts or purchases. Of these the largest was the Pettaquamscutt Purchase, a tract approximately twelve miles square containing some of the richest land in Rhode Island.[9] The private acquisition of this vast area by four Rhode Island merchants and John Hull of Boston who intended to profit from agriculture, pasturage, mining, and land sales had at least the tacit consent of the Rhode Island government. But by 1658 it had become clear that if there were many more such transactions Rhode Island would lose control of most of its land. In that year the General Court of the colony ruled that no purchases from the Indians would be legal without the express approval of the Rhode Island authorities.[10] This law did not prevent the Atherton Company, a newly formed group of Massachusetts and Connecticut merchants, from proceeding with their plans. In 1658 they bought from the Indians two strips of land along Narragansett Bay, north and south from the Smiths' trading house at Wickford. In 1660, despite the sharp protests of Rhode Island, the company gained title to the unsold land of the whole Narragansett Country by buying up a mortgage the Indians had been forced to grant the United Colonies in lieu of a fine levied on them for violence.[11]

All this was most promising to the merchants, except that in the eyes of Rhode Island both transactions were illegal. To the company, therefore, it became most important that the Narragansett Country be placed within the bounds of Connecticut, a matter of special interest to the purchasers who came from that colony. At the Restoration both Connecticut and Rhode Island, negotiating in London for royal charters, instructed their agents to make sure that the Narra-gansett Country was clearly incorporated in their territories.

The Atherton merchants were confident of success, for John Winthrop, Jr., one of their members, was Connecticut's agent. For his edification they wrote an elaborate justification for extending the Connecticut border to Narragansett Bay, and at the same time en-trusted their specific agency to Scott.[12] Winthrop, doubly instructed, had no hesitation in asking that the border be fixed at the Bay, and so it was inscribed in the new charter of Connecticut. The Rhode Island representative, Dr. John Clarke, thereupon petitioned the king for a review of the question of borders since the Connecticut charter "hath injuriously swallowed up the one half of our Colonie." Winthrop, though he stood to profit from the new arrangement both as governor of Connecticut and as a leading member of the Atherton Company, was a fair-minded man as well as a good friend of Roger Williams and other Rhode Islanders. He agreed to submit the dif-ferences between the colonies to arbitration. The final award was that Rhode Island would maintain jurisdiction over the Narragansett Country but that "the proprietors and inhabitants of that land about Mr Smithes trading house . . . shall have free liberty to chuse to which of those colonies they will belong." [13]

This decision stripped the company of its legal right to the huge area contained in the Indian mortgage. John Scott was hardly satis-fied with such an arrangement. Nursing a grievance against Winthrop for having been "averse to my persecuting" the affair, he waited until the governor left London and then went to work. First, he added to the membership of the company one Thomas Chiffinch who, as comptroller of the excise and new imposts, page of the backstairs, and keeper of His Majesty's closet and pictures, could be relied on to help arrange things to the company's desire. For good measure Scott distributed gifts where they would be most useful. His reward was a letter from the king addressed to the New England colonies which stated that since the king's loyal subjects, Thomas Chiffinch, John Scott, John Winthrop, etc., had a just right to certain Narragansett lands which they intended to "improve into an English colony and plantation," they were to be left undisturbed and receive the aid of the neighboring colonies. With this, for the time at least, the Atherton Company had to be content.[14]

Other claims against New England were also brought before the

Plantation Board in these years. The undertakers of the defunct iron-works petitioned for help against the seizure of their property by Massachusetts for "supposed" debts. The heirs of Mason and Gorges sought the restitution of their rights to Maine and New Hampshire. And from all sides came complaints that an organization known as the New England Company, chartered by Parliament in 1649 as a fund raising organization to finance charitable and missionary work in New England, had become corrupt and that its large annual income was finding its way into "private men's purses." [15]

3

While responding to immediate pressures with *ad hoc* decisions, the Plantation Board and Privy Council also considered more permanent policies. As petitions, claims, and accusations continued to flow in, it became clear that an extensive investigation would have to be made, and the king in council instructed a royal commission to visit New England. Its purpose was to draw the colonies closely under English rule by insisting that the obligations and the liberties, secular and religious, of Englishmen be maintained. The commission was told not to sit in judgment on any matter within the jurisdiction of the colonies "except those proceedings be expressly contrary to the rules prescribed by the Charter, or . . . arise from some expressions or clauses contained in some grant under our Great Seale of England." This was a wise consideration, especially as a guard against the excessive zeal of one of the four commissioners — Samuel Maverick, "Esquire." [16]

Insofar as the commission aimed to draw the New England colonies more fully into the British political scheme its career in New England was unsuccessful. Where the existing conditions were satisfactory, it met with little opposition; where it discovered abuses and tried to correct them, it was challenged and frustrated. In the three southern colonies of Plymouth, Rhode Island, and Connecticut the commissioners were welcomed both for the protection they offered against the encroachments of Massachusetts and for their support in maintaining the colonies' chartered liberties. All three colonies made what slight changes in their institutions were necessary for complete agreement with the royal demands. [17]

The first difficulty the envoys encountered was the problem of the Connecticut-Rhode Island border and the status of the Atherton claims. This they solved by following their instruction to capitalize on a twenty-year-old deed made out by an Indian sachem of the Narragansett Country "who had submitted that country to the K. Ch. I. of blessed memory." After receiving the sachem and his people "into the King's protection," the commissioners made the whole region a separate royal province but allowed the present magistrates of the district to remain as "Justices of the Peace in the King's Province." As for the Atherton Company, the commissioners declared its purchases void and ordered it to vacate the Narragansett Country forthwith.[18]

In its efforts to come to terms with the Massachusetts authorities the commissioners met with a type of obstinacy for which not even the warnings of Breedon could have prepared them. Excited rumors of Maverick's presence on the commission had brought Puritan hostility to a pitch.[19] By the spring of 1665, when the commissioners presented their credentials to the General Court, they had become devil figures, incarnations of evil to the inflamed Puritans. The General Court declared their commission invalid on the ground that the authority it conveyed conflicted with that of the Massachusetts charter, and refused to authorize their activities within its jurisdiction.

Denied access to the Massachusetts legislature, the commissioners announced their intention of holding a court of appeals in a private dwelling and summoned a number of litigants. To this the General Court replied with an official declaration to the effect that submission to the commissioners' authority was "inconsistent with the maintenance of the laws and authority here so long injoyed and orderly established under the warrant of His Majesties Royall Charter," and that it would not "countenance any" who chose the mission's jurisdiction over its own. At this proclamation, published "with sound of trumpet" in three centers of Boston, one of which happened to be directly under the windows of the commissioners' lodgings, "the Commissioners," as one witness put it, "gave up."[20]

In Maine and New Hampshire they were offered a warmer hospitality, but here too they met with opposition from Massachusetts which had assumed control of both colonies. The commissioners made Maine, which gave evidence of strong opposition to the domination of the Bay Colony, a temporary royal province like the Narragansett Country; despite protests from Massachusetts, they appointed local justices of the peace, "leaving the final determination to his Majesty." In New Hampshire the commissioners attempted to initiate the fortification of the Piscataqua as instructed by calling together an assembly of the inhabitants of the nearby towns. But Massachusetts sent a peremptory order forbidding the meeting and in a curt letter charged the commissioners with having exceeded their authority. Replies by the commissioners to the effect that the General Court's communication was "full of untruth and wanting grammar construction" were to no avail. There was little else they could do and they withdrew from the Piscataqua and from New England, venting their frustration in angry reports to London and elaborate schemes for reducing Massachusetts to subservience.[21]

Thus from the point of view of political organization the commission failed in its attempt to draw Massachusetts closer into the English empire. Yet in a deeper sense the commission had a far-reaching effect on the development of that stubborn colony and on the rest of New England as well. Its presence made unmistakably clear some of the consequences of the political intrusion of empire into the New England scene. It acted like a magnet on the society of the ports, drawing together men of certain common interests, separating others hitherto united by the attraction of conformity and the fear of compulsion. It helped crystallize the social character of the merchant group.

Though the commissioners had been instructed to maintain an impartial position among "the great factions and animosityes" in New England, they soon discovered that if they were to proceed at all it would be necessary for them to rally the support of some part of the population. Maverick took special delight in seeking out and organizing the dissident elements in Massachusetts. On the very afternoon of his arrival in America he wrote to Thomas Breedon in Boston, on whose sympathy he could surely rely, ordering him to reprimand the General Court for its action in an admiralty matter.[22] He attempted to lay the groundwork for the success of the commission's efforts in Massachusetts by making a three-week tour of the port towns, renewing old friendships, managing, he later boasted, to "undeceive both Majestrates, Ministers and other considerable persons." Upon their arrival in Boston the commissioners made Breedon's house their headquarters, which became the meeting place for their sympathizers and for the enemies of the ruling magistrates. It was here that they attempted to assert their authority by sitting as a court of appeal. Never was a political commission less suited for the judicial role. The main case they chose to call never came to trial; it foundered on the rock of Puritan intractability. Yet it was important, for it symbolized the subtler effects of the commission in New England.[23]

The dispute they futilely attempted to reopen centered on the charge of the merchant Thomas Deane that Joshua Scottow, another merchant, was dealing in smuggled French goods, hence violating the navigation acts.[24] In reviving this old dispute which had been dropped by the General Court for insufficient evidence in 1661 the commissioners added impetus to important divisive forces at work in New England. Deane and Scottow were at opposite extremes in the spectrum of merchant personalities and interests and stood at opposite poles in the social and political geography of New England.

Scottow, then fifty years old, had immigrated in the Puritan wave of the 1630's and had been accepted into the First Church before the decade was out.[25] Like Keayne, profoundly devout, drawn by tensions that could best be relieved by writing passionate moral exhortations, he rose slowly to a prominent position in Boston. He kept as sharp a watch for opportunities in business as he did for moral lapses, and during the fifties became involved with La Tour in the development of the Acadian trade. His French contacts probably date from this period. To him the Restoration was the catastrophe it was for divines like John Davenport; the new restrictions on trade appeared to him no less evil than the religious settlement.

Deane, on the other hand, twenty-four years old, had arrived in Boston just after the Restoration along with his friends Thomas Kellond and Thomas Kirke who were also starting out in trade. All three of them were zealous in the royal cause and conceived of New England as a dependency inconveniently full of mulish nonconformists, yet a place where a quick profit might be turned. As an eligible young Englishman Deane probably had his pick of the marriageable girls, and in 1665 he selected the daughter of the merchant William Browne of Salem, an heiress whose dowry was well over £800.[26]

The careers of these two men continued to diverge after 1665 and concluded in complete and significant contrast. Deane applied himself to trade in Boston assiduously, flourishing as a factor for London exporters who "filled my hands with businesse," he later wrote, because of his willingness to accommodate them with advances out of his own funds. In 1678, a widower with capital and excellent connections in America, he returned to England where he set up as a London merchant in the colonial trade. Successful there as in New England, he ended his career a wealthy man and died in the same Hampshire countryside in which he had been born.[27]

Scottow, meanwhile, ever restless, bought land in Scarborough, Maine, and settled in that near-wilderness spot in 1670. There he engaged in the fisheries, became something of a public man, and played a notable if controversial part in King Philip's War.[28] All the while he was consumed by remorse as he saw about him the decay of the Bible Commonwealth which had all but justified his existence to him. As characteristic of Scottow as were cautious, self-satisfied business letters characteristic of Deane was the tract he published in 1691 entitled *Old Men's Tears for their own Declension mixed with Fears of their and posterities falling off from New England's Primitive Constitution.* In this enthusiastic lament Scottow cursed the evils of the day as mockeries of the Puritans' original purposes.

New-England is not to be found in *New-England*, nor *Boston* in *Boston;* it is become a lost Town (as at first it was called) we must now cry out, our *Leanness*, our *Leanness*, our *Apostacy*, our *Atheism, Spiritual Idolatry, Adultery, Formality in Worship, carnal and vain Confidence* in Church-Privileges, forgetting of GOD our Rock, and Multitude of other Abominations. . .[29]

For him there remained only to record for posterity this descent from virtue, a task which he accomplished in 1694 in his *Narrative of the Planting of the Massachusetts Colony. . .*[30]

Thus rekindling the embers of the Deane-Scottow case, the commissioners brought into public controversy representatives of two opposing types within the merchant group. Their power to make manifest certain latent social divisions was more broadly displayed a year later when the Bay Colony balked at the king's order to send representatives to England to answer the reports of the commissioners.[31] To the Court's chagrin a petition from a number of Massachusetts towns was submitted warning against further antagonism to the king, recalling that the charter by which Massachusetts justified its intransigeance had defined the Bay Colony as a royal dominion, and requesting that the agents be sent. At least 134 signatures were attached, though "hundreds more might have been had." [32] An analysis of the twenty-five names from Boston reveals the characteristics of the royalist party in that town. Of the twenty-three whose occupations are known, eighteen were merchants, three were artisans, and two were physicians.[33] Of the full twenty-five, only three had been freemen before the arrival of the commissioners; three others had been granted that status since 1664. Ten of the nineteen signers whose date of immigration is known reached Boston in 1659 or after. Only six of the petitioners are known to have been church members in 1666.[34]

Thus sympathy for and outspoken support of the commissioners in Boston centered in the recently arrived merchants without church affiliation or the franchise. As the commission worked its way through the northern New England towns and villages it continued to attract and repel, separating the Deanes from the Scottows. In Maine and New Hampshire it defined mercantile family groups whose rivalries dominated local politics for the next half-century. Their appointees as justices of the peace in Maine, led by Francis Champernowne and Robert Cutts of Kittery, gave recognition to the large number of settlers of little sympathy for Puritanism, men largely from the west country of England, fishermen, fishing merchants, and the surviving servants and agents of Mason and Gorges.[35]

The division they caused among the New Hampshire merchants was particularly sharp. Trade in the towns along the Piscataqua, based on the timber and fishing industries, had grown rapidly in the fifties and Maverick's report that "There is usually loaden thence above twenty ships yearly" was not exaggerated.[36] The merchants of the region were being recruited from two main sources. A number of established merchants of the Bay Colony like Valentine Hill or younger Massachusetts men like William and Richard Waldron had moved north to Dover and Strawberry Bank (Portsmouth), New Hampshire, to join in the new developments there.[37] By virtue of the limited franchise and the General Court's power of public appointment these men had come to dominate the political life of the infant communities. Meanwhile, west-country fishermen and other non-Puritan settlers had moved from the coastal islands and the northern villages into the same region. Some of them rose quickly as mill-owners, timber merchants, and fish wholesalers. By 1665 they stood in defiant opposition to the Massachusetts group.

The presence of the commissioners in New Hampshire touched off their flammable resentments. Twelve of the anti-Massachusetts group in Portsmouth appealed to the royal officers, complaining of their forced subjection to Massachusetts "under which power five or six of the richest men of this parish have ruled and ordered all offices, both civil and military, at their pleasure, and none durst make opposition for fear of great fines or long imprisonment." Begging for the right to worship in the Anglican ritual and for the benefits of the franchise, they singled out as the leading offenders Reverend Joshua Moody, the Puritan leader of Dover, and the merchants Richard and John Cutts, Elias Stileman, Nathaniel Fryer, and Bryan Pendleton. Among the twelve signatures were the names, now linked in a public document for the first time, of a number of New Hampshire merchants for whom the issues of 1665 were the first of a series in which they found a common position between London and Boston: Francis Champernowne, John Sherburn, Sam Fernald, John Partridge, Mark Hunking, John Frost, Joseph Atkinson, and George Walton. The same men headed a second petition, this one from all the towns of New Hampshire, in which the signers described themselves as "transported with joy" at His Majesty's interest in the colony and prayed that their government be joined to that of the new royal province of Maine.[38]

The departure of the commission from New England did not put an end to the animosities. The Puritan magistrates, uninclined to show charity to their enemies, indulged in a fit of anger against those who had sided with the commissioners. The General Court's summons to Abraham Corbett, the Portsmouth distiller, "to answer for his tumultuous and seditious practices against this government" and its orders to the leading Massachusetts petitioners "to attend this Court in October next, to answer for the same," further animated the controversy. When the petition was debated in the Court it developed that sympathy for the signers had seeped into the very heart of that body, for the legislators Dennison, Bradstreet, Pynchon, Browne, Corwin, and Davis — all merchants — came to their defense.[39]

To the Puritan stalwarts it must have seemed that God's blessing lay on them and on their policy of stubborn independence. For, as in the case of the Laud Commission a full generation earlier, the crown was unable to support its representations with force. Convulsed by the plague of 1665, the great fire of 1666, war, and the fall of Clarendon, the home government could spare little time for the affairs of New England. Massachusetts, freed from the fear of immediate punishment, continued the campaign against its critics and resumed the government of Maine.[40]

One important aspect of the commission of 1664 was hidden from the eyes of contemporaries. The commissioners, particularly Maverick and Sir Robert Carr, believed that the government of the colonies was part of the system of patronage and sinecures that had its center in London. All four commissioners expected to be rewarded for their services by governmental posts, perquisites, or gifts in the colonies. Carr's need or greed was more evident than that of the others, and, disappointed in his expectations of large personal gain in the conquest of the Delaware region, he reminded Lord Arlington of the king's promise to him "in your owne house, at a private musicke," and requested a portion of the Narragansett Country. Maverick, who seems to have found New York more congenial than Boston after the commissioners' departure from New England, wrote thanks to the Duke of York for "the guift of the house in the Broadway." The positions in the colonies that were becoming available to the government for patronage, being necessarily connected with the enforcement of trade regulations or endowed with the power to grant land and economic privileges, were of vital concern to the merchants. The New Englanders would quickly learn, if they did not already know, that the path to such favors stretched across the Atlantic and wound through the maze of English government and London society.[41]

4

The commission of 1664 helped introduce New England to the political meaning of empire. In the same decade its economic meaning also became clear as the merchants learned the importance to their business enterprises of membership in England's Atlantic community.

Before 1676 circumstances tended to exaggerate the benefits of operating as colonials in the new British commercial system. The immediate effect of the navigation laws was negligible. For the most part, the trade that had been built up by the New England merchants conformed to the requirements of the laws of 1660 and 1663. Nothing in these regulations restricted the merchants' exports of fish, provisions, and lumber to the Atlantic islands and Europe.[42] The ban on foreign merchants engaging in the English plantation trade was a boon as it eliminated competition.[43] The Staple Act of 1663 which prohibited colonials from importing goods directly from Europe was only slightly if at all injurious to them since their imported manufactures came mainly from England. Moreover, the act had exempted from the ban on direct foreign imports salt, vital for the New England fisheries, and wines from Madeira and the Azores, which had become standard returns from the adventures to the Wine Islands.

Thus the heart of New England's commerce was mercantilistically sound. But were its extremities? Was it legal to import wines from the Canary Islands which, unlike Madeira and the Azores, were Spanish, not Portuguese? Were Ireland and Scotland actually to be considered outside the home islands for the purpose of trade? If so, the New Englanders were violating the staple act by importing from those northern dependencies anything but servants, horses, and provisions, and were flouting the enumeration clause by exporting tobacco to them. Were the Channel Islands — Jersey and Guernsey — between England and France to be considered foreign territory despite the fact that they were British possessions? If so most of the traffic with those places was illegal. No more tobacco was to be shipped to Holland, and no more manufactures were to be imported from Dutch markets.[44]

The Canaries, Scotland, Ireland, the Channel Islands, Holland — these were the fringes of the New Englanders' commercial system and these were the parts of it which could immediately have been affected by the navigation laws. But before 1676 New Englanders were not disturbed even in these relatively minor parts of their trade, for enforcement of the navigation laws had to await a more tranquil period in English affairs than that from 1660–1675. Orders were sent to the governors to enforce the laws in every detail, but until the Dutch wars were over the English government could do no more than write instructions and exhort the colonial magistrates.

One way, however, in which the new political control of commerce affected the New England merchants adversely before the middle of the eighth decade soon became apparent. It lay in the fact that the merchants' economic activities were now at the mercy of diplomatic decisions made by European statesmen motivated by considerations utterly unrelated to New England or its merchants.

Thus it was that within ten years after the Restoration the profitable trade of Nova Scotia, built up by the efforts of Temple, Breedon, and their associates, was wiped out at a stroke. Temple had returned from England the uncontested possessor of the governmental rights to Nova Scotia; but he was in debt to the merchants who had financed his operations and had taken care of the trade in his absence. Breedon was still the financial master of the situation, and by 1665 he, together with his brother John, of London, and the well-known merchant Thomas Bell, also of London, had increased their hold over Temple to the extent of £5,500.[45] That Temple managed to pay off this debt in a few years was no fault of these creditors, for they used every device available to squeeze him and the trade, profiting, according to Sir Thomas, 100 per cent on the goods they sold him and charging him £180 to transmit the yearly £600 to Elliott. After ridding himself of this set of leeches, Temple turned to the Bostonians Hezekiah Usher and Samuel Shrimpton for financial aid; by 1668 he owed them £2,700. But the end of his troubles and the merchants' profits was at hand for, in the Treaty of Breda of 1667, Charles II ceded Nova Scotia to France in return for the West Indian islands of Antigua, Montserrat, and the conquered half of St. Christophers. Temple protested vehemently against this betrayal of his interests as did the Massachusetts government, mindful of the dangers of French control of the Nova Scotia fisheries and fur trade. It was useless. They had no choice but to concede to a decision made 3,000 miles away by men concerned with dynastic and strategic problems.[46]

Thus the few merchants concerned with the Nova Scotia trade had reason to regret New England's lack of autonomy. Yet even they, with many irons in the fire, stood greatly to profit by England's mercantilism. The West Indian trade soared and, if Hezekiah Usher could justly have complained of the Treaty of Breda, he must at the same time have attributed not a little of his large success in the West Indian trade [47] to the navigation act that banned foreign vessels from the plantations. The islanders, in fact, were becoming increasingly dependent on shipments of goods and provisions from New England. In 1668 a petition from Nevis stated that when the New England merchants, fined for selling above set prices, withdrew their trade saying that the islanders should "suck their paws as bears did in their country in the winter until those usages were forborne," the inhabitants of Nevis had been faced with a famine. Three years later the governor of the Leewards begged the home authorities for shipments of goods direct from England, complaining of the profiteering of the New Englanders.[48] By 1677 the New England merchants dominated the inter-plantation trade of the West Indies.[49]

The flourishing trade in Caribbean products fed not only the merchants' European trade but the local New England market as well. This was particularly true in the case of sugar which was now put to a new use in the manufacture of rum. Distilleries, introduced in New England perhaps by Emmanuel Downing of Salem,[50] multiplied rapidly to cope with the demand for the liquor. Their proliferation was so great that by 1661 the overproduction of rum was declared by the General Court to be a menace to society, and in 1667 that body had to take action against the innkeepers who had been selling beer watered with the cheap sugar drink.[51] Most important to the merchants was the fact that rum was becoming a prime ingredient in the new and extremely profitable Newfoundland trade.

The New England merchants had sent trading vessels to Newfoundland as early as the first years of the Puritan settlements, but until the end of the Commonwealth period no great advances were made in the traffic with that island. In the fifties and in the first decade after the Restoration, with the local fishery safely in their own power, the New England merchants expanded their interests in the northern grounds. To some extent they sought the fish available there and engaged in buying up boatloads for sale either to European shipmasters or to their usual buyers in the Wine Islands, Spain, and the West Indies. But of more value to them in this period was the excellent market they found in Newfoundland for their provisions, timber products, and imported tropical goods. The growing number of settlers as well as the transient fishing population were eager for the bread, peas, flour, beef, pork, butter, tar, lumber, sugar, molasses, and tobacco the merchants could supply. In return the New Englanders received bills of exchange on England, which they could sell at home for 25 per cent profit, as well as coin, fishing equipment, and European goods, not all of them from England. Their cheaply produced rum became a valuable commodity in this trade, and as early as 1677 England instructed the commodore at Newfoundland to ascertain to what extent the liquors sold by the New Englanders were responsible for the debauchery of the fishermen.[52]

This suspicion of the New Englanders' motives in entering the Newfoundland trade was general in London circles. The colonials were becoming interested in the region at a time when control of the Newfoundland fishing industry was contested by two groups of Englishmen: the London merchants, seeking the profits from transporting fish prepared by a permanently settled colony of fishermen on the island; and the west-countrymen, striving to discourage settlement in order to preserve the preëminence they still had in the yearly fishing fleets. To both, the New England merchants were a threat. The westerners, who had not so long before been forced out of the New England waters, complained that the Americans were corrupting their fishermen with liquor, entangling them in debts, and encouraging them to desert to easier lives in New England. They argued that a settled colony in Newfoundland would eventually come under the complete control of New England just as the Maine settlements had — a sentiment in which the Privy Council concurred. The Londoners feared the competition of New Englanders both in the provision and the carrying trades. Both groups suspected the New England merchants of using Newfoundland as a base for smuggling operations since contact could be made there with French and Dutch shipmasters willing to dispose of foreign manufactures.[53]

Despite these criticisms New England's trade with Newfoundland not only was perfectly in accord with the navigation acts but also was encouraged by the merchants' situation within the British community. Though strict mercantilists like Josiah Child objected to New England's participation in the commerce on theoretical grounds, others, like the London merchant John Gould, pointed out that if provisions came to the fishermen from one of the colonies instead of from England nothing was lost, for eventually the trade

The Saugus Ironworks in 1650 (Restoration)

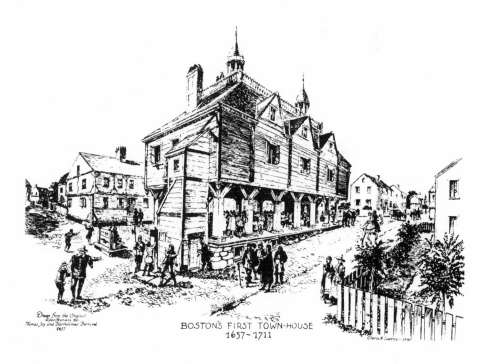

Drawn from the Original
Specifications by
Thomas Joy and Bartholomew Barnard
1657

BOSTON'S FIRST TOWN-HOUSE
1657~1711

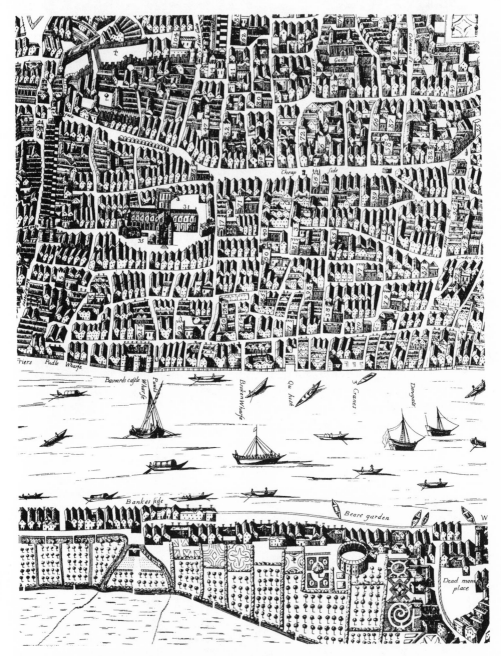

The Cheapside-Cornhill District of London in 1658

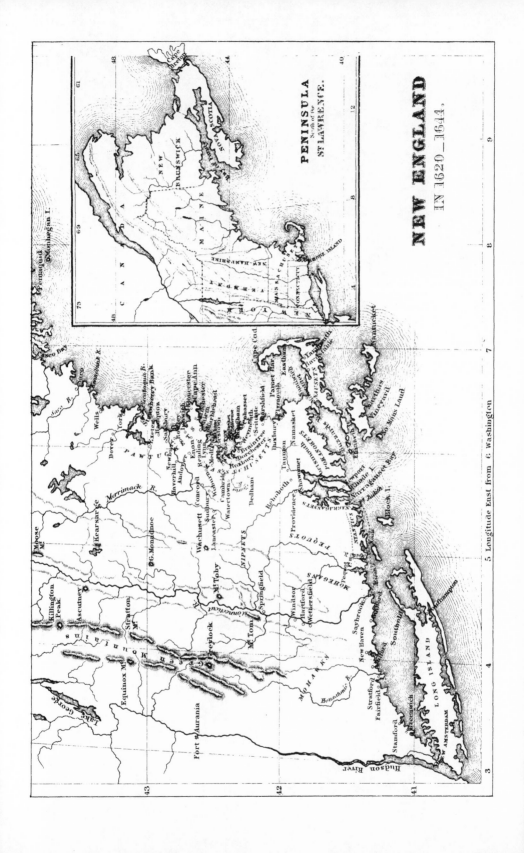

NEW ENGLAND
IN 1620-1644.

PENINSULA
North of the
ST. LAWRENCE.

Longitude East from G. Washington

"circles to England." If the island and the fishing banks had been in the control of the French, English colonials would have been denied access to the trade. Britishers, the New Englanders were free to enter the northern dependency.[54]

Newfoundland was but one of the many points in the Atlantic world where the rival European state systems conflicted. Unattached colonials were quickly absorbed by the European powers, and unsettled or unprotected places in the western hemisphere where wealth was easily extracted were fair game for all. When, in the early 1670's, the New England merchants, led by one of the Cutts brothers, joined with other Englishmen in invading the Gulf of Campeche, weakly held by the Spaniards, to cut and remove the valuable logwood trees, they were following the accepted pattern of mercantile warfare.[55] In this almost continuous maritime conflict the offensive was taken by privateersmen, against whom coastal fortifications and convoys were not always adequate protection.

In such a situation the ambition of the Puritans to make of New England an independent, semi-isolated American commonwealth was impractical. With its merchants capitalizing in every way possible on their membership in the English community, New England moved steadily, if reluctantly, toward full participation in the conflict of nations. In 1666, during the second Dutch war, when privateers infested the American coastal waters, the governor and Council issued a commission to Benjamin Gillan of the *Mary Ruth* to seize what French and Dutch vessels he could and bring them to Boston to be judged as prizes. Sympathy for the Puritan cause and antipathy to the new regime in England did not bind merchants to neutrality in international affairs. John Hull complained that in their sea warfare the Dutchmen "make no difference between New England and Old," but he himself did not refrain from investing in privateer voyages. During the third Dutch war pressure on the General Court to support the merchants by freely issuing letters of reprisal rose sharply after seven heavily loaded New England vessels were lost to the enemy within a single year. If Freke, Deane, Wharton, and Paige were the more readily refused such permission because of their declared disaffection for the Massachusetts government, they could, like Joseph Dudson, operate on commissions issued by such English officials as Sir William Stapleton, governor of the Leewards.[56]

None knew better than the merchants how important it was that England's wars were New England's too. Even if their shipping had been untouched by enemy freebooters and if they had had no temptation at all to join in the business of privateering, they would have been deeply affected by England's conflicts. The extension of European wars to the colonial world meant ruined crops, incomplete cargoes, and broken voyages, but it also meant huge orders for provisions which the merchants were particularly eager to supply after Massachusetts promised to pay the bill with tax money.[57] Above all, wars meant ships, and ships meant masts, spars, and tar — naval stores of all sorts — of which New England had the finest natural supply available outside the Baltic.

The importance to England of New Hampshire's magnificent stands of timber had been made clear during the first Dutch war when Nehemiah Bourne, the ex-Boston merchant, then a navy commissioner, agreed to furnish three cargoes of American masts. Though the first of these arrived after the main fighting was over, there was no doubt that a major source of naval timber had been uncovered. Thereafter New England masts arrived regularly to ease the chronic shortages in the navy yards.[58] New England masts were among those supplied to the Navy by the first post-Restoration contractor, William Wood, as well as by his successors, Pepys' friend Sir William Warren, Captain John Taylor, Sir Josiah Child, and Sir John Shorter.[59] In 1666, when the supply of naval stores was completely exhausted, a panic in London was quieted by the announcement of the arrival of a number of New England masts, "a blessing," wrote Pepys, "mighty unexpected, and without which, if for nothing else, we must have failed the next year." [60]

The Massachusetts legislators, hoping to counteract the effect of the commissioners' report and their own failure to support a military expedition against Canada, could not have chosen more wisely than they did in 1666 when they sent the king a gift of twenty-eight New England masts.[61] Shrewd dealers started to pile up reserves of American timber. In 1670, when it was reliably reported that ten shiploads of masts were being exported every year from Portsmouth, New Hampshire, Warren had 259 New England masts, worth at least £135 each, ready for sale to the Navy. By 1672, when the third Dutch war was beginning to reduce all naval supplies to disaster levels, New England timber, despite its high price, had become vitally necessary for the functioning of England's Navy.[62]

The mast trade was big business — bigger than any yet seen in New England. Its organization depended on two groups of men, the London entrepreneurs who made the contracts with the government and the New England merchants who furnished the timber. The former were necessarily powerful merchants, for dealings in timber tied up large amounts of capital and entailed risks beyond the capacity of small jobbers.[63] These contractors operated with all the arts of high-pressure negotiators, from cornering the supply to cultivating friendships with government officials like Pepys. Of the colonial merchants engaged in the American end of the business, the most successful were those with the best connections in London, especially with the London contractors. The appearance in New Hampshire after the Restoration of William Vaughan, brought up in the household of the merchant-banker Sir Josiah Child, was undoubtedly related to the fact that Child was at that time deeply involved in the mast business.[64] But though Vaughan immediately assumed a large role in the affairs of New Hampshire he does not seem to have been able to put his relationship to his "master" [65] to full use. It was, instead, Peter Lidget, who moved from Barbados to Boston after 1651, partner of Thomas Deane and a man of standing in the London business community, who seems to have gained the greatest part of the naval contractors' orders. In 1668 he was supplying three of the four main mast dealers, including Vaughan's patron, Child, and at his death a decade later his accounts showed balances with every London merchant known to have been engaged in the American mast trade up to that time.[66]

Even in these years it was clear that the greatest profits would be extracted from the mast trade by the merchants who could obtain a complete monopoly of the navy contracts and fill them with the aid of personal agents who held the exclusive rights to the mast trees in New Hampshire. Such a tightly controlled mast trust did develop at the end of the century,[67] but in these earlier years the necessary monopolies on both sides of the Atlantic could not be maintained. In England the rivalries among governmental and business cliques were too intense and the system of awarding contracts too susceptible to a variety of pressures to allow long-term monopolies. In New England also the time was not ripe for such exclusive control, as Richard Wharton discovered in 1670 when a company

he organized was granted a ten-year monopoly of all naval stores
production in both the Massachusetts and Plymouth colonies; little
if anything came of this early attempt.[68] The governmental mecha-
nisms necessary to enforce such a monopoly were not yet effective;
influence in the local government by men such as Wharton was
insecure; and the timber trade in New Hampshire was still competitive and loosely organized.

By the end of the Dutch wars the mast trade had become a conspicuous element in the social as well as the economic life of New
Hampshire. In those who enjoyed its benefits it helped nourish a
growing sense of distinctiveness. Like the commission of 1664 it
became a precipitant of the emerging social structure of New
England.

5

By the middle of the eighth decade it was clear that the merchant
group, emerging from the constrictions of a medieval social order,
was an effective agent of change in the nascent society of colonial
New England. Not all the merchants, to be sure, had separated
themselves from the Puritan style of life; a few of them, vestiges of
the past, clung to the old ways, struggling as champions of God in
daily battle with Mammon. But now, a half-century after the Great
Migration, such men were becoming archaic types among the New
England merchants.

John Hull, a prototype of the Puritan merchant, survived into his
sixtieth year, 1683, and left both his material and spiritual legacy to
his famous son-in-law, the diarist Samuel Sewall. The long career of
the latter, a third generation merchant, reflects the passing of the
Puritan tradition. In all outward ways Sewall kept the faith. He per-
petuated the forms as well as the ethics of Puritanism. In his early
years, undecided between trade and the ministry, plagued by dreams
of the "*sedes beatorum*," he endured inward struggles capable of
transforming a "proper fair" morning into one "metaphoric, dismal,
dark and portentous, some prodigie appearing in every corner of
the skies." [69] But the intensity of his spiritual life slackened as the
years passed. He died neither sunk in a convulsion of brooding
introspection like Robert Keayne nor uplifted in grim rectitude like
the elder Winthrop but evenly at peace with God and man, a genial
patriarch, honorable and old-fashioned.

With Sewall were others of similar interests and tempers who, like Joshua Scottow, saw only evil in the ways of the younger generation. Yet their numbers were diminishing rapidly, and the continuity of such types was ended in the fourth generation. Of the fourteen children born to Hannah Hull Sewall nine reached maturity, but none of their lives were cut to the pattern of her father's or husband's.

Hull, Sewall, and Scottow were exceptions among the commercial leaders of New England. The majority of the merchants, socially as well as economically oriented toward England, felt common bonds drawing them together, distinguishing them from other settlers in the New England communities. Important differences among them were suppressed as they stood together in opposition to the reigning magistrates.

This sense of separateness and group identification among the merchants revealed itself most dramatically in conflicts with authority. But its most profound effect on the development of New England society could not easily have been observed by contemporaries. In the genealogy of the merchant families lies a true indication of the force of this growing sense of distinctiveness.

The most important fact embedded in the genealogy of the merchant families is the extent of intermarriage among the descendants of the successful first generation tradesmen.[70] Eligibility for marriage, in fact, seems to have been effectively restricted to other children of merchants or to the sons and daughters of clergymen. By the third generation the merchants in each locality formed what amounted to a single interrelated family; the bonds of marriage united almost every merchant with every other merchant in the same immediate vicinity. Thus, for example, by the marriages of the ten children of the immigrants William and Edward Tyng those venerable merchants became related to the Bradstreets, Whartons, Brattles, Dudleys, the Searles of Barbados, the Savages, Ushers, and Gibbonses — all merchant families. The Winthrop, Jr. children married into the Palmes and Corwin families, the latter already connected to the Browne, Lynde, and Wolcott clans. Elizabeth and Charles Lidget, children of the mast merchant Peter Lidget, married respectively John Usher, son of old Hezekiah the bookseller-merchant, and Bethiah Shrimpton, daughter of the immigrant brazier Henry Shrimpton. Through the Ushers and the Shrimptons

A PARTIAL RECONSTRUCTION OF THE TYNG-USHER CONNECTIONS IN THE SECOND GENERATION

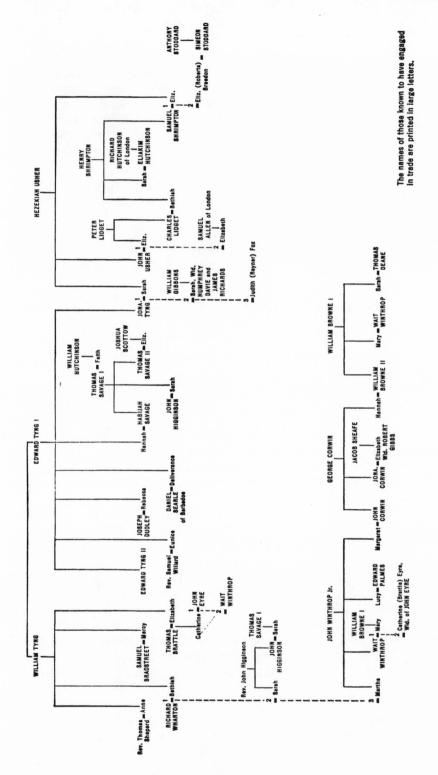

The names of those known to have engaged
in trade are printed in large letters.

the Lidget family gained kinship associations with the Tyng tribe as well as with the Hutchinsons, Breedons, and Stoddards. The Sheafe and Gibbs families were linked with the Corwins, Brownes, and Winthrops by the marriage of Captain George Corwin's son Jonathan to Elizabeth Sheafe Gibbs. The alliance between the Vaughans and Waldrons, leaders of the Massachusetts faction in New Hampshire, was cemented by the marriage of Richard Waldron to Eleanor Vaughan, the former having been married earlier to Hannah Cutts, daughter of the merchant John. John Hinckes was Nathaniel Fryer's son-in-law; Champernowne married Robert Cutts' widow by whom he became related to the Humphreys and Eliots. By the end of the century the three leading merchant families of Kittery, Maine — the Frosts, Brays, and Pepperells — were also intermarried.

The extent of intermarriage among the merchant families may in part be accounted for by the frequency of remarriages by widows and widowers. Thus, for example, Richard Wharton in the course of his thirty years in New England married successively daughters of the Tyng, Higginson, and Winthrop families. John, the graceless, grasping son of Hezekiah Usher (who himself had taken no less than three wives), increased the wealth brought him by his first wife, Elizabeth Lidget, by that of his second, Elizabeth Allen, whose father had bought the proprietary rights of New Hampshire from the Masons. John Usher's sister Sarah was followed as the wife of Jonathan Tyng by Sarah Gibbons, already widowed by the merchants Humphrey Davie and James Richards. She, in turn, was succeeded by Judith (Reyner) Fox. By the last two of his four marriages Lawrence Hammond, the Charlestown merchant, became related to the Willoughby and Gerrish families.

Forming in the two decades after the Restoration a group of increasing social cohesiveness, the merchants unmistakably and relentlessly were breaking through the lines of the existing social organizations.

For most of them the importance of church membership was disappearing. The commissioner who had said that the New Englanders "will marry their children to those whom they will not admit to baptisme, if they be rich" [71] had exaggerated, but he had exaggerated the truth. Of the four Tyng sisters, for example, Anne married the distinguished minister Thomas Shepard; Mercy chose

Samuel Bradstreet, son of the magistrate Simon, who had spent four years in Europe and had come back to sign the petition supporting the commissioners; Bethiah married none other than Richard Wharton; and Elizabeth, the merchant Thomas Brattle, another petitioner. Anna Keayne, the granddaughter and heiress of old Robert, survived a fantastic marriage arranged for her by an unscrupulous pair of local fortune-hunters to settle down happily as the wife of the newly arrived merchant Nicholas Paige, another signer of the petition of 1666 and a man who in his long stay in the colonies did not associate himself with any nonconformist church.[72]

Not only had membership in a Puritan church ceased to be a criterion of social acceptability among the merchant families, but by the third generation the interrelated merchant group showed signs of moving toward the still officially anathemized Church of England. Outspoken Anglicans like Wharton married freely into the group, and there is no indication that that outstanding entrepreneur felt discomfort in being related by marriage to Reverends Thomas Shepard and Samuel Willard. Marrying the heiress daughter of a nonconformist colonial seems, in fact, to have been a normal procedure for ambitious young Englishmen making careers for themselves in American trade, and their eligibility was not diminished by their Anglicanism. On the contrary, by the mid-seventies they seem to have had the balance of social influence with them. More frequently than not they were able to maintain their Anglicanism, if not blatantly, like Breedon, then quietly, like Paige. Peter Lidget pursued his mast business in utter disregard of his standing among Puritans like Scottow. His daughter Elizabeth took her husband John Usher with her into the Anglican communion, and his son Charles, married to one of the richest heiresses of the old Puritan group, Bethiah Shrimpton, led Boston in the establishment of an Anglican Church before returning permanently to England.[73]

Among New Hampshire and Maine merchants Anglicanism was still identified with the proprietary faction led by Champernowne; consequently as yet it had little attraction for the friends of Waldron and Vaughan. However, in Connecticut Episcopacy found numerous sympathizers, especially among the traders of Stratford and Fairfield in continuous contact with royalist New York and other mercantile centers.[74] Rhode Island, still a babel of dissenting sects, nourished the seeds of its famous eighteenth-century Episcopal institutions in the sympathies of the two Richard Smiths and in the beginnings of a sudden interest in the colony by recently arrived English merchants like Thomas Brinley and Stephen Burton who saw greater opportunities in the undeveloped Narragansett Bay area than in the relatively crowded Boston Bay region.[75]

If the mercantile group cut across the lines of the once powerful institution of the Puritan church, so too did it ignore the differences between freemen and non-freemen. The newcomers among the merchants valued the franchise as a means of forcing decisions that favored their interests. Yet many waited years before claiming such a right, and there is no indication that Maverick's frantic concern over the franchise was widespread among them. Some, in fact, found its obligations more onerous than its privileges beneficial and refused to accept the rights of freemen when they were offered to them.[76] In 1689 a number of Connecticut merchants including Winthrop, Jr.'s son-in-law Edward Palmes refused to become freemen in protest against the resumption of the charter government.[77]

Thus the social distinctions derived from the early institutions of church and state were no longer effective among the majority of the merchants. This fact in itself constituted a threat to the guardians of the old order, for the merchants were now in a position to challenge their authority. Though the merchants' influence did not yet extend over the political system, it reached into those subtle, fundamental attitudes and assumptions which ultimately determine institutions.

In the larger port towns of provincial New England, particularly those in continuous touch with Europe, the business community represented the spirit of a new age. Its guiding principles were not social stability, order, and the discipline of the senses, but mobility, growth, and the enjoyment of life. Citizens of an international trading world as well as of New England colonies, the merchants took the pattern for their conduct not from the Bible or from parental teachings but from their picture of life in Restoration England. To the watchmen of the holy citadel nothing could have been more insidious.

Though the strong right arm and the spiritual vision of pristine Puritanism weakened and fell, its voice remained, rising ever more clearly from the orthodox pulpits.[78] The ministers of the gospel saw about them the evidence of a decay of piety, a "declension" in spirituality, and the calamitous failure to perpetuate the ideals and standards of the Founders. Instead of devotion to the life of the spirit they saw only a mad pursuit of gain by a people rotten with the sin of pride. Horrified and disgusted, they denounced the wicked, exhorted the sluggish, and threatened the stubborn. At trade and its propagators they hurled their bitterest invective, for in them lay one of the deep roots of malignancy.

Again and again, at every opportunity, and especially when called to preach before the General Court of Massachusetts, the ministers reiterated the theme that New England had forsaken its original purpose and now ran idolatrous after new gods. No one voiced this belief more powerfully than John Higginson in his 1663 election day sermon, *The Cause of God and His People in New England* . . . The Salem minister, two of whose sons became important merchants and whose daughter Sarah was within the decade to marry Richard Wharton,[79] cried out against the notion that the purpose of God in establishing New England was to further separatism, toleration, or "the getting of this World's good." On the contrary, Higginson said, "when the Lord stirred up the spirits of so many of his people to come over into this wilderness, it was not for worldly wealth, or a better livelyhood here for the outward man," but rather for the furtherance of the "Reformation of Religion according to God's word."

My Fathers and Brethren, this is never to be forgotten, that *New-England is originally a plantation of Religion, not a plantation of Trade.*
Let Merchants and such as are increasing *Cent per Cent* remember this, Let others that have come over since at several times understand this, that worldly gain was not the end and designe of the people of *New-England*, but *Religion.* And if any man amongst us make Religion as *twelve*, and the world as *thirteen*, let such an one know he hath neither the spirit of a true *New-England man* nor yet of a *sincere Christian.*[80]

Higginson's *Cause of God* intoned what became a familiar note in the jeremiads trumpeted by the ministers at a fallen people. Year after year it was heard, and in 1676 it received a full orchestration by Increase Mather:

It was in respect to some worldly accomodation that other Plantations were erected, but *Religion and not the World* was that which our Fathers came hither for . . . *Pure Worship and Ordinances* without the mixture of humane Inventions was that which the first Fathers of this Colony designed in their coming hither. We are the Children of the good old *Non-Conformists* . . . And therefore that woful neglect of the *Rising Generation* which hath bin amongst us, is a sad sign that we have in great part forgotten our *Errand* in this Wilderness; and then why should we marvail that God taketh no pleasure in our young men, but they are numbred for the Sword, the present judgment lighting chiefly upon the *Rising Generation.*

Mather included this charge in the *Necessity of Reformation* he wrote for the synod of 1679.[81]

If the purpose of New England had fallen from the perpetuation of God's word to the furtherance of trade, its outward life — "carriage," manners — had plummeted to the depths. The modest, humble garb and conduct of the Fathers had been succeeded by fearful extravagances: "Laying out of the hair, Borders, naked Neck and Arms, or, which is more abominable, naked Breasts, and mixed Dancings, light behaviour and expressions, sinful Company-keeping with light and vain persons." Instead of looking to the Bible and the past for the proper style of life, the younger generations were looking abroad to the English Gomorrah seeking "*Courtly Pomp and Delicacy*." "A proud Fashion no sooner comes into the Country," said Increase Mather,

but the *haughty Daughters of Zion* in this place are taking it up, and thereby the whole land is at last infected. What shall we say when men are seen in the Streets with monstrous and horrid *Perriwigs*, and Women with their *Borders and False Locks* and such like whorish Fashion, whereby the anger of the Lord is kindled against this sinful Land![82]

And do you think you will succeed, shrewdly asked John Oxenbridge of Boston's First Church? Are you able to "fashion your selves to the flaunting mode of *England* in worship or walking" even if you sinfully want to? No indeed; "you undertake a vain thing, for you can but limp after them . . . and if you have a minde to turn your Churches into Parishes, and your Ministers into Priests and Prelates, I cannot think the Lord will ever endure it . . ."[83]

This fear, that a generation bent on reproducing the corruptions of England would turn to the Anglican Church, gnawed at the souls of the faithful and led preachers like Higginson to warn,

Our Fathers fled into this Wilderness from the face *of a Lording Episcopacie, and humane injunctions in the Worship of God: now if any of us their children should yeild unto, or be instrumentall to set up in this Coun-*

*try, any of the wayes of mens inventions, such as Prelacie, imposed Leitur-
gies, humane Ceremonies in the Worship of God, or to admit ignorant and
Scandalous Persons to the Lords Table, this would be a backsliding indeed.*[84]

A backsliding indeed, yet one that would appeal to important
merchants like Higginson's future son-in-law, Wharton. It was no
doubt true that "God will rather have his people poor and humble,
then rich and proud . . . rather distressed and oppressed, then enlarged to wandring and security." [85] But were these the only alter-
natives? The sons and grandsons of the first generation merchants
did not believe so. Now the rising leaders of New England, though
not yet fully in control of the civil power, they sought to live like
their London friends. The charge that their lives were sinful, their
ways alive with "that spirit of Covetousness and inordinate love of
the world, that is so inconsistent with the love of the Father," [86]
may have given them pause; but it could not alter the conditions for
succeeding in the mast trade, obtaining the support of an influential
courtier, or attracting the correspondence of powerful London
firms. The desire to succeed in trade and to live the full life of
English merchant-gentlemen was stronger than any counterforce
the clergy could exert.

VI

Elements of Change

SUDDENLY, AT the end of the eighth decade, the full effects of the changes set in motion by the Restoration of the Stuarts were felt in the colonies. It appeared to the New England merchants that the balance of their trade had been upset. Victors in commercial skirmishes, they found themselves victims of distant maneuvers.

But "the heavinly King," as John Hull said, "knoweth Easily how to make all worke for our best good." [1] Certain of the leading merchants, whose social orientation had shifted from the parochialism of rural and Puritan New England to the cosmopolitanism of commercial Britain, found in the altering political relationship between England and the colonies a long-sought path to political power. Advancing toward positions of public authority, they grasped the support of a royal agent in the colonies, one of the men in England's new colonial administration. Representing an emerging colonial officialdom, this agent, Edward Randolph, rallied the merchants whose search for political authority created a momentary harmony between his interests and theirs. Though now, in the late 1670's, a unifying force among the New England merchants, Randolph and the group he represented would ultimately precipitate vital differences among the colonials, differences that would shape the social character of the merchant group.

Accepting whatever assistance was offered them, the merchants moved forward as the ninth decade opened to protect their commerce and to seize the reins of government so long denied them. From their efforts in these directions would come a final definition of their interests and of their place in British society.

1

A sudden rush of events in the late 1670's marked the convergence of two developments affecting the merchants that had been in motion since the Restoration: the widening of commercial contacts and the tightening of the British mercantilist system.

Commercial contacts in seventeenth-century New England were relationships between individuals whose personal lives played important roles in their economic activities. The creation of new ties was less an impersonal economic transaction than the actual coming together of men interested in similar types of enterprises.[2] Innovations in New England commerce, therefore, depended to a large extent on the movements of men. And since commercial relations with the English-speaking world had been outlined by the first generation of merchants, new types of contacts tended to link New England to England's main rival in the colonial world, France. The men who introduced New England to this alien world included not only immigrants with different backgrounds from those of the first settlers, but French freebooters, merchants, and commercial agents as well.

When, precisely, Philippe L'Anglois, a shipmaster from the Channel Island of Jersey, first appeared in New England is not known, but by 1665 he had changed his residence to Salem and his name to Philip English.[3] His quick success as a Salem merchant was based as much on the uniqueness of his business connections as it was on the capital he may have brought with him. His acquaintances were scattered over the coasts of Europe, from Spain to Sweden, and in the 1660's, sailing into their ports as an independent New England shipmaster, he entered into business dealings with them. He bought all sorts of continental goods in exchange for the fish and produce of New England and the tobacco of the southern colonies. Like New Englanders before and after his time, he found it profitable to import indentured servants from Europe, but his main enterprises turned on the unusual products he could bring to the New World and on the multiplicity of his exchanges.[4]

In 1677 at St. Malo, the French port opposite Jersey, Philip English signed a contract with the Malouin agent of Sire Moïse Coubel of this Channel Island. Coubel, the document states, was investing £208 in a voyage English was to undertake in his ketch, and was promised by the Salemite that his money would be returned to him with about 30 per cent profit when the voyage was completed. The contract specified that English was to sail from St. Malo to Boston, whence to

Bilbao, Spain, the Bay of Biscay, Bordeaux, the coast of England, and finally to Jersey or St. Malo where Coubel or his agent would be waiting to collect the return on the investment.[5] St. Malo, Nantes, La Rochelle, Bordeaux — centers of the new French West Indian trade — Oporto in Portugal, as well as Jersey itself were familiar ports to English, and he helped introduce New England to their merchants.

He was not alone. In 1675 a French commercial agent in Boston reported a temporary glut of French goods in the Boston market because of the activities of the Flemings and the Malouins who trafficked in New England under the banner of Jersey.[6] This representative, Henri Brunet, might have added that the New Englanders paid for the goods mainly with tobacco which they were carrying to Jersey in increasing quantities in the 1670's.[7] Brunet found the presence of French goods in Boston something of an embarrassment as his purpose in visiting the colonial metropolis was in part to start up a trade in such commodities on behalf of members of the *Compagnie du Nord*. This organization, founded in 1669 by Colbert to exploit the resources of Nova Scotia, found its commercial monopoly of the region challenged by the New England merchants who had been accustomed to trade and fish there under licenses from Thomas Temple. Brunet, sent in 1672 to inspect the situation in Nova Scotia, reported back that the Englishmen infesting the waters found the trade so profitable that they would be willing to pay for the privilege of continuing it. He recommended that the *Compagnie* reinstitute Temple's system of licenses.[8]

It was in the course of investigating this problem that Brunet looked into the question of sending French goods to New England. Though he thought poorly of the land and its people he understood the possible value of its market, and despite the present competition he decided to leave a consignment of goods with one of the Boston merchants. He instructed the individual he selected, William Taylor, to dispose of the goods only on orders from himself or his principal in France, a man with the rather unusual name of Faneuil.[9]

This correspondence between the Bostonian and the first of the famous Faneuils to engage in New England commerce may explain why Taylor was chosen in 1678 by the notorious French privateer Bernard Lamoyn to be one of his attorneys when he had to defend certain of his captures in the Massachusetts courts. The burden of

Lamoyn's defense, however, was borne not by Taylor but by another Boston merchant whose stake in the French trade was greater than Taylor's.[10]

Richard Wharton's involvement in the French trade seems to have originated in his connection with a London merchant named Robert Bendish. Acquaintance between the two men may have dated from before Wharton left England; more likely it was made through Thomas Bendish, undoubtedly a relation of Robert, who arrived in Boston in the early 1670's. Robert Bendish was one of the Londoners engaged in the profitable triangular trade between London, the continent of Europe, and Newfoundland, exchanging manufactures and fish for French and Spanish commodities. It was an obvious convenience for him to have the American end of the business handled by someone well acquainted with conditions in the New World. By 1672 Wharton had become his agent and a partnership between Wharton and Thomas Bendish had been arranged.[11] Through his connections with the Bendishes, Wharton established business relations with Jean Bailly of La Rochelle, who became interested enough in the possibilities of the New England trade to send a West Indian connection of his, Augustine Mellot, to Boston as his factor. By 1674 Wharton was well known in certain parts of the French colonial trading world, and in that year with Thomas Bendish he decided to back a serious undertaking in this area. It was well known that the French West Indies were starved for provisions despite the efforts of Colbert to have them supplied from France, Canada, or Nova Scotia. The ban on foreign traders in the French islands was strict and effective. No doubt a few sloops a year could slip into the ports, but large operations could be conducted only with passports issued in France. Wharton and Bendish received these indirectly from Bailly who sent them via a relative of his in Martinique, one Clerbaut Bergier.[12]

The partners sent a shipload of provisions to Mellot and Bergier in the Caribbean, who led the vessel on a peddling voyage among the French islands in order to pick up a full load of sugar. The cargo was then dispatched to Bailly and others at La Rochelle where its yield was credited to the partners' account with Robert Bendish in London.[13]

Other contacts with French merchants followed. By 1676, when the effects of King Philip's war were still felt, Wharton and Bendish were importing grain as well as liquor and vinegar from Michel

Boucher of La Rochelle, whom they discouraged from sending linen, silk, and other dry goods to Boston. The partners informed Boucher, as Brunet had told Faneuil, that the Boston market was glutted with such commodities.[14]

The French trade had much to recommend it, but it involved the New Englanders in uncertainties of a kind they could avoid in the English trade. Wharton was obliged to build up his system of correspondences by a series of personal recommendations: Thomas Bendish recommended Robert Bendish, who recommended Bailly, whose factor was Mellot, and so forth. The Bendishes came from London where Wharton was able to check on a man's reliability, but when he sought a responsible correspondent in the French West Indies he had to trust Bailly's recommendation of Clerbaut Bergier. It happened that Bergier was a relative and protégé of Bailly who by his letters and instructions led the Bostonians to believe that Bergier was "of great account, and reputacion," the only man capable of getting the necessary passports for them. Closer acquaintance, however, proved this to be false. Bergier paid Wharton and Company for certain goods in bills drawn on Michel Boucher, who refused to accept them for the very good reason that Bergier had no assets on account with him. Their disillusion was complete when Bergier turned up in Boston "without any estate," insisting that goods were being sent him from France, "which," Wharton wrote Boucher, "also faild." All this "great Damage and loss to our Selves, and Sundry of our friends" resulted from the simple "want of acquaintance with Mr Bergier . . . And wee Canot Thinke that Mr Bayly hath been [Kind] unto us, in recomending Mr Bergier . . ." The fact was, he added, that "wee have been insnared for want of good advice from Mr Bayly and Mr Mellott." [15]

At the same time that contact was being made with the French and goods were beginning to flow between Boston and the French ports, the New England merchants were expanding their commerce further in the English-speaking world. For a full generation they had been accustomed to ship tobacco from Virginia and Maryland to the English market either directly or by way of Boston or the Caribbean. To this familiar traffic was now added the production of the new settlements in Carolina.

New England seamen had been in touch with Carolina at least as early as 1663 when a group of New Englanders had attempted to launch a settlement near the mouth of the Cape Fear River. They had

shared in the profits of transporting and supplying the first settlers at
Charles Town, and more recently — in the early 1670's — had gained
a monopolistic control over the yearly product of Albemarle County.
Behind the barrier of shifting sand bars that blocked Albemarle Sound
to all but the most shallow-draft oceangoing vessels lived approximately three thousand settlers: farmers, coastal backwoodsmen, many
of them tough, stubborn refugees from better organized communities.
Their one cash crop was tobacco of which they prepared nearly one
million pounds a year. A number of New Englanders sent their small
coasting vessels to the sound where they easily gained control over
almost all the tobacco produced, for to the settlers the New Englanders were the only possible buyers of their crop. In 1679 an observer described the control of the northerners as so complete that
anyone in the region hoping to produce or trade in tobacco "must
become Bostonized or relinquish Dealing. . ." [16]

If sources of supply multiplied, so too did the markets visited by the
New Englanders within the British empire. Ireland and Scotland became important new outlets for the merchants' goods. In the ports of
Cork and Dublin new correspondences sprang up quickly with the
English Protestant townsmen. Tobacco and other colonial goods
could be exchanged for manufactures as conveniently in Ireland as in
England, and probably more profitably in Scotland. Symbolic of the
new interest of the New Englanders in these northern dependencies
was the fact that in 1676 Thomas Breedon had taken up residence
in Dublin, where he was sent tobacco from Virginia by Richard
Wharton.[17]

2

Uppermost in the minds of the New England merchants who led
this movement of entry into the French commercial world and into
new corners of England's Atlantic empire was the fact that they personally and New England as a whole profited by their enterprise.
But to the merchants and the mercantilist-minded politicians who controlled the English government these innovations seemed to threaten
England's interests as defined in the navigation acts. The act of 1660
had specifically forbidden exportation of enumerated goods, including
tobacco, direct to the continent of Europe or to the dependencies
of foreign powers. But the merchants, trading now to France as
well as to Spain, paid for their purchases as much in tobacco as in non-

enumerated goods like fish, lumber, and provisions. Moreover, the act had made clear that neither Scotland, Ireland, nor the Channel Islands were to be considered part of England for commercial purposes, and hence shipments of tobacco to these places were illegal. The staple act, which had directed European goods intended for the colonies to be carried first to England where duties were to be exacted, had also considered Scotland and Ireland foreign lands and had permitted only servants, horses, and provisions to be shipped from their ports to the plantations. The only other exceptions that affected the New Englanders were those of salt from the continent to New England for the fisheries, and wines and fruit from Madeira and the Azores, possessions of England's ally, Portugal. Legally, all the French goods that Brunet observed in Boston, all the Irish and Scottish manufactures, and all the Spanish and Canary wines and fruit in New England were liable for seizure unless they had come by way of England. Only in the case of Canary wines could the merchants have defended themselves, for the Canary Islands had not yet been clearly assigned by geographers to either Europe or Africa. The staple act had banned from direct importation only "commodities of the growth, production, or manufacture of Europe. . ." A legitimate claim might be made that the Canaries were in Africa.[18]

To these long-standing regulations applicable to New England's new trading contacts was added in 1673 a law which affected the New Englanders more deeply than either of the other two main navigation acts. This law was passed, in fact, largely in response to complaints received in England against the New England merchants.

Criticism of Massachusetts' failure to enforce the navigation acts had not ceased with the departure of the commissioners of 1664 from New England. Repeated accusations were made that certain merchants in the colonial trade were evading the enumeration clause of the act of 1660 by taking advantage of its ambiguous wording. This regulation was twisted by the merchants — it was charged — to justify their shipping the goods in question directly to Europe once they had entered them in a plantation port other than the port of the goods' origin. The merchants, particularly those of New England, it was claimed, argued that reshipping enumerated goods from a plantation port was equivalent to reëxporting them from England and consequently they saw nothing wrong in taking sugar and tobacco from the places of growth or manufacture to New England, making up composite cargoes there, and sending them off directly to France, Holland, or Spain.[19]

By 1673 such allegations had convinced Parliament that steps had to be taken to stop this practice, and the problem was dealt with in an important piece of legislation enacted in that year. Its purpose was to cut down the profits being made on goods sent illegally from the plantations to the continent of Europe. It levied at the port of clearance a tax on enumerated goods roughly equal, in most cases, to that imposed on the same goods upon entrance into England. And it required shipmasters to deposit a bond obliging them to take the goods only to another colony or to England. Exception was made only in the case of vessels already bonded to take enumerated goods directly to England. Moreover, and of great importance to New England, the law provided for the appointment by the English customs commissioners of agents to enforce the navigation laws in the colonies and to collect the new duties.[20]

Though the New England colonies were in no hurry to put this law into force, others, more easily controlled from England, complied with its demands. Before five years had passed the New Englanders came to realize that the plantation duty, ostensibly aimed at stopping a leak in the enumeration law, threatened their ordinary and legal commerce. The tax on sugar, tobacco, and the other enumerated goods could be interpreted to mean that unless New England merchants took these products immediately from the port of lading to England they must pay tariff on them twice over, once at the port of origin and, after the usual stopovers elsewhere in the colonies, again in London. The English merchants, on the other hand, whose practice it was to send vessels out to the colonies in order to bring these commodities directly back to England, had to pay a duty only at the home port. Moreover, the refunding of part of the English tariff upon reshipment of colonial goods from England to Europe reduced the total duties still further for the English merchants. Since mid-century prices of sugar and tobacco had fallen steadily as production had risen and the limited English markets had been assured a steady supply. A double duty on tobacco and sugar would make a noticeable difference in profits to the New England merchants.[21]

This was but one point among many. As the merchants spread their network of correspondences into new areas, English officials began to enforce other parts of the navigation acts besides the duties of the act of 1673. Agents were appointed to attend to the details of surveying and controlling the movements of goods. Orders were sent out to colonial magistrates containing detailed instructions about shipping. Gradually these efforts were rewarded.

Feeling the limitations of mercantilism, the New England merchants protested sharply against what struck them as gross discrimination. In 1677 John Hull informed the Massachusetts agents in London that their "orphant Plantation" was being crushed by the enforcement of the plantation duty.

. . . iff we carry our Provitions (which we heare Raise with great difficultyes becase of long winters etc.) to the west Indies we pay custom for our cotton wool and sugere there and the bulke of them are sent to England againe from hence and Pay custome theyre a second time.

The Massachusetts government joined merchants like Hull in protesting against this invidious tariff, and eventually its London representatives listed this complaint as the most important of a number of obstructions to New England's commerce which they desired the Lords of Trade to remove.[22]

Patience in the face of declining profits was not a common virtue among the merchants. Many sought ways of evading payment of the duties. The law of 1673 had made avoidance of customs difficult in ports where reliable officials were stationed, but in Carolina the temper of the people and the tightness of the New Englanders' monopoly of the trade made the collection of the duty almost impossible. In 1677 the settlers, fearing an increase in the prices of goods if the New England merchants were forced to pay the penny a pound tax on tobacco, forced the governor to remit to the traders three farthings in every penny taken. In 1677 the appointment of an imperious collector of customs determined to enforce the laws led to a rebellion of the settlers headed by John Culpeper and supported by the New England merchants. Until the proprietors of the colony could regain control Culpeper acted as collector, formed a temporary government, and barred the royal comptroller and surveyor of the customs at Albermarle from the exercise of his office. The rebellion was soon quelled and the main culprits brought back to England for trial. Culpeper's rebellion, backed if not instigated by the New England merchants trading to Carolina, had no permanent consequences. But it was an important sign of the tendency of events.[23]

Other points in the tightening mercantilist system drew sharp if not violent reactions from the merchants. To Hull the staple act was as invidious as the plantation duty. In December 1677 he wrote to the agents complaining bitterly of the effect of this law.

If that wee send our fish to Bilboa and Carrie the Produce thereof into the Streights at great charge and Hasard and procure fruite, Oyle, sope, wine, and Salt, the bulke of our Loadings [being] Salt . . . and because we have a little of the other goods (for our nesesity call not for much) wee must goe to England to Pay his majestys customs, which is as the cutting off our hands and feete.[24]

By February 1679 Hull was appealing to the king to remember his role as father of his people. Instead of injuring New Englanders who "by great diligence and Industry" had managed to work up a decent trade, the king should be interested in subsidizing their efforts. "I doe not see how it is Possible the Acts of navigation Can be attended to here. The Merchant People will be occationed to bid farwell to the Country and Com to England." But if the English monarch would not aid them, wrote Hull, the Heavenly King would surely come to their assistance. Their course, which he outlined in a strikingly prophetic passage, would be clear. God, he stated, knew how to turn adversity to advantage. He would lead them to

fall Close to all sorts of manifacture and forbeare trading by the sea: and so Enable us to live . . . without Such dependencies, if we Cold be so low and content in our Spirits as then wold be our Condition, to Eate noe fruite, sugar, Spice, and drinke noe wine but our owne Cyder, and weare no Clothing but of Or owne making. I doe not know what we might be as helthy and as warme as we now are, and It may be more holy, righteous, and humble.[25]

At the same time that Hull and other New Englanders were protesting against the operation of the navigation acts they were being charged at Whitehall with flagrantly violating them. Reports flowed in accusing them of holding the staple act in utter contempt and ignoring its provisions completely. In January 1676 the Lords of Trade were sent a petition signed by twenty-four London merchants engaged in the export trade to America in which they stated that the New Englanders were carrying on illegal commerce with Europe, importing goods to sell cheaply all over the colonial world. Not only were the petitioners' own businesses being ruined, they stated, by this illegal competition of the colonials, but New England was quickly making itself "the great Mart and Staple" of Atlantic commerce to the prejudice of England and His Majesty's revenue. In April of the same year the Lords of Trade read two more petitions which the mercers and silkweavers had submitted. They estimated the loss to His Majesty's customs occasioned by New England's smuggling trade with Europe to be £60,000 a year.[26]

Official confirmation of these charges was supplied shortly after the receipt of these petitions when a committee of the Lords of Trade summoned before it a number of New Englanders then in the City and London merchants whose usual habitat was "the Exchange upon the New England Walk" to testify on the matter. When pressed by the committee "some were shy to unfold the mystery, others pretended ignorance," but most of them finally agreed that a smuggling trade with the continent of Europe did exist, and that it enabled the New Englanders to obtain goods which could be sold with profit 20 per cent cheaper than commodities imported from England. At the same time Sir Joseph Williamson completed a thorough study of the clauses of the navigation acts affecting New England and reported his findings to the plantation authorities.[27]

During the same period another long-standing complaint against Massachusetts was being brought to the attention of the Lords of Trade as the heirs of both Robert Mason and Ferdinando Gorges attempted to revive their inherited claims to the control of New Hampshire and Maine. Robert (Tufton) Mason had refused to abandon the hope of reaping a harvest from his title to New Hampshire even after the failure of the commissioners of 1664 to shake off Massachusetts' control. He had continued to receive reports from agents and relatives in the province and with Gorges had petitioned the Council for Trade and Plantations repeatedly for official action in support of his claim. Though by 1671 his confidence in being able to regain his province was so slight that he was willing to sell his patent to the king for the right to import 300 tons of French wines duty-free, he nevertheless continued to seek a solution to the problem that would satisfy himself, the New Hampshire settlers, and Massachusetts. After the conclusion of the Dutch wars, Mason who then occupied a position of influence at court submitted his full "Considerations" of the question to the Lords of Trade. When the legality of his title to New Hampshire was satisfactorily established his claims were added to the growing number of New England issues that demanded a final settlement.[28]

Pressed on all sides to take action against the stubborn colonies and freed from the immediate pressure of military and political problems, the Lords of Trade in 1676 launched a full investigation of the situation. After studying the complaints and reports that had come to hand and consulting with the best informed people in London, they agreed that New England's subordination to the home country, politically and economically, was incomplete. But they postponed action to a future time, observing that the obvious ways of dealing with stubborn colonists — imposing taxes or other burdens on them, or sending out "a Governor to raise a fortune from Them" — would be of little service to His Majesty. For the moment they were content to relieve the immediate pressure of Mason's influence by sending a royal messenger to New England to demand in the king's name that Massachusetts delegate agents to confer in London on the claims to New Hampshire and Maine. The messenger was also to make a firsthand report on actual conditions in New England, especially on how well the colonials were complying with the trade laws.[29]

3

Never was there a less disinterested public servant than Edward Randolph, the man selected to perform this task. A relative by marriage of Robert Mason, he had been employed through his influence as early as 1661 in buying up timber for the Navy Commissioners. In 1666, threatened with prosecution for a debt of £205 10*s*., he had been rescued by the affluent Mason who obtained work for him in Scotland, again as a timber purchasing agent, this time in the employ of the Duke of Richmond. Managing somehow to pay off his old debts and having accumulated new obligations in Scotland, Randolph had returned to England where, until his appointment as emissary to New England, he had worked in the office of the commissary of the Cinque Ports.[30] Ambitious, intelligent, and well-connected, he might have been a successful placeman and government official like his friend William Blathwayt or like Samuel Pepys, but his compelling need to overcome his poverty and his utter lack of judgment in handling people made him offensive to everyone with whom he came in contact. Arrogant to his inferiors, both importunate and obsequious to those in authority, he was constantly frustrated in his desire for security. An Anglican and staunch royalist by conviction, he viewed the colonies as the undoubted possessions of Englishmen, fruit ripe for the plucking.

This attitude was characteristic of a new group of Englishmen now coming out to the colonies. Minor placemen and petty bureaucrats, these officeholders were finding lucrative positions in the colonial service. Their presence in America not only signalized England's determination to exert control over colonial commerce but also introduced an important element into the emerging form of American society. Randolph's experiences in New England epitomize the problems that accompanied their settlement into the colonial scene.

Carrying with him detailed instructions from the Lords of Trade as well as the king's message to Massachusetts and letters from Mason and Gorges to the northern inhabitants, Randolph embarked at the end of March 1676 and arrived in Boston after a voyage of ten weeks. Within a few hours of his arrival he delivered the king's message to the Council and demanded that the magistrates draw up a reply for him to carry back to England. His arrogant bearing as well as the message he conveyed touched the tender pride of the Puritans who asked to see his authorization for making such a request. Randolph replied curtly that "what I had there demanded I would answer [for] at Whitehall." This first exchange with the Massachusetts magistrates set the tone for all his future dealings with the Puritan government.[31]

Waiting in Boston for the reply to England, he had ample time to study the people, their government, and trade. Within a week his opinion of all three was formed, never thereafter to change. To him the leaders of the colony were "inconsiderable Mechanicks" who gave expression to the wishes of the real power in the region, which was a faction of fanatical dissenting ministers and religious zealots "generally inclined to Sedition being Proud Ignorant and Imperious." Their practice, he stated, was to keep "whole herds of the meaner Inhabitants" in a state of cowed obedience by circulating dreadful rumors of the fate of English nonconformists like John Owen "and others— eiusdem Farinae."[32]

In his first week of residence in Boston he satisfied himself that violations of the navigation acts abounded. He marked the arrival of two vessels directly from France with cargoes of brandy and three with wines from the Canaries, and recorded a report of the arrival of two other ships a month earlier loaded with wine from Spain as well as from the Canary Islands. When he asked Governor Leverett for an explanation of this illegal commerce he was told "that the Laws made by Our King and Parliament obligeth them in nothing but what consists with the Interest of New England. . . " Foreign merchants and English factors of foreigners, he wrote back to London, were allowed to reside freely in Boston and on the Piscataqua, protected by a despotic government which acknowledged no real tie to the mother country.[33]

A brief visit to the northern districts and to Plymouth confirmed Randolph in his first impression of New England. In New Hampshire, reading a message from Mason to those inhabitants who would listen and receiving complaints from Maine against Massachusetts' rule, he stirred up discontent. In Plymouth he encouraged Governor Josiah Winslow in his antipathy to what Randolph represented as the aggrandizing, bullying policies of the Bay Colony.

Randolph, like Maverick and the other commissioners of the previous decade, looked about him, even in these first days of acquaintance with New England, for individuals who would be of use in forcing issues against the Massachusetts government. The Anglican opposition in Maine and New Hampshire he knew he could count on, and Governor Winslow was surely worth cultivating. But more important to him were sympathetic men within Massachusetts' mercantile community. The social composition of the group he would seek most avidly to rally to his support, despite apparent contradictions between their interests and his, was forecast by his singling out Thomas Savage and Fitz-John Winthrop, both men of Puritan background in the business community, for special praise and even admiration. The former, he stated in his first communication to the home authorities, was "a Gent of a very good family in England and Loyal Principles," and Winthrop he declared to be not only a courageous and beloved military commander, but, more important, a man who "upon good occasion will freely act for his Majestys service." [34]

These same attitudes and opinions characterized the full reports Randolph submitted to the Lords of Trade upon his return to England. He listed in detail the ways in which Massachusetts brazenly insulted England's sovereignty and supremacy, and attributed such irreverent, not to say treasonous, conduct to the leadership of the fanatical faction of nonconformist ministers and laymen. On the other hand, he stated to the Lords of Trade, there were many "who only wait for an opportunity to expresse their duty to his Majesty." In general, these "men of good principles and well affected to his Majestie" were "the most wealthy persons of all professions" in a society where the "chief professions are merchants . . . and wealthy shop-keepers or retailers. . . ." Most of these presumed loyalists must have been among the thirty or so leading merchants whose wealth Randolph estimated at between ten and twenty thousand pounds each. He named fourteen prominent men who could be relied on to side with royal authority in an emergency, and of these nine were well-known merchants.[35]

Having excepted these leading merchants from his general charges against the New Englanders, Randolph proceeded with jarring inconsistency to discuss the disloyalty of the New England merchants in their willful disregard of the navigation laws. They kept up a constant smuggling trade with the French in Nova Scotia and they imported direct from the continent of Europe goods in such quantities "that there is little left for the merchants residing in England to import into any of the plantations, those of New England being able to afford their goods much cheaper than such who pay the customes and are laden in England." Then, linking his observations to what he knew of the charges being brought by the English exporters, he assured the Lords that this clandestine trade of New England caused England to lose "the best part of the western trade, there being very little exported hence but only such commodities as are properly the product and manufacture of England and cannot be had in other parts." The whole truth of the matter, he concluded, was that

There is no notice taken of the act of navigation, plantation, or any other lawes made in England for the regulation of trade. All nations having free liberty to come into their ports and vend their commodities, without any restraint; and in this as well as in other things, that government would make the world believe they are a free state and doe act in all matters accordingly, and doe presume to give passports to ships, not only belonging to that colony but also to England, without any regard to those rules prescribed by his Majestie.

The more he thought about the matter the more serious these violations of the navigation acts appeared to him. In May 1677 it seemed to him that they were the cause of New England's engrossing "the greatest part of the West India Trade." After ten months of separation from the American scene he discovered the full extent of New England's illegal trade. There was no doubt in his mind that it was costing His Majesty in lost customs over £100,000 a year.[36]

Randolph's reports were among the most important items consid-

ered by the Lords of Trade and the Privy Council in a second complete review of the New England problem. This time they were
determined to force a clear statement of intentions from the Massachusetts government. The series of replies they received to their
demands for an explanation confirmed Randolph's report and their
worst suspicions. The laws of England, the Massachusetts General
Court declared,

. . . are bounded within the fower seas, and doe not reach Amerrica. The
subjects of his majestie here being not represented in Parliament, so wee
have not looked at ourselves to be impeded in our trade by them, nor
yett wee abated in our relative allegiance to his majestie.

Nevertheless, Massachusetts hastened to add that it had voluntarily
embodied the English navigation laws in statutes of its own passed in
October 1677 and, despite the inconvenience that would result, would
enforce them in the future.[37]

The agents who bore the burden of expounding the official Massachusetts view before the English government saw the futility of trying
to maintain such a doctrine of independence, and, apologizing for the
few merchants who, they conceded, were violating the laws "by
reason they have not understood those Acts," stressed the measures
Massachusetts was taking to obey the letter of Parliament's law. At
the same time the agents wrote back sharply to the General Court in
an effort to make the legislators appreciate the seriousness with which
the English government considered the matter of trade regulation.

The country's not taking notice of these acts of navigation to observe
them, hath been the most unhappy neglect that we could have fallen into,
for, more and more every day, we find it most certain, that without a fair
compliance in that matter, there can be nothing expected but a total
breech, and the storms of displeasure that may be.[38]

Supplied with Randolph's reports, the testimony of the London
witnesses and the colonial agents, the official replies of the colonial
governments, as well as the opinions of the attorney general and the
commissioners of the customs, the Lords of Trade gradually came to
a permanent solution to the problem of New England. Though in
July 1677 they were content to lecture the agents on Massachusetts'
remissness and to order better compliance in the future, by April 1678
they were agreed that only a revocation of the Massachusetts charter
and the establishment of a royal governor would bring the colony into

a proper relation to England. While further dispatches were sent to New England demanding obedience to the existing orders, steps were taken to start a suit against the charter. At the same time, the Lords of Trade acted on an old recommendation of the commissioners of customs and ordered the governors of the New England colonies to take an oath to enforce the navigation acts in every particular.[39]

It was in ordering this governors' oath that Randolph's selection of a loyalist nucleus in Massachusetts was first used. On September 3, 1678, the Lords of Trade ordered the commissioning of Randolph, the councillors of Massachusetts, and a number of private citizens to administer the oath to Governor Leverett. The fourteen individuals named, chosen presumably for their loyalty to the crown and their interest in seeing the navigation acts enforced, included no less than twelve merchants, many of whom must have been participants in the very commerce they were being commissioned to help eliminate.[40]

4

Randolph was not a fool, nor had he been deceived by these merchants during his stay in New England. His inconsistent attitude to them reflected their own conflict of interests. Though the enforcement of the navigation acts was beginning to make clear to them the price of membership in the British empire, it did not outweigh the benefits of that connection. For most of them a growing social orientation to England and a deepening involvement in British trade went hand in hand with an increasing resentment at their subordinate role in politics. For though they had advanced to the point where their importance to the economic welfare of New England was outstanding and their social influence a challenge to the authority of the Puritan leaders, they were almost completely excluded from the upper levels of government.

It was not so much that some of them were disfranchised by the religious requirement of the suffrage act of 1664. Even if the merchants had had fifty votes each they still would have lacked political power commensurate with the common English estimation of their real importance to society. The difficulty lay not in the narrowness of the franchise but in its width. Church membership as a qualification had opened the vote to a large number of farmers and townsmen who, for lack of property, would have been denied suffrage in almost every community in the western world. As a consequence, the merchants who represented the part of society accustomed to wield political power in England could be outvoted on every issue.[41]

The Puritan countrymen brought to power friends who saw things as they did or familiar leaders who represented to them the stable ways of the Founders. By 1678 thirty years had passed since the death of the elder Winthrop, but during that whole period only four men had enjoyed the governorship of Massachusetts: John Endecott for fourteen years, Richard Bellingham for nine, John Leverett for six, and Thomas Dudley for one term. With the single exception of Leverett none of these men had been particularly sympathetic to the trading community. Of the deputy governors only the shipwright Francis Willoughby, who returned to New England in 1662 enhanced in prestige by his service as Navy Commissioner, had more than a passing interest in commerce. The few merchants like Richard Russell, Edward Tyng, and Thomas Clarke who had been elected to the Council had never controlled the upper house. The deputies overwhelmingly represented rural or Puritan interests.[42]

By the end of the eighth decade, therefore, the merchants welcomed any help they could get in gaining an amount of political power proportionate to their economic and social influence. That this aid came to them in the form of the same English officials whose ultimate purpose threatened their economic welfare was perhaps unfortunate. Yet considering the importance of their friends and correspondents in England they were not without hope of easing the worst effects of the navigation acts. In Randolph's needs and the intentions of the Lords of Trade they saw an opportunity to gain their immediate political goal. The larger problem would be dealt with when circumstances were more favorable.

For Randolph the situation offered a means to the long sought end of wealth and influence, and he moved quickly to assure his position. He formed his plans along two lines. First, there was his connection with Mason. If his kinsman could regain possession of New Hampshire Randolph would at least be entitled to a number of minor but lucrative posts in the reorganized government. It was not improbable that he would also have access to free land, timber rights, and trade privileges. Secondly, the Lords of Trade were about to appoint officials to enforce the navigation laws in New England, and men in such positions were entitled to fees not to be scorned by one of Randolph's needs. Moreover, a complete revamping of that colony's government would undoubtedly reveal a variety of ways for an ambitious English official on the scene to make his fortune, especially if he had support in Whitehall.

By the spring of 1679 Randolph's plans had matured. His petition for the post of collector of customs for the plantation duty in New England had been endorsed by the Lords of Trade, and, despite the opposition of the Massachusetts agents, he was appointed to this important post as a "reward for his Services." [43] He may even have brought one of the Massachusetts agents over to his side by an arrangement concerning the Atherton Company's claims to the Narragansett Country. Randolph kept this agent, William Stoughton, informed of the progress of his efforts to obtain orders supporting the company, and when at one point his hopes dimmed he wrote the colonial to "feare not but I will gett you into some place of profitt and advantage." And to assure his power of patronage he petitioned the king for the right to appoint not only deputy collectors in the lesser ports but also officers of the forts and castles guarding the harbors. [44]

As the time for his departure for New England approached he redoubled his efforts to gather authority into his hands. He suggested to the Lords of Trade a plan for the complete reorganization of the Massachusetts government, and though this was rejected, he worked successfully with Mason to complete arrangements for the new proprietary government in New Hampshire. In May 1679 the Lords of Trade ordered Massachusetts to withdraw all its officers from Mason's territory, and then came to an agreement with Mason that his government would consist of a president, nine councillors, and an assembly which would be convoked in order to make a settlement of the land rent problem. Mason promised to forget all past rents due him by the settlers and grant them full title to the land they had improved on condition that they become his tenants and in the future pay him a quitrent not to exceed sixpence in the pound on all improved land and housing. All timber lands were to remain in Mason's hands. [45]

In appointing the first councillors the Lords of Trade consulted a number of New Englanders then in London and also Sir William Warren, the timber dealer, who had been in touch with the New Hampshire merchants since the Restoration. Their suggestions were used, with the result that the new Council of New Hampshire was made up largely of the Massachusetts or Puritan group of merchants. Though headed by the disaffected John Cutts it included William Vaughan, Richard Martin, and Richard Waldron. Randolph was ordered to see that this government was duly installed. [46]

The newly appointed collector of New England took care of other details before he left London. He argued successfully, in this year of the Popish Plot, that all disabilities placed upon Anglicans in New England should be removed and that an orthodox minister should accompany him to New England and set up a church there in the Anglican form. He arranged to have his salary of £100 a year made retroactive to 1676, though he could not keep his wages from being paid "out of the Custom." [47]

5

Carrying instructions from the commissioners of the customs, the Lords of Trade, and Robert Mason, Randolph arrived in New York early in December 1679. Before the month was out he had taken possession of the Narragansett Country for the king, visited Connecticut, Rhode Island, Plymouth, and Boston briefly before going to New Hampshire where he delivered the commission of government to the "old and infirm, but just and honest" John Cutts. [48]

Resistance to the Mason commission headed by Waldron and Martin immediately flared up. Five of the six men appointed to the Council, encouraged by the Massachusetts government, refused at first to serve. Second thought suggested that together they could control the new government and that if they declined the commissions they would be powerless against whomever Cutts decided to appoint in their places. And so after efforts to get Cutts to refuse the presidency failed, they took their places as magistrates in the proprietary government. [49]

Pleased with his success, Randolph returned to Boston at the end of January 1680 where he was greeted by a "paper of scandalous verses" which lampooned him as "that hector, / Confirmed at home to be the sharp Colector," whose intention it was "To play the horse-leach; robb us of our Fleeces, / To rend our land, and teare it all to pieces." The poem, hyperbolic and crude, contained at least this truth which must have caught Randolph's attention:

> If Merchants in their traffique will be Faire,
> You must, Camelion-like, live on the aire.
> Should they not trade to Holland, Spaine and France,
> Directly you must seeke For maintenance.
> The Customs and the Fees will scarce supply
> Belly and back. What's left for's Majesty?

For the moment, however, there was little likelihood that the merchants would stop their illegal commerce and that Randolph would go begging for maintenance. In fact, if the change of governors was an indication of trends, circumstances would favor Randolph, for after the death of John Leverett in 1680 the aged merchant Simon Bradstreet was elected to the high magistracy. Though devoted to many of the old ways, he was yet realistic enough to understand the necessities of the times. In March 1680 he ordered the marshals and constables of Massachusetts to aid Randolph in seizing vessels or goods for trial.[50]

Clothed in high authority and exuding an arrogant superiority to everything colonial and provincial, Randolph proceeded to the serious work of collecting the plantation duty and enforcing the navigation acts. His actions during the ensuing nine months and the reactions of the colonials to them forced into bold relief the outlines of unexpected difficulties that would impede his pursuit of gain in the colonies. Between March and December 1680 he attempted sixteen or seventeen seizures of goods or vessels and managed to bring ten of these before the local courts. In each instance the juries decided in favor of the defendants, although on one occasion the court imposed a £40 fine on a defendant for insubordinate conduct to a royal officer. Not content with taking advantage of the prejudices of the jurymen, the merchants filed countersuits against the collector. His servant acting on orders "was sett upon by 4 or 5 persons [and] very much beaten"; he was himself derided and cursed. Even such a man as Nicholas Paige, the elegant, English-born husband of Anna Keayne, flared in anger and threatened to have Randolph "knock'd at head" if he boarded one of his vessels.[51]

Such threats and the loss of each suit increased Randolph's ire against the colonials and heightened his ruthlessness in dealing with them. He claimed that the juries were packed with partisans who would vote against him no matter what the evidence was. In this he was not entirely mistaken. Public feeling was high against him. In four of the ten trials there is no reason to doubt his assertion that the juries had cleared ships and goods which ought to have been forfeited; but in the other six Randolph exceeded his powers and victimized the merchants involved.

In two of these instances the vessels concerned were out of the legal limits of Boston harbor when he seized them; they should not have been molested.[52] In another, Randolph acted as both informer and prosecutor, but since the violation was against the staple act, not the law of 1673, he was not legally empowered to prosecute.[53] In the case of the *Gift of God* of Kittery, Randolph simply misconstrued the law in demanding that a New England coasting vessel without enumerated goods aboard enter with him before unloading.[54] His suit against the *Two Sisters* was of no greater validity, as the only French commodity he mentioned as having been smuggled in it was salt, which had been specifically exempted from the prohibitions of the staple act.[55] His seizure of a parcel of Irish yarn in a warehouse without a search warrant violated local law.[56]

Yet these were cases in which Randolph felt his claims justified. In others he had to confess that his grounds for confiscation were weak or his methods unjustifiable. His seizure of seventeen butts of Samuel Shrimpton's brandy rested on such flimsy evidence that he was obliged to declare publicly that his action was indefensible. His belief that the *James* of Londonderry was loading tobacco clan-destinely was based only on the word of a disgruntled sailor, and he ought not to have been surprised at finding himself threatened with rough treatment when he attempted to board the vessel. Nor could he back up his charges against Nicholas Paige, Josiah Cobham, or the *Batchelor's Delight*.[57]

The fact of the matter was that Randolph was using the real illegalities of trade as an excuse to fleece the merchants. He did so not merely because he was avaricious or ruthless or because to him colonials were an inferior breed of men. The logic of his situation demanded that he indulge in what has been called "customs rack-eteering," and he had no scruples in doing so.[58] The navigation acts could be enforced only if the collectors in the colonies were efficient, and in a period when the colonial bureaucracy was in its infancy and when perquisites, fees, bribes, and gifts — not salaries — were the main financial reward for public service, efficiency could be ensured only if close attention to duty was repaid by such benefits. For Randolph the salary of £100 a year out of the customs was poor payment for his troubles. He was after a large and steady income which he ex-pected to receive not in the form of salary but from fees like the 50 per cent of confiscated goods due him as informer.

Randolph was right in believing that trade violations were ordinary occurrences. However, New Englanders did not share his opinion that colonials were lesser Englishmen, and they were prepared to defend their property by all devices known to English law. With the instinctive litigiousness of the Puritan Fathers, the merchants fought each case through the courts, using every wrinkle and twist of the law that happened to favor them. And they were prepared to justify violence by the higher law that protected the individual against the tyranny and oppression of those in positions of public authority.

By the end of the year it was evident to Randolph that his powers would have to be enlarged if he was to proceed in the face of the merchants' evasions or of their infuriating use of legal entanglements. As early as June 1680 he wrote home requesting greater jurisdiction; in the first weeks of 1681 he returned to England determined to increase his authority.[59]

In London he poured out his complaints against the colonials to his immediate superiors, the commissioners of the customs, submitting to them a number of requests for powers he considered necessary for the fulfillment of his duties. The commissioners forwarded the list to the Lords of Trade, together with their own analysis of it and their recommendations concerning its particular points.

Randolph desired, first, to make it obligatory for all ships bound both inward and outward to enter with him and to report their cargoes on oath. The commissioners found this surprising and advised the Lords that "noe masters are by Law obliged to make Entry of their ships upon Oath, but such only as come to New England with any of the Ennumerated plantacion Goods, Or there Load them for some other place . . ." [60] They made no objection to Randolph's suggestions concerning the limitation of the legal ports of entry, but answered shortly and sharply his request to force every ship clearing New England harbors to be visited and certified by royal officers: "Wee doe humbly informe your Lordshipps, That the Officers have noe such power here in England." [61] Randolph's next point was more important and drew a lengthy response from his superiors. He attributed a large part of his failure in New England to his inability to search at will for hidden goods. Governor Bradstreet's order to the constables was no more than a warrant to aid in seizure. What Randolph wanted was a full writ of assistance, that is, a general search warrant. He requested that the royal officers should

... have Liberty at all times in the night to attend their Duty without disturbance, and that none be sued or molested to prevent their performing of their Trust; and that they may be impowered to demand aide of Constable or Officer to assist in opening Doores, and to seize, and search for prohibited goodes, and secure them till a Tryall.

To this the commissioners replied by informing the Lords that the issuance of such search warrants was neither the law nor the practice in New England. But they added that the Fraud Act of 1662 had made it legal at least in England for anyone authorized

... by writt of Assistance under the Seale of his Majestys Court of Exchecquer, to take a Constable ... and in the day time to enter, and goe into any house, shop, Cellar, warehouse or roome, or other place, and in Case of resistance, to breake open doores, Chests, Truncks, and other package, there to seize, and from thence to bring any kinde of Goods or merchandize whatsoever, prohibited and uncustomed, and put and secure the same in his Majestys Storehouse, in the port next to the place where such Seizure shall bee made. . .

They left it up to the Lords to judge whether or not it would be advisable to demand "the same Ayde and Assistance" of the New England government.[62] Randolph's request that he and his deputies be empowered "to go off to sea aboard Shipps comeing within the Capes, and to bring such into Port who refuse to produce their clearings" met the sharpest reply of all from the commissioners: "Wee know of noe such practice as this in England, and what the Consequence thereof may bee cannot bee foreseen, and wee cannot recommend of it to your Lordships Approbacion." Similar treatment was given his suggestion that foreign ships claiming distress should be allowed into New England ports only with the permission of a royal officer and with an English functionary aboard.[63]

The importance of these requests made by Randolph lay in the attitudes they reflected and the assumptions behind them. Randolph presumed that colonial merchants were inferior Britishers, that they were important only insofar as they contributed to his own and England's welfare, and that in dealing with them certain ordinary protections of English law might be suspended.

Randolph's first year as collector of customs in Boston and his request to the commissioners for extended authority mark an important turning point in the history of the New England colonies. His manner of enforcing the trade laws and of dealing with the colonials reflected, of course, his own personality. But his behavior was not unique. It was, in fact, characteristic of a whole class of Englishmen now beginning to arrive in the colonies. These men — customs functionaries, lesser bureaucrats, fortune hunters in official positions — found careers for themselves in the quickly expanding colonial administration. Together with the widening scope of commerce and the tightening of trade regulations they were the main new elements in the changing situation of the New England merchants.

VII

The Merchant Group at the End of the Seventeenth Century

IN THE turbulent decade of the 1680's the merchants, twisting and turning with circumstances in an effort to keep their goals in sight, found the limits of their vital interests. Thereafter, so long as New England remained within the same system of economic and political pressures the basic needs of the merchants remained constant. When, almost a century later, economic changes and new colonial policies altered the conditions of their prosperity, they sought in drastic measures means of perpetuating their familiar world.

The permanence of the merchants' interests was part of the more general stability of the mercantile community. Just as specific economic issues flowed within unchanging limits, so the individual merchants with their myriad ambitions, their particular desires and abilities, lived within a framework of group organization. The permanent structure of the merchant group, like the definition of the merchants' interests, emerged in the last years of the seventeenth century. It was altered only by the convulsion of revolution that transformed so much of American society three generations later.

1

The sequence of political events in New England during the 1680's forms the background for the final development of the merchant group.

In the six years after Randolph's return to America in 1683 the New England governments underwent a series of transformations that came to an end only in the general settlement of colonial affairs after the English Revolution of 1688. The first colony to succumb to innovation was New Hampshire, which in 1683 was placed in the hands of a needy court favorite, Edward Cranfield, as governor, and a

Council composed of Randolph, Mason, and a number of resident royalists. Cranfield summoned an assembly of town representatives to come to terms with Mason on the question of land rents. In this as in other matters he discovered how stubborn colonial Englishmen could be in defending their property. The new government could not force the settlers to accept Mason's title to the land. Opposition to Randolph's attempts to enforce the navigation acts flared repeatedly. Later events in Massachusetts were foreshadowed when a number of merchants joined with the Puritan faction to form a common front against the new governor and Council. The conflict over property and political control deepened when Cranfield identified his leading antagonists as fanatical nonconformists. The approaching crisis indicated by an armed outbreak led by one Gove and the forced ejection from the province of the Puritan leader Reverend Joshua Moody was averted only by Randolph's return to England and Cranfield's departure for the more salubrious climate of the West Indies.

Meanwhile, the opponents of the Puritan government in Massachusetts had succeeded in obtaining an annulment of the Bay Colony's charter and the appointment of a temporary council and president to rule both Massachusetts and New Hampshire. In this arrangement the imperialist-minded Massachusetts merchants completely satisfied their political ambitions, for the new Council, though presided over by Joseph Dudley, the politician son of the Founder Thomas Dudley, was dominated by Richard Wharton and was composed almost exclusively of the interrelated mercantile leaders whose rise to prominence had been the most important social development in the two decades after the Restoration. Entirely unopposed in their authority, free even from the limitations of a popular assembly, they proceeded to enjoy a feast of political privilege.

For twenty months during 1685 and 1686, as rulers of the northern New England colonies, they used every device of government to advance their personal interests. Yet such independent, unfettered local power could not survive long in a mercantilist empire. The Dudley Council was a temporary arrangement, meant to last only until the advisers of James II completed plans for an important reorganization of colonial administration. In 1686 they replaced Dudley with Sir Edmund Andros and expanded the Council to include representatives from all the New England colonies and later from New York. This new government, the Dominion of New England, whose jurisdiction eventually extended from Nova Scotia to the Delaware River, no longer embodied the interests of the Massachusetts merchants alone. In its short career, in fact, it ruled against them in a number of important measures.

The Puritan faction in Massachusetts, now completely excluded from the direction of public affairs, found popular support against Andros' policies and new allies in most of the very merchants who up to 1685 had been among their most outspoken opponents. Animosity against Andros and his Council turned to hatred when the governor established an Anglican church in Boston and threatened the colonists' title to their land. The growing crisis came to a head in April 1689 when news of the overthrow of James II was received in Boston. The Puritan faction, with broad popular backing, rose against Andros and his closest associates, overpowered his armed supporters, and seized the reins of government. A council of safety ruled the colonies while agents negotiated in London for a new settlement of the New England governments. The outcome was the restitution of the charters of Connecticut and Rhode Island, the permanent establishment of a royal government in New Hampshire, and the reorganization of Massachusetts' politics by the terms of a new charter that went into effect in 1691.

Woven into the fabric of this familiar history is the less conspicuous story of the emergence of the permanent interests of the New England merchants. For them the vicissitudes of politics sifted vital needs from unqualified desires, separated individual from group aims, isolated the necessary conditions of their prosperity.

2

The merchants discovered, first, the extent and nature of their dependence upon highly placed individuals in England. The occasional practice of seeking support for their plans from Londoners became a fixed policy as they realized that they could not carry through a single large commercial operation without the coöperation of business and governmental leaders in the home country. Nor was this merely true when the merchants lacked control of local affairs. It was as necessary for them during the Dudley administration when they themselves directed the colonial governments as it was during the Puritan or Dominion regime.

Thus at the beginning of the decade when the heirs of the original members of the Atherton Company set out to capitalize on their claim to the Narragansett region, they first sought the assistance of the Pettaquamscutt proprietors. Then in the face of strong opposition from the actual settlers in Rhode Island they petitioned the king to place the district within the jurisdiction of Connecticut and to grant them full possession of the land under a royal charter.[1] But such a petition would have been cast aside in London unless actively promoted by someone capable of influencing the Privy Council. To win such support the company in 1680 added to its membership Thomas Lord Culpeper, then absentee governor of Virginia and a man of importance in the government of Charles II. Culpeper, who had probably been approached as early as 1675 when he had visited New England, agreed to back the company's petition. In April 1681 he suggested to the Lords of Trade that a committee be appointed to investigate the Atherton claims on the spot and to recommend future action. He provided also a list of "substantial, able and (as I was informed in the place) uninterested persons fit to be Commissioners in the Narragansett affair." As Culpeper probably knew, the group he suggested, though it did not include actual members of the company, was made up entirely of the stockholders' relatives and friends.[2]

Culpeper's proposal was accepted in 1682 and a commission was duly appointed to investigate the problem. It was headed by Edward Cranfield, governor of New Hampshire, who saw in the company and its troubles a means of profiteering at the expense of the colonials.[3] He did not work alone. His appointment to the commission, as to the governorship, had been obtained with the help of two men: William Blathwayt, secretary of the Lords of Trade, and Francis Gwyn, son-in-law of Sir Robert Southwell and clerk of the Privy Council. Gwyn was also a cousin of the Earl of Conway, then secretary of state for the northern department; both he and Blathwayt were the Earl's personal secretaries.[4] Cranfield's obligations to these two men were large and he was not likely to forget this fact. In February 1683 he wrote Blathwayt that if he and Gwyn would entrust the affairs of New England entirely to Randolph and himself "I do give you my faith that you two shall come into an equall part of every thing that tends to proffitt." His scheme for fleecing the Atherton proprietors and their opponents was part of a general plan for making his stay in the colonies worthwhile. First, he explained to Blathwayt,

... as to the Settlement of the Province of Maine wee shall att least make 3000li: The Narragansett Countrey lyes betwixt severall claimours. Both partys have mony and 3 or 4000:li will not be felt in the disposeing those Land's, and as for Boston there are some person's to bee Exempt out of the pardon who will buy their pardon att 8 or 10,000 li price. Besides there are severall graunts of Towne land's, which will in a yeare or two come to bee renewed to pay above 2000 li upon their new leases. The Excize and custom's yearly paid come to above 1500:li and there is above 5000: mony which was collected for the Evangelizeing of Indians, now out att use in the Countrey which by commission may bee inspected into and regulated with other advantages, which will arise in the Settlement ...

How much he managed to extract from the Atherton Company is not known, but when in October 1683 he reported to Blathwayt the commission's complete endorsement of the company's claims he informed the secretary that the merchants "doe all intend to complement you with a parcel of land within their claime." [5]

By this time the company had not only stirred up new discontent among the Rhode Island colonists but had stimulated other Englishmen to think longingly of the rich Narragansett lands. Randolph, though an original member of the Cranfield commission, was always available for new "jobs," and in 1684 he suddenly appeared as agent for the Duke of Hamilton who had resurrected an ancient title to the lands. Petitions from the settlers against the company continued to flow into Whitehall as the Atherton proprietors sought the validation of their claim in the form of a royal charter. But though they were confident enough to parcel out the land for sale to prospective settlers, they met with little success in their final and most important dealings with English officialdom. With the accession of James II, who knew well the importance of the southern New England region from his days as proprietor of New York, the company's plans came into conflict with the grand design of the Dominion of New England. The long-sought royal charter was withheld and all hopes for it vanished in 1687 when Andros advised Whitehall that the Atherton Company's claims were fraudulent and that both land and government belonged to Rhode Island. Members of the company who had actually improved some of their land were compensated for their loss, but since the merchants could not exert sufficient pressure in London to overcome Andros' influence the career of the Atherton Company came to a sudden end. [6]

All of the extravagant plans projected by the merchants in the

1680's followed the same pattern of development. Wharton, whose appetite for commercial adventure was matched only by the fertility of his imagination, launched at least a half dozen major schemes in as many years and each of them eventually turned on his ability to influence the right people in London. Among his land schemes was the Million Purchase, a plot about six by ten miles including a section of the Merrimac River which he, Dudley, and Samuel Shrimpton bought from the chief Indian of the region together with all rights to the river, its islands, fish, and all the privileges of the land. The purchasers transferred the property to a company of twenty stockholders among whom were a number of Englishmen whose help was vital in gaining the necessary royal confirmation. One of them was the inevitable William Blathwayt whose fingers seem to have been in nearly every large commercial pie prepared in New England during the 1680's. To him the Million Purchasers revealed their intentions and hopes in a letter in which they explained the value of the land and river and added, ". . . if you please so farr to Countenance us as to allow us your equall partnership we will at your Direction Transmitt the Papers that we may obtain his Majesties Ratification thereof." Blathwayt went along with the proposal and forwarded the petition to the proper authorities. The Lords of Trade, reluctant to make such grants, referred the matter to Andros who, opposed to the "engrossment of large tracts of land," reported adversely. Again Wharton and his friends lacked the force to counter Andros' influence in London and the plan was laid aside.[7]

Time after time Wharton failed in his projects for want of the proper support in Whitehall. By grants and purchases he accumulated a personal estate in Maine which may have totaled half a million acres, and he petitioned the crown to bestow on him the power of government over the whole region. His plan was to turn this Pejebscot Purchase into a manor over which he would rule as lord. But he could not overcome the reluctance of the Lords of Trade to recommend the creation of such an imposing lordship. Andros' disapproval on the grounds that it would hinder settlement provided the *coup de grâce* to the moribund enterprise.

Wharton was learning from these disappointments, however, and for his grandest scheme he took great pains to have himself properly represented in England. In the middle years of the decade he laid the foundations for a joint-stock company which by royal charter would be empowered to develop mines, foundries, and the manufacture of saltpeter, salt, drugs, dyes, and naval stores. Leaving nothing to chance, he went to England himself and enrolled a number of important Londoners in the company, among them Sir John Shorter, the Lord Mayor. When the plan was well under way he sought even higher levels of influence and succeeded in gaining the support of one of the Lords of the Privy Council who was known to carry particular weight with the king. In February 1688 Wharton petitioned for a comprehensive grant of privileges for the company. He had the aid of the English merchants in advancing his request through the channels of the Board of Trade, the Treasury, the customs offices, and the attorney-general's department. Again he was disappointed. The Revolution of 1688 upset all plans, and Wharton, exhausted by his never-ending, fruitless activity, died before his petition could be revived under the new monarchs.[8]

The importance of ties to men of influence in England was brought home to the merchants not only by the difficulties they faced in attempting to launch large plans without their help but also by the obvious advantages in trade the new functionaries and governing officials in the colonies had by virtue of their connections with the home authorities. Randolph, in whom duty and desire were indistinguishably blended, with the help of Southwell and his other patrons obtained a contract from the Navy Commissioners in 1685 to supply a number of New England mast trees. His sudden interest in this trade was doubtless increased by his appointment in the following year to the position of surveyor of the king's woods in Maine.[9] Cranfield also attempted to put his official connections to good use in trade, arriving in New Hampshire in 1683 with a cargo of goods he expected to sell at considerable profit.[10]

3

In attempting schemes like Wharton's and in observing the business advantages men in official positions enjoyed, the merchants came to realize that the maintenance of connections with people in England close to the sources of political power was the first of their permanent interests. Of the second, less need be said. It flows from the fact that under the Dudley regime and the Dominion of New England the merchants controlled the New England governments for the first time in the century-long history of the region. Their authority centered in a particular political unit from which their influence radiated in all directions. Since access to this governmental body was confirmed to them in the charter of 1691 it remained throughout the colonial period the institution through which they could best gain their political ends.

On the day in May 1686 when the Governor and Company of the Massachusetts Bay, stubborn to the last, dissolved itself by adjourning "to the second Wednesday in October next," the merchants came into immediate control of the colony's Council. It was this body, which once had been the stronghold of the Puritan oligarchy, that ruled the northern New England colonies during 1686 and 1687. No assembly was called and Dudley was a willing confederate of his relatives who directed the decisions of his government. Through their control of the Council the merchants made up for the lean years of exclusion from governmental power. Not only did they grant each other title to large stretches of unoccupied land, but they assigned to themselves and their friends all the offices, high and low, which promised the slightest emolument or influence. They gave Dudley himself control of the Massachusetts probate records, made John Usher treasurer of the royal "Incomes and Revenues of this Government," Richard Smith, Jr. and Edward Palmes justices of the peace, John Richards and Simon Lynde judges of the Suffolk County Court of Pleas, and Richard Waldron, Jr. clerk of the County Court of New Hampshire, probate of wills, and deputy register to Randolph. They determined the legal fees to be charged by officials as well as the imposts and duties, appointed a large committee to investigate the decay of trade, assigned ports of entry, exempted themselves from town taxation, and rewarded themselves handsomely for all services they rendered each other or the public.[11]

In so doing they were neither corrupt nor unusually greedy. The controversy with the intransigeant Puritan faction was safely behind them and ahead lay the prospect of continued enjoyment of the power they now held, though qualified, as even they realized it would have to be, by an elected assembly. For them, as for the political leaders of eighteenth-century England, there was "nothing to do but to govern," and their attention was entirely directed to the uses of government, to the questions of patronage and advantage. Andros alienated most of them by denying them the controlling influence in the Council. Though he continued in office the same merchants who had served on Dudley's Council and was obliged to fill certain vacancies with others of the same group, he created a majority whose interests clashed with those of the New England merchants.[12]

He appointed not only a number of men like John Palmer who were dependent upon his favor for their livelihood, but also the prominent New Yorkers Steven Van Courtlandt and Nicholas Bayard. For his ex-colleagues in the Manhattan government like the lieutenant governor, Francis Nicholson, and the former acting governor and commander-in-chief of the British troops in New York, Major Anthony Brockholls, he also found seats on the Council. He gradually shifted the lucrative appointments from the merchants to his friends. Randolph, who had his own grievances against Andros, was not exaggerating when he wrote in 1688 that "the Governor is safe in his New Yorke confidents, all others being strangers to his councill." [13]

It was this Council, dominated by royal appointees and confederates of the governor, which ruled against the fiscal policy advocated by the New England merchants. Andros identified his own interests and those of his friends with the desire of King James to consolidate and regulate the northern colonies. He effectively removed from the New England merchants a decisive voice in the one organ of local government they felt they needed to control. The victims of the rebellion of April 1689 were the officeholders appointed by Andros. Of the twenty-four men jailed with the governor, only four were New Englanders. The rest were military and civil officers like Palmer, Brockholls, James Graham, the attorney general, and the new secretary and register of New England, John West. Merchants like John Richards, John Foster, Peter Sargeant, John Nelson, Samuel Shrimpton, William Browne, Jr., and Bartholomew Gedney joined the revolution not to overthrow royal government as such but to eliminate a governor and council they could not control.[14]

The Massachusetts charter of 1691 and the appointment of a royal government in New Hampshire reinstituted the council as the political voice of the merchants in the centers of New England commerce. In Massachusetts the Council was to be elected by the General Court composed of the members of both houses elected by the forty shilling freeholders. But since the governor was allowed to veto the selections for the Council the elective power of the General Court was reduced to that of nomination. The effective power of appointment rested with the governor, who was to be chosen by the king. With the assembly representing the lesser property owners, especially the more prosperous farmers and artisans, the merchants would have to rely for their political influence on the support 'of the governor. The selection of this magistrate, whom the merchants would have to control or at least come to terms with if they were to maintain a strong grasp on the upper level of government, now became the object of their intense concern. Their later success in dealing with this problem was forecast by the designation as first royal governor of Massachusetts the New England adventurer Sir William Phips, together with a council composed mainly of second and third generation New England merchants.[15]

In New Hampshire the continuing influence of the proprietary party delayed the consolidation of the political position of the local merchants. Samuel Allen, a London merchant, bought out the Mason claims to the land in 1691 and managed to have himself appointed the first royal governor of the province. But in this arrangement the future political power of the New Hampshire merchants was anticipated, for Allen remained in England as absentee and appointed as his lieutenant governor none other than John Usher who had propitiously married the new governor's daughter.[16]

4

Even if the merchants succeeded in maintaining connections with powerful individuals in England and in dominating the councils of the commercial colonies, they could not consider themselves fully in control of their destinies until they solved the problem symbolized by the presence of Edward Randolph.

Though Randolph had little success in obtaining the extraordinary powers he sought in 1681, he was able to advance himself in the growing colonial bureaucracy. Lord Culpeper and his other patrons had his appointment as customs collector renewed in the form of a royal commission rather than the usual and more vulnerable warrant from the commissioners of customs. His salary in this post, moreover, was doubled. Blathwayt made him his deputy surveyor and auditor of royal revenues in New England, except for New Hampshire. Within the next four years he maneuvered himself also into the positions of secretary and register of the New England colonies, surveyor of the woods and timber in Maine, and deputy postmaster in New England. All of these offices had fees and perquisites which made them worth the attention of a penurious placeman. From them and his shares in confiscated vessels and goods Randolph hoped to find the means to secure himself and his family.[17]

He calculated, however, without sufficient regard for the interests of the New England merchants. Though up to 1686 they still had to rely on Randolph to help them gain the political influence they desired, they had no hesitation in blocking his confiscations at every turn. In this they were supported by the Puritan magistrates who, refused to allow Randolph to search without a warrant from themselves. Nor did they intend to issue such warrants to him. Moreover, in 1682 Massachusetts set up its own naval office whose functions duplicated in several ways those of the royal collector.[18] The result was a long series of conflicts between Randolph on the one hand and the magistrates and merchants on the other.

Time and time again Randolph was kept from boarding and searching suspected vessels for lack of the armed support he could have commanded with a search warrant. He was reduced to such expedients as following the local naval officer into warehouses which the latter happened to be inspecting. It was with a tone of satisfaction that Randolph reported on one occasion that he had seized some Scotch goods in a warehouse, "the doors being left open." The financial success of his collectorship seemed to depend on his obtaining the power to search and seize at will. By June 1682 he wrote the customs commissioners flatly that "A writ of Assistance is necessary." But such was not forthcoming, and for the moment at least Randolph had to be satisfied with reaching the suspected merchants through technicalities of the law. If he could not prove that goods had been imported or exported contrary to the navigation acts he could sue their owners for loading or unloading them before entering with him or for failing to give bonds on enumerated goods.[19]

Randolph's presence was a constant threat to the merchants' trade, legal or illegal, for the collector, being primarily interested in the emoluments of his position, was far from punctilious in his accusations. However, the merchants themselves were not without resources and, together with the Puritan faction, they made life as difficult for Randolph and his "Rogues" as they could. Besides winning almost every case at law Randolph chose to bring forward, they filed countersuits against him, had his assistants thrown in jail at the slightest excuse, warned them out of town, and boycotted them from entertainments and employment. Randolph himself was taxed by the Boston magistrates, his wife and daughters were subjected to a campaign of vilification, and though he remained outwardly a friend of the merchants who still needed him, he was the object of universal contempt and hatred.[20]

The merchants and their allies were so effective in blocking Randolph's efforts to confiscate suspected vessels and goods that by January 1685 the collector had to confess to Southwell that "Its true: I have of late slackned my prosecutions." He explained his remissness as the result of his failure to gain favorable decisions from the courts and of his being "tyred out with tedious journeyes and no profitt. . ." But this was not the end of his efforts to reap a harvest in the colonies. His salary continued as did a small income from fees due him in his various positions. And there were at least two directions in which he could still proceed in securing the welfare of his family.[21]

He petitioned the crown for 300–400 acres of land in Salem, a plot that was part of the estate left by Hugh Peter who had been executed in 1660 for abetting the regicides. "Tis forfeited by his treason," Randolph wrote Southwell, "and the Grant of it would be a kindness to my children." His recollection of the pitiful indigents he had met at Whitehall, dependents of men who had spent their lives and fortunes in His Majesty's service, "obliges me," he explained, "for my childrens sake to engage my freinds in their behalf in case of any accident befalling me." Later, during Andros' administration, he petitioned for the whole of Nahant Neck, which belonged to the town of Lynn, as well as 700 acres situated between Watertown and Cambridge, a parcel of land near Portsmouth, Rhode Island, and about 250 acres at Newport. In each case his petitions were contested by the towns or individuals who held claim to the land.[22]

If he encountered opposition in fleecing the merchants and in reaching for free land, he could not be prevented from appointing whom he wished as his own assistants. In 1683 he appointed his brother, Bernard, deputy collector, who, receiving "many affronts" in a few months in office, returned home before the year was out. Randolph replaced him by still another brother, Gyles, who served as deputy until his death in 1684 and was eventually succeeded by his predecessor, Bernard.[23]

All his schemes — his connivance with Blathwayt, Cranfield, and Mason, his efforts to accumulate a tidy sum from informing and confiscating, to gather together a landed estate in New England, to place his brothers in the customs service, and in every way to squeeze the perquisites of his various offices for every farthing they were worth — emphasized the conflict of interests between himself and the merchants. His profit was largely their loss, for out of their pockets came the informer's moieties, the multiplying fees, and in some cases even the land he sought. For the illegal traders his presence was an obvious menace. But so long as he was of use to the merchants in their struggle for political power he was tolerated. The break came in 1686 when the merchants took over the Massachusetts government.

The Council that convened for the first time on May 25, 1686, consisting mainly of an interrelated group of Massachusetts merchants, had been selected by Randolph with the advice of the new president, Joseph Dudley.[24] By the middle of the summer Randolph realized that he was a victim of the merchants' strategy. In July he wrote Southwell that the new president and Council were "still but the Governor and Company." Dudley, whom he had himself correctly sized up as a man who "hath his fortunes to make in the world," used his office to gain advantages Randolph coveted. He appointed his sixteen-year-old son clerk of the Suffolk County Court, a job Randolph estimated as worth about £100 a year. He made appointments to the deputy recorderships and secretaryships without reference to Randolph, the secretary and recorder, thus depriving him of "all fees, rights, privileges, profitts, perquisites and advantages [belonging] to the said places and offices. . ."[25] Wharton, the most powerful individual on the Council, angered at Randolph's disposal of at least two minor positions he wanted as well as disagreeing strongly with him on the proper conduct of trade, openly accused the collector of intending "to inthrall this people in vassalage." The Councillors gave Randolph no support in setting up an Anglican church, kept him from certain sums he claimed as informer, and refused even to let him inspect the records of their new land grants. Most important, the Council, some of whom, as Randolph belatedly discovered, "are traders, and others by marriage or otherwise . . . nearly related," blocked his efforts to make "strict orders to prevent the irregular trade of this place." By the end of the year he was denouncing his erstwhile friends roundly and looking forward to the arrival of the royal governor who he hoped would restore him to his rights and privileges.[26]

In this as in almost all his other hopes he was disappointed. Andros, who in 1680 had been relieved of the governorship of New York because of charges of racketeering in fees and perquisites, parceled out all available jobs to his own underlings and dependents. His men West and Palmer descended on the settlers in Maine with demands for large fees for the confirmation of their land titles and carved out a few choice lots for themselves. Randolph was forced to lease his secretaryship to West, whom he promptly turned upon with charges of taking "extravagant fees." "The harpies themselves," as Hutchinson later wrote, "quarreled about their share of the prey." [27]

In the two years of Andros' reign the merchants fell victim to the same abuses that Randolph had tried to subject them to. And from Andros' appointees they heard still more of a now familiar kind of argument. To the merchants who signed the *Declaration* defending the revolt of 1689 it seemed that Andros' officeholders considered the New Englanders "*Slaves*, and the only difference between them and *Slaves* is their not being bought and sold." They quoted these "abject Persons" as demanding to know whether they expected the privileges of Englishmen to follow them to the ends of the earth. Palmer, indeed, believed that New England was a possession of the king of England, to be ruled by him "without any regard to *Magna Charta*." [28]

Randolph's extortionate use of his offices the merchants might have considered merely the offensive behavior of an avaricious man, but in the rapacity of Andros' followers they could not help but see evidence of a permanent influence that worked to their disadvantage. Excessive fee-taking and other abuses in the customs service would continue as long as New England remained within England's mercantilist empire. Having neither the desire nor the ability to separate themselves from the British community, the merchants at the end of the seventeenth century sought ways of controlling this new, permanent force.

The solution of this problem became a major interest to them thereafter. In most cases they would attempt to guide the appointments to the royal offices in New England or come to terms with the men who filled them. If the incumbents owed their positions to the resident merchants they would not readily victimize them. And if these lesser officials were native New Englanders instead of hungry English placemen there would be even less likelihood of trouble from them. If they turned against their countrymen they would be treated not merely as bullies and thieves but as traitors as well.

By every means available to them — by the influence of their English connections, by their own power in the colonial governments, by bribery, trickery, or the manipulation of public opinion – the merchants would seek to restrain these functionaries. They did not fail to do so. Randolph's successor as collector in New England was Jahleel Brenton, son of the Rhode Island merchant William Brenton. And when it developed that this wealthy, ambitious colonial chose to behave like an ordinary English factotum, Governor Phips, a merchant himself, acted in behalf of the mercantile community when he claimed local jurisdiction over the customs collection and threatened to break every bone in the collector's body and cut off the ears of his witnesses if he failed to release a confiscated vessel. Phips was recalled to London for his opposition to Brenton and to his colleague Captain Short, commander of the royal frigate *Nonesuch*. He obeyed, but not before he had broken his cane over Short's head and had him thrown in prison.[29]

5

Like the desire to keep a firm hand on the agents of British officialdom serving in the colonies, the final basic interest of the merchants to emerge at the end of the seventeenth century originated in the connection with England. Mercantilist theory was based on the assumption that a right ordering of imperial affairs would result in a continuous flow of wealth from the colonies to the home country. The natural balance of trade and the enforcement of the navigation acts had made this theory a reality, and by the ninth decade of the century the New England merchants were faced with the consequences.

The difficulty of finding returns for manufactures which was the central problem of New England commerce throughout the colonial period had been increased by the plantation duties of 1673 which tended to narrow the merchants' profit margin. In 1685 this burden was increased by an additional tariff on tobacco and sugar which had so harmful an effect on trade that even Randolph questioned its wisdom. Moreover, the gradual elimination of piracy, the tightening control of trade with the bullion-producing Spanish colonies, and a decade without war and privateering in the Atlantic world dried up other familiar sources of coin. Yet the necessity to pay the English exporters of manufactures continued, as did the need for a convenient form of currency in the commercial centers. Specie and bills flowed continuously from the colonies to Europe, and Massachusetts' attempts to stabilize the money supply by legislation banning the exportation of coin failed completely. The merchants who managed to accumulate small stores of bullion were in a most advantageous position. Sewall's occasional shipments of metals, like that consisting of 435½ ounces of plate "in one entire Piece in a Bagg" to John Ive in London, show him acting as temporary banker to other New England merchants.[30]

The balance of trade was so heavily weighted in favor of the home country that only by ingenious and complicated devices could the merchants make coin or exchange flow directly from England to New England. One such arrangement was the New England Company, which had been organized before the Restoration to collect and transmit charity moneys from Puritan sympathizers in the British Isles to New England. By 1679 control of this organization was in the hands of its treasurer, the London merchant and alderman Henry Ashurst, who later served as Massachusetts' agent in England. The use which the merchants made of the company may be seen in a letter dated December 17, 1679, written by John Hull to Ashurst. The Boston mint-master applied to the latter for the right to avail himself of the company's banking facilities. Ashurst's "kindsman my loving neighbor" Peter Sergeant had informed Hull, he wrote, that as treasurer of the company the Londoner was "wonted to pay moneyes in London and to receive it here with such advance as you Judg meet." Sergeant had indicated that in the coming year he would not be using his usual share, and so Hull asked Ashurst if this sum might be made available to him.

Ashurst's reply is not known, but if he had been willing to accommodate the Bostonian he would have deposited the money to Hull's credit with a London merchant who would then have allowed Hull to draw bills as payment to London creditors. In return Hull would have distributed goods to the recipients of the company's bounty in the colonies to the extent of the exchange value of the money Ashurst had deposited to Hull's credit — plus interest. The severity of the money shortage in the colonies and the consequent difficulty the merchants faced in paying off their English debts is indicated by the fact that the interest rate for such transactions was commonly set, and accepted, at 20 and 25 per cent.[31]

Even at this price such funds were hard to come by, and the resources of the New England Company could satisfy at best only a fraction of the needs of the New England merchants. Feeling in the ninth decade the full effect of mercantilism and the imbalance of trade, the merchants looked about for monetary schemes by which to improve their situation.

The first proposal that came to their attention was that of the Reverend John Woodbridge of Newbury. Though this cleric protested his lack of skill in *"merchantile Affairs . . .* being better acquainted with *coelestial Dealings,"* it was he who introduced banking to New England. While still in England during the Commonwealth period he had learned the details "of a *Bank* of *money"* which he communicated to "divers Country Gentlemen, Yeomen and others" after his arrival in New England in the 1660's. The idea spread quickly, was considered by the Massachusetts Council, experimented with in a small way in 1671, and put into trial operation in the fall of 1681.[32]

The resulting bank, called the Fund and organized by a few Bostonians, emitted bills to those who deposited with the Fund security in the form of land mortgages or personal property. This paper was to be accepted in payment of debts by other members of the Fund who noted on the bills the amount involved in the particular transaction. For the few individuals concerned in the Fund of 1681 the bills served certain immediate needs, but the more important intention of the managers was to demonstrate to the general public how fully the bills would *"supply the defect of* Money" and to convince them of the value of accepting the "Fund-Pay." The experiment lasted about six months and attracted at least seven subscribers in addition to the three known Fundors. By 1682 its projectors considered it successful enough — despite the arguments of its detractors decried by Woodbridge as *"broad-sides of Pot-gun-pelletts, chained with Fallacies and buffoonry"* — to propose its expansion into a larger enterprise.[33]

Leadership of the banking scheme was taken by Captain John Blackwell, a recently arrived merchant "of much piety and worth." Under his direction Woodbridge's simple banking device broadened into a complicated plan for a "Bank of Credit, Lumbard, and Exchange of Moneys by persons of approved integrity, prudence, and estate in this country. . ." Provision was made for a managerial hierarchy consisting of assessors, twenty-one managers, and a number of deputy managers from whom were to be chosen a master and assistant master, three trustees, and two treasurers. A team of clerks was to

complete the staff. The capitalization of the bank was to be at least
£10,500.[34]

However cumbersome and impractical the proposal for the new
bank was, it served the main purpose of suggesting a way of providing
the currency so badly needed by the merchants. By September 1686
the scheme was far enough advanced to be proposed for approval to
the Dudley Council. This body referred it to its "grand and standing
Committee" on trade and maritime affairs, which included most of the
commercial leaders in New England. Though the committee and
subsequently the Council officially endorsed Blackwell's petition, a
major difficulty suddenly appeared. The merchants, though willing to
have the government approve the scheme, were not eager to invest in
it themselves. Their lack of support doomed the bank to failure. By
the end of the year the managerial staff had dwindled to four assessors,
and in July 1688 Blackwell reported that the whole enterprise had
been abandoned. The press for printing the bills was returned to
England and all assets were liquidated.[35]

There were two causes of the merchants' disinterest and the consequent collapse of the bank of credit. The first was the realization by
the merchants that their needs were not really served by Blackwell's
proposal. The second was the feasibility of another approach to the
problem of currency.

The merchants engaged in importing manufactures from England
came to believe as the date of launching the bank approached that
the bills of credit would benefit only the farmers, debtors, and inland tradesmen. The large supply of bank paper, certain to depreciate
even within New England, would be of little value in payment of debts
to the London merchants. The importers, therefore, would be forced
to pay in hard coin or expensive bills on London but would receive in
payment for their commodities a local currency of uncertain value.
The most important merchants trading with England never at any
time associated themselves actively with the bank. Of the twelve men
known to have been involved in the scheme five were not merchants
at all. One of the others had been in New England only a single year
and, though the other six were members of the mercantile community
by marriage or occupation, none was a leading importer. One of them,
Elisha Cooke, became the first leader of the "country party" in later
Massachusetts politics.[36]

For the majority of the merchants a more attractive way of solving the currency problem was to manipulate the valuation of coins and to continue the operation of the Massachusetts mint.

Seventeenth-century Americans acted on the belief that specie could be attracted from abroad by the simple expedient of legal over-valuation. It was assumed that Spaniards, pirates, and others with bullion would rather dispose of their money where pieces of eight were declared by law to be worth six shillings than where they were rated at only five shillings. Similarly, it was believed that one way to block the outflow of New England coins was to enhance their value so that, presumably, they would buy more in New England than elsewhere and merchants would not be tempted to dispose of them abroad. The principle was clearly stated by Hull, the mint-master:

> If our own coin be carried out of the country, it is a sign that it is not so light as it may be, and that it would be for public advantage to make it lighter, unless we had some public income by mines as the Spaniard hath.[37]

Massachusetts, in fact, had long been accustomed to manipulate coin valuation in order to increase the money supply. As early as 1632 the colony by legislative fiat had raised the legal value of the piece of eight above its intrinsic worth. In creating the mint ten years later, however, this provision had been rescinded, and for twenty years thereafter foreign coins had been allowed to circulate freely at market valuation. The local money, meanwhile, though declared to be the equal of English coin, was being lightened by the introduction of alloys at the mint and by the seigneurage allowed the minters. Merchants preferred to pay their foreign debts with the harder pieces of eight because they believed the pine tree shillings were most valuable in New England where by 1672 they were officially valued at 25 per cent more than their intrinsic worth. Foreign coin left New England in increasing quantities until the agitated merchants in the Bay Colony forced through a law setting the legal prices of pieces of eight and pine tree shillings equal for the same quantity of silver content.[38]

The authorities at the English mint had never been satisfied with either local mints or debased moneys in the colonies, and after the revocation of the Bay Company charter they fought to have the closure of the Massachusetts mint made permanent. The Dudley Council of merchants in 1686 protested against such a move, and, observing that "wee haveing no staple commodities to pass current in payments as in other Plantations, by which our Trade for want of money is much perplexed and decayed," begged Blathwayt to petition the king "for establishing a Mint in this his Dominion, with an allowance of such alloy, or abatement in weight as may secure our money from Transportation . . ." In this they had the support of Andros who favored both the continuation of the mint and the inflation of coin valuation. But the English officials thoroughly discussed the matter with Andros before he left for America, and it was decided that the Massachusetts mint would not be opened, though the Dominion governor was to have the power to regulate the value of coins.[39] Consequently, Andros' arrival at the end of 1686 was the signal for the merchants toying with Blackwell's bank scheme to concentrate upon obtaining the proper valuation of coins from the Andros Council. The issue was fought out in February and March 1687.

A group of merchants led by Richard Wharton, fearing a further depletion of the coin supply, proposed to fix the value of the New England shilling at fourteen pence, the sixpence at seven, the three pence at four, and the twopence at three — a level considerably higher than the pre-1684 valuation. They suggested, further, that all foreign coins and metals be priced not by piece but by weight at the very high rate of seven shillings six pence per ounce.[40]

Wharton's proposal touched off a heated debate in the Council. Some argued that such a pricing would attract only light coins from the Caribbean instead of the usual "Sugar Mellasses Rhum etc.," thus ruining the shipping industry and eliminating familiar returns to England. And it was further suggested,

that the Raiseing mony would help only the Merchants [,] and the Country Inhabitants [would] not be the better for they would not advance upon their goods and So would be a great Inequality in Trade and Suddainly the Country would be ruined.[41]

The problem was difficult and the merchants were not in agreement among themselves. On March 10 a second group led by Simon Lynde proposed that New England money be continued "at same rate as now it is," that exportation of it be strictly forbidden, and that all foreign money pass at six shillings ten pence per ounce instead of the sterling silver rate of six shillings eight pence per ounce. Andros called in the local goldsmiths and quizzed them on the real value of the standard Spanish piece of eight. After receiving the goldsmiths' opinion the Council entered on a long debate about the money problem in the course of which Andros "found out the designe of the Merchants to [consider] mony a Commodity, and not to make it Currant mony at a price." The decision that was reached was a defeat for the merchants on the matter of foreign coins, for the Council ruled that the piece of eight would be rated thenceforth not by weight but by piece and that the standard coin of this denomination would pass at six shillings. But the Lynde group at least won its point on the local money, for it was ruled "that the present New England mony do passe for value as formerly." [42]

In 1688 the ratio between Spanish and New England coin was still an open question, and in 1692 the Massachusetts government responded to pressures similar to those that had operated in 1672 and raised slightly the legal value of the piece of eight. Except for this change the decision of the Andros Council remained in force during the rest of the century. But it did not, of course, solve the money shortage. The rating of the piece of eight, Randolph wrote in May 1687, "does not answer the end, money grows very scarce and no trade brings it in." The bank advocates, though reduced to a mere handful of politicians, were still active enough to publish a pamphlet in 1688 entitled *A Model for Erecting a Bank of Credit. . .* Since they could not now hope to succeed unless they could counter the merchants' arguments in favor of the overvaluation of coin, they included in this publication an eight page "Supplement *or* Appendix" in which they attempted to show "the many Prejudices that will Inevitably ensue, as well to His *Majesty* as to his Subjects by enhansing the value of Spanish *Coynes* etc. above his *Majesties*." But their audience had vanished. There is no indication that the pamphlet had the slightest effect. [43]

This resolution of the coinage and banking problems was only temporary, for the difficulty of operating in a money-short economy was not lessened. When in 1690 the Massachusetts government was faced with the economic consequences of Phips' abortive expedition against Quebec it was unable even by the most rigorous taxation to raise the money necessary to pay the soldiers and sailors and the merchants who had furnished the supplies. Failing to obtain a hoped-for loan from the merchants, the government resorted for the first time to the expedient of issuing paper bills of public credit, which it declared to be legal tender in payment for all debts. The money, to be backed and retired by future taxation, was emitted first in the quantity of £7,000, and when this was found to be entirely inadequate £40,000 more was printed. Despite vigorous endorsement of the paper by merchants like Elisha Hutchinson, it was received with distrust and rapidly depreciated. Some of the recipients were so eager to get rid of the bills that, despite the General Court's pledge to receive them at a premium of 5 per cent, they sold them for only 60 per cent of their face value. They were still in circulation, badly worn and heavily discounted, as the century closed.[44]

Thus the years between 1681 and 1691 were as revolutionary in economic as in political matters. In attempting to solve the problem of the money supply during this decade when its full severity was felt for the first time in New England the merchants became acquainted with the three devices that would dominate all thinking on the subject throughout the following century: the overvaluation of coin, banks of issue, and government paper money. None of these methods were wholly satisfactory, and by 1700 the merchants were far less sure about what to do than that something had to be done. The war at the end of the century brought a sudden influx of English money into New England, and the resumption of privateering also tended to lighten the burden temporarily. But eventually the merchants would have to deal with the problem in a permanent way. They had discovered another of the continuing interests of their group.

6

These were the fundamental interests of the New England merchants at the end of the seventeenth century: to maintain connections with highly placed individuals in England; to dominate the colonial councils; to control the English functionaries in the colonial service; and to find a solution of the money problem which had been created by the enforcement of the navigation laws and the imbalance of trade. All the merchants, of whatever personal background, status, and social ambitions, felt these needs, for they were demands imposed by a common occupation. So long as New England remained within the British empire and so long as that empire was regulated according to the theories of mercantilism, these interests would remain. The need to pursue them in one way or another was inescapable for any New Englander — whatever his origins or social condition — who engaged in the wholesale importation, exportation, and distribution of goods.

But a community of economic interests does not necessarily determine a social unit. By the end of the seventeenth century it was clear that the merchant group was not socially homogeneous. It was not an undiversified social unit. The merchants, despite their common interests, formed not a singular social entity, but a spectrum; not a clearly defined bloc of like-minded individuals with similar attitudes and styles of life, but a combination of people as different as Charles Lidget and Samuel Sewall, John Usher and Elisha Hutchinson, Nicholas Paige and Anthony Stoddard, Humphrey Luscomb and William Vaughan. The later history of the New England merchants lies rooted in these differences as well as in the interests common to the group.

The merchants were divided deeply by the very needs they held in common. For if their interests were the same their ability to satisfy them was not. Every important merchant trading overseas had connections of some sort in the home country which brought him into indirect contact with the economic and political leaders of the realm. But, especially in the heated political atmosphere of late Stuart England, all ties to leading personages were not equal.

Most of the politically informed colonists in New England of whatever occupation identified their own welfare with that of the Whig-Puritan party in England. They considered each blow struck at dissenters to be an attack on themselves and rejoiced at every victory of Whiggism. To them the acquittal of Shaftesbury was a glorious event and the revocation of the city of London's charter a threat to their own liberties.[45]

To some of the merchants the same simple alignment was possible. Many of their business connections in England were with the dissenting Whig merchants whose predecessors had sent the first shiploads of manufactures to Puritan New England. For Samuel Sewall ideology and interest merged in his sympathy for one of his chief London correspondents, Thomas Papillon, whose leadership of the London Whig merchants ended in forced exile.[46] Most of the merchants, however, were not as strongly motivated by religion or as closely tied to the English dissenters as this staunch Puritan. For the majority of commercial leaders the effective principle of association with English party groups was more complicated and more permanent. For them the chief consideration was the relation of their most powerful supporters to the exercise of power. No ideology, no religious belief, no abstract political principle or party loyalty separated Richard Wharton and Charles Lidget, but in 1689 they were on opposite sides of the political fence. Lidget ended up in the Boston jail with Andros because his connections, inherited from his father who had built the family fortune on the timber he sold to the navy mast contractors, linked him to the men in authority under James II in both England and America. Wharton died in the midst of his fight for the removal of Andros whose favor, like that of the Lords of Trade and the Privy Council, he had been denied. The fact that Lidget was one of the founders of the first Anglican church in New England does not indicate a religious or ideological orientation different from Wharton's. The latter, if he was not an active Anglican, certainly was not a dissenter. Both men married heiress daughters of nonconformist New Englanders.[47]

The Boston merchants who participated in the revolt against Andros did so because they had been unable to control the decisions of his Council and had suffered for this lack of influence. They joined the rebellion in the name of liberty, and they were undoubtedly sincere in believing, like the English Whigs in 1688, that their actions were aimed at the elimination of tyranny. But as soon as the dust of insurrection had settled most of them busied themselves with seeking another royalist government in New England, which, like the councils of England itself — Whig or Tory — they hoped to use for their own purposes.[48] As for the merchant loyalists in this early American revolution, no one could have understood their position more fully than their eighteenth-century counterpart, the merchant governor Thomas Hutchinson. Anticipating his own attitude to the revolutionary movement that was to sweep him and his family into exile, he wrote in his *History* in 1764 that the rebels of 1689 had acted too rashly. The fate of New England depended upon that of the Old. If William succeeded, wrote this famous merchant whose wealth and political position flowed from his connections with the ruling men of England,

. . . they might have assumed the government without any hazard. If he failed, had they remained quiet, they would have been in no worse state than before; but the consequence of an insurrection would have been death to the principal actors, and a still harder slavery than before to all the rest of the inhabitants.[49]

The merchants of whatever political affiliations agreed that English liberties of life and property were jealously to be guarded and carefully preserved for future generations. But their calculation of the extent of the threat to those liberties — in 1689 as in 1776 — varied with their proximity to the sources of privilege and power. Neither the jailed Charles Lidget nor the merchants like Nicholas Paige, John Nelson, Francis Foxcroft, Nathaniel Byfield, Richard Sprague, David Jeffries, Edward Palmes, Francis Brinley, and John Pynchon, Jr. — all of whom in 1690 petitioned the crown to send over another royal governor to rule New England — thought less of freedom than did Sewall. But as a result of their particular relationships to the new leaders of England or their prospective influence on the proposed magistrates of New England they considered the advent of a second royal governor less an abridgment than a guarantee of their liberties.[50]

7

The variety of relationships to governmental authority in England and America was part of a more general differentiation among the New England merchants. At one end of the merchants' social scale were men whose situation, attitudes, and style of living are best exemplified in the life of Samuel Shrimpton. This son of the immigrant brazier Henry, who had died in 1666 worth £11,979, lived a life far different from his father's. Heir to one of the largest fortunes in New England, he expanded his land investments, and by 1687 he was the richest man in Boston. In that year he paid the town's largest tax. His assessed wealth in trade was 1.7 per cent of the total assessed mercantile property in Boston: his estimated real estate holdings in that town alone totaled .6 per cent of the entire value of the principality's land and buildings. And he owned property in Chelsea, Dorchester, and Brookline as well. He was the proprietor of Beacon Hill and both Noddles and Deer Island in Boston Bay. His trading operations extended into the logwood trade, the importation of manufactures, and the Newfoundland-to-Europe fish commerce.[51]

Shrimpton thought of himself as an elegant, fastidious English gentleman, a man whose wealth made him a proper trustee of the country's welfare. He scorned the Puritan government. As soon as he heard of the revocation of the Massachusetts charter he refused any further allegiance to the Commonwealth government. In 1686 he flatly rejected the jurisdiction of the Massachusetts courts and defied the legislature. He welcomed the arrival of Randolph with the commission for the Dudley government. By the end of the Dominion period he had become one of the leaders of what might be called Anglican officialdom. This faction, formed around the royal governor and the English naval and military officers in Boston, included a number of merchants like Shrimpton and Lidget. These men, if not actually Anglicans like Lidget and Luscomb, sympathized with the Church of England as did Shrimpton, in whose house Randolph's chaplain performed his first Anglican marriage ceremony in New England.[52]

To Samuel Sewall, however, as active a merchant as New England could boast,[53] these men lived in a world apart. Next to them Sewall, born into a family of yeoman status, was provincial. To him they were the *haut monde*, living lives of frivolous and wicked extravagance. "Mr. Shrimpton, Capt. Lidget and others," Sewall reported in his *Diary*,

come in a Coach from Roxbury about 9. aclock or past, singing as they come, being inflamed with Drink. At Justice Morgan's they stop and drink Healths, curse, swear, talk profanely and baudily to the great disturbance of the Town and grief of good people. Such high-handed wickedness has hardly been heard of before in Boston.

He was not invited to their dinner parties, nor they to his, and he concluded his description of the pomp and ceremony of Humphrey Luscomb's funeral with the remark, "None of our family were invited." [54] Their fashions revolted him, and none more so than the wearing of those symbols of Restoration sophistication, perriwigs. To some they were important articles of dress, carefully selected and proudly worn; to Sewall they were the height of artificiality, and he had no hesitation in saying so. When he found that Mr. Hayward, the notary public, had cut off his hair and was "wearing a Perriwig of contrary Colour," he harangued him so vociferously, supporting his arguments with "the words of our Saviour . . . and Mr. Alsop's Sermon," that the poor man had to take refuge in the excuse that "The Doctor advised him to it." To Sewall, it was a fitting end that came to Mr. Clendon, the Boston barber and perriwig maker, who died, the merchant wrote in his *Diary*, "being almost eat up with Lice and stupified with Drink and cold." [55]

Yet Sewall had considerable respect for these men of fashion, whatever he said of their moral lapses. They were close to Governor Andros whom Sewall found a somewhat awesome figure in his "Scarlet Coat Laced." When, on a memorable occasion, Sewall was introduced to Andros, he concealed his hostility to him and "thankfully acknowledged the protection and peace we enjoyed under his Excellencie's Government." Shrimpton, on the other hand, was an intimate of Andros and his friends. In 1687 on Randolph's recommendation he was added to Andros' Council, with which he broke only when the governor challenged his title to certain parcels of land.[56]

Shrimpton was a high-living colonial Englishman whose pride would never have permitted him to write as Sewall did on a trip to England that he was "a Stranger in this Land." [57] Only one generation removed from the immigrant Henry, Samuel Shrimpton had traveled far on the span that separated the social extremities of the merchant group. At his death in 1698 he stood near the summit of the mercantile community where a merchant lived in a superior world, linked closely to the powers that ruled in America and England, a member of an elegant, mannered society of gentlemen, English as only British colonials can be English.

Yet most of the men who engaged in trade were closer in attitudes and style of life if not in religious enthusiasm to Samuel Sewall. The scale of merchant types descended from the high-church officialdom group to the wellborn natives with less wealth and poorer overseas connections but with equal social ambitions — men like Fitz-John and Wait Winthrop — to the successful first generation merchants like John Bray of Kittery and Andrew Belcher of Boston, who were still part of rural, provincial frontier society, to the lowest reaches of the group where tradesmen, peddlers, shopkeepers, mariners, and fishermen gathered together their resources, invested in a few voyages overseas, and gradually came to think of themselves as merchants. The base of the merchant group was hidden in the obscurity of occasional voyages in small ships, the jumbled shops of port towns, and the isolated trading shacks of backwoods Connecticut where, as Madam Knight remarked in her famous *Journal*, "They give the title of merchant to every trader." At this level there were no distinct boundaries of the merchant group. There were no institutional limits which could prohibit an ambitious shipmaster from calling himself a merchant, just as there was no way to prevent the well-known mariner Captain Cyprian Southack from describing himself as "gent." [58]

In New England in the 1690's, as indeed throughout the eighteenth century, the occupation of trade, though it defined an area of common interests for the men engaged in it, did not delimit a stratum of society as it did in England. It was not so much a way of life as a way of making money; not a social condition but an economic activity. It was the most important single vehicle for social ascent. By the wealth and connections it offered as by nothing else one could traverse the slope of colonial society.

By the end of the century the pattern of social ascent through trade was clear. An unknown, hard-headed colonial tradesman, sailor, or even farmer becomes a successful merchant, competes for the political and economic favors of the official group, attains power on the colonial Council, creates friendships with influential people in England, and passes on a fortune to his son. The heir grows up in a different society from that of his father, solidifies the family position in English officialdom, uses his family connections to advance in trade and to receive important political appointments, and becomes a colonial member of the British ruling class. Having reached through different channels the social and political position of the Englishmen who left the home country for careers in the colonial governments, he is tempted to end his career in the English countryside. But what is a return to his colleagues is an arrival for him, and most often he ends his career as a colonial merchant prince.

So it was with the Belchers, whose lives illustrate the pattern of mercantile ascent through British society with classic perfection. At what point did Andrew Belcher become a merchant? The son of a Cambridge settler, he started probably as a country peddler or innkeeper, progressed as an inland provision wholesaler, and, inheriting some money from his wife's father, bought a vessel and became an independent shipmaster-merchant. The economic upheaval of King Philip's War offered him the opportunity to branch out into large-scale commerce in provisions. Gradually, almost imperceptibly, he inched upward across the surface of colonial society, finding a few firm footholds in successful voyages, slipping and stumbling on poor risks and hard luck, dashing through the open stretches of political favors. The measure of his success was less his eventual wealth or the fact that his equipage at the governor's reception in 1702 included a Negro footman, than that twelve years after serving as master on one of Samuel Sewall's vessels he had become the main provisioner of the royal ships that touched at Boston harbor.[59]

The road he traveled was long, stretching from the obscurity of rural New England to the company of Governor Lord Bellomont and a commercial correspondence with the London alderman Sir Ambrose Crowley.[60] But no first generation merchant could go the whole distance himself. It was not Andrew but his son Jonathan who reached the next stage of ascent when'he attained the security of colonial officialdom. The son of a man who had spent his best years searching for markets and supplies in remote colonial America, Jonathan spent his own youth largely in Europe, visiting twice at the Court of Hanover where he was given a gold medal by Princess Sophia. In England he made lasting friendships "among the ministry and nobility; the principal of whom was Lord Townsend, by whose influence he obtained his commission" as Governor of Massachusetts and New Hampshire. The final stage of the journey was attempted only by *his* son, Jonathan, Jr., who viewed the summit of English society in the perspective of a provincial governor's son. He was brought up and educated among people for whom home meant England and establishment among the landed county families the goal of all endeavor, but his best efforts and all the family wealth failed to win him a secure place in English society. Though in his profligate living in London he aped the manners of the fashionable London rakes, and though he erased one vestige of the family origin by joining the Anglican church, he failed in his ultimate ambitions. Disappointed in his hopes of marrying an English heiress, he returned to the colonies where he fell into the pattern of his father's life, going from one position in the colonial administration to another.[61]

The Belchers were prototypes of the ascending merchant families in the late seventeenth and early eighteenth centuries. There were many variations. Few of them, even in the third generation, attempted and fewer still succeeded in making the final transference from the colonies to the English gentry. Many found sufficient satisfaction in lifting the social level of their own dissenting churches rather than in changing to the Anglican communion; certain of the Congregational, Presbyterian, and Quaker churches became as prestigious as the Anglican. Some of the merchants, like the Wentworths of New Hampshire, founded veritable dynasties. The ultimate product of this powerful family, the princely Anglican and loyalist Revolutionary governor John Wentworth, was the direct descendant of the Puritan immigrant Elder William Wentworth, whose grandson, the shipmaster John, left a mercantile fortune, excellent connections in England, and fourteen children as a basis for the family's ascendancy.[62]

The Belcher and Wentworth families rose to the top of the merchant group in almost the same years at the turn of the seventeenth century. With them were a number of other merchant clans which together came to form a large part of the ruling aristocracy of eighteenth-century New England: the Apthorps, the Bowdoins, the Faneuils, and the Olivers in Massachusetts; the Ayraults, the Bernons, the Lopezes, and the Malbones in Rhode Island; the Pepperells, the Partridges, and the Sherburns in New Hampshire. But from below came the continuous challenge of other merchants who demanded entrance to this privileged group. Charles Apthorp, a proper Englishman in every way, for whom "being in the same social set as Governor Shirley and the British admiral [led to] being given most of the contracts in company with other favorites such as the son-in-law of the general commanding the New England army," — Charles Apthorp had to withstand the competition of Thomas Hancock, the ambitious son of a penniless Puritan minister of Lexington, Massachusetts. Eventually the Hancocks and the Apthorps stood together as "the two richest merchants in Boston made so by the publick Money and now wanton in . . . insolent demands." But this came only after a battle that was part of a campaign which the country-born nonconformist Thomas Hancock could not hope to win by himself. Even his nephew and heir John could not close the social gap that separated the two families.[63]

Thomas Hancock accomplished what Andrew Belcher and the first John Wentworth had. He came close enough to the peak of colonial society to consider following the example of a few of his wealthy neighbors and "sell all and Go to England and spend my days in quiet, and Mrs. Hancock is quite willing."[64] What Hancock did in Massachusetts the Browns and the Hopkinses were attempting to do in Rhode Island.[65] But by the middle of the eighteenth century society in the New England port towns was solidifying; mobility was slowing down as the successful families tightened their control of trade and politics. When in the decade after 1765 the merchants discovered that they could no longer satisfy their fundamental interests they rose in protest against the new imperial policies and demanded the rights of Englishmen. The conviction that these were being denied them led to a crisis such as had not occurred since 1689. And this time, too, as in those distant days when Randolph and Andros had darkened the horizon, the New England merchants reacted not as a unit but as individuals whose social differences were at least as strong as their common interests.

Abbreviations

A.A.S. *Procs.*	*Proceedings of the American Antiquarian Society*
A.H.R.	*American Historical Review*
Cal. S. P. Col.	*Calendar of State Papers, Colonial Series, America and West Indies*
Cal. S. P. Dom.	*Calendar of State Papers, Domestic Series*
D.N.B.	*Dictionary of National Biography*
Essex Instit., *Hist. Colls.*	*Historical Collections of the Essex Institute*
M.H.S. *Colls.*	*Collections of the Massachusetts Historical Society*
M.H.S. *Procs.*	*Proceedings of the Massachusetts Historical Society*
N.E.Q.	*New England Quarterly*
N.E. Register	*New England Genealogical and Historical Register*
N.Y. Col. Docs.	*Documents Relative to the Colonial History of the State of New York*
Pubs. C.S.M. (Trs.)	*Publications of the Colonial Society of Massachusetts . . . (Transactions, . . .)*

NOTE: This book is based on a heavily annotated doctoral dissertation. Since printing costs and the reader's convenience have required considerable reduction in documentation, reference has occasionally been made in the notes to the Dissertation Copy, which may be consulted in the Harvard College Library.

$\mathcal{N}$otes

CHAPTER I. ORIGINS OF TRADE

1. William Strachey, *The Historie of Travaile into Virginia Britannia* (Hakluyt Society ed., London, 1849), p. 180.

2. Astrid Friis, *Alderman Cockayne's Project and the Cloth Trade* (Copenhagen and London, 1927), p. 152, chap. iii.

3. John Aubrey, *Brief Lives and Other Selected Writings* (ed. Anthony Powell, London, 1949), p. 185.

4. Alexander Brown, *The Genesis of the United States* (Boston and New York, 1890), I, 34.

5. William R. Scott, *The Constitution and Finance of English, Scottish and Irish Joint-Stock Companies to 1720* (Cambridge, England, 1910–1912), II, 288, 299; John Latimer, *The Annals of Bristol in the Seventeenth Century* (Bristol, 1900), p. 27; John Latimer, *The History of the Society of Merchant Venturers of the City of Bristol* (Bristol, 1903), p. 148; James P. Baxter, *Sir Ferdinando Gorges and his Province of Maine* (Boston, 1890), III, 122, 124–126.

6. These accounts are reprinted in *Forerunners and Competitors of the Pilgrims and Puritans*, ed. Charles H. Levermore (Brooklyn, 1912), I, 25–68, 308–351. See Dissertation Copy, pp. 9ff.

7. Compare the diagram of the Sagadahoc fort in Brown, *Genesis*, I, facing page 190, with the photographs of the English fort-factory at Surat, India, in H. G. Rawlinson, *British Beginnings in Western India, 1576–1657* (Oxford, 1920), facing pages 41, 43, 120.

8. Baxter, *Gorges*, III, 154, 161.

9. That the west-country merchants lacked neither the finances nor the interest to continue in colonial enterprise is proved by the fact that, only a year after the failure at Sagadahoc, several Bristol merchants were instrumental in the chartering of the Newfoundland Company and led its first settlement at Cupers Cove. Charles M. Andrews, *The Colonial Period of American History* (New Haven, 1934–1938), I, chap. xv; Daniel W. Prowse, *A History of Newfoundland . . .* (London and New York, 1895), pp. 93ff. Their establishment of Bristol's Hope on Newfoundland in 1617 indicates further that they simply preferred the less exotic but safer investment in the fisheries near shores long familiar to them to the dubious riches of New England.

10. John Smith, *Works* (ed. Edward Arber, Westminster, 1895), I, 188; II, 697; *Baxter, Gorges*, I, 207; II, 17; Charles K. Bolton, *The Real Founders of New England . . .* (Boston, 1929), p. 25; Levermore, *Forerunners*, II, 439.

11. *The Farnham Papers 1603–1688*, ed. Mary F. Farnham (*Documentary History of the State of Maine*, VII, Portland, Maine, 1901), 25; The President and Council of New England, *A briefe Relation of the Discovery and Plantation of New England . . .* (London, 1622), reprinted in Baxter, *Gorges*, I, 199–240.

12. Baxter, *Gorges*, I, 222.

13. Charles Francis Adams' remark that the membership list reads "like an abstract from the Peerage" (*Three Episodes of Massachusetts History* [Boston and New York, 1892], I, 122) seems to have obscured the fact that a number of wealthy and powerful financial manipulators were charter members. Among them were Sir Nathaniel Rich, of Virginia Company fame; Matthew Sutcliffe, Dean of Exeter, who had contributed a fortune to colonizing projects; Admiral Sir Robert Mansell, the glass monopolist; and the infamous Sir Giles Mompesson.

14. The text has been published by Miller Christy, "Attempts toward Colonization: the Council for New England and the Merchant Venturers of Bristol, 1621–1623," *A.H.R.*, IV (1898–1899), 678–702.

15. *The Records of the Virginia Company of London*, ed. Susan M. Kingsbury (Washington, 1906–1935), I, 277, 321; *N.Y. Col. Docs.*, III, 4; *Proceedings and Debates of the British Parliaments respecting North America*, ed. Leo F. Stock (Washington, 1924–1941), I, 35. Richard A. Preston, in "Fishing and Plantation: New England in the Parliament of 1621," *A.H.R.*, XLV (1939), 29–43, argues that the Parliamentary opposition to the Council's monopoly did not take shape until 1624. In 1621, he writes, the Free Fishing Bill was meant to apply to Newfoundland rather than to New England, and the Virginia Company was satisfied once its particular claim was upheld.

16. Christy, "Attempts toward Colonization," p. 693. The fishermen could avoid the direct fee by transporting and landing in America one man for each thirty tons of shipping "with the value of tenne pounds to bee layd out in such provision as should bee appointed, only the charge of the man's goeing over to be deducted."

17. *N.Y. Col. Docs.*, III, 5, 11; Charles Deane, ed., "Records of the Council for New England," A.A.S. *Procs.* (April 24, 1867), p. 70.

18. "Records of the Council," p. 61. Compare Scott, *Joint-Stock Companies*, II, 302.

19. "Records of the Council," pp. 64–65, 96^2, 65.

20. The commonly accepted view that the Council's monopoly was the cause of a commercial slump in New England during the 1620's is false. This theory is particularly attractive to Whig historians who identify opposition to James' patents with laissez-faire liberalism (for example, Henry S. Burrage, *The Beginnings of Colonial Maine* [Portland, Maine, 1914], p. 159). Its supporters claim that the fishing licenses wrecked the industry in New England. But Preston has proved that the "actual cost of fishing licenses was not excessive." *A.H.R.*, XLV, 40. Furthermore, the Council failed to enforce the use of the licenses. The evidence that George L. Beer and Charles B. Judah, Jr. use to prove their case — complaints against interlopers and Captain West's efforts to police the New England waters — proves exactly the opposite. Charles B. Judah, Jr., *The North American Fisheries and British Policy to 1713 (Illinois Studies in the Social Sciences*, XVII, nos. 3–4, Urbana, 1933), 58ff.; George L. Beer, *The Origins of the British Colonial System 1578–1660* (New York, 1908), p. 276.

Another point usually made is that the Parliamentary debates for free fishing were attempts to recover for fishermen valuable waters which had been closed to them. But John Smith wrote that "within these few last years [of the 1620's] more have gone thither than ever." *Works*, II, 892. And Bradford complained repeatedly of "the irregular living of many in this land, who without either patent or license, order or government, live, trade, and truck." *Gover-*

nour Bradford's *Letter Book* (M.H.S. *Colls.*, III), p. 56; see also pp. 62–64. Sabine, who blames the Council for a decline in the Newfoundland fishery as well as in that of New England, attributes the removal from Monhegan Island of a party starting to plant there to the same cause. Lorenzo Sabine, *Report on the Principal Fisheries of the American Seas: Prepared for the Treasury Department of the United States* (Washington, 1853), p. 45. This is surely incorrect, as the main merchant involved, whom Sabine does not identify, was at that time a patentee of the Council and hence hardly one to be injured by its monopoly. The merchant was Abraham Jennens. William Bradford, *History of Plymouth Plantation 1620–1647* (ed. Worthington C. Ford, Boston, 1912), I, 341n, 447n; "Records of the Council," pp. 61, 75, 82.

It is impossible to measure the decline, if there was any, in the New England fisheries during the 1620's. However there was an evident failure of commercial companies to maintain colonies in New England. The causes for this, discussed in the following pages, have nothing to do with the Council's monopoly.

21. Such as the Jennens group behind the Monhegan plantation, 1622–1626 (above, note 20); their successors led by Robert Aldworth and Gyles Eldridge of Bristol; and John Beauchamp and the Castine post (Bradford, *History*, II, 80–81).

22. Christopher Levett, *A Voyage into New England* (London, 1628), reprinted in James P. Baxter, *Christopher Levett . . .* (Portland, Maine, 1893), p. 125.

23. Phinehas Pratt, "A Decliration . . . [1622?]," *M.H.S. Colls.*, 4th series, IV, 477; Bradford, *History*, I, 108, 115.

24. Edward Winslow, *Good News from New England* (London, 1624), reprinted in *The Story of the Pilgrim Fathers*, ed. Edward Arber (London, 1897), p. 514.

25. Levett, *A Voyage*, p. 139.

26. John White, *The Planters Plea* [London, 1630] (facsimile ed., Rockport, Mass., 1930), p. 73. The combination of hope in fishing profits and the need for self-sufficiency created the requirement that the planters find fertile soil along the beaches of fishing grounds. In 1630 John White listed as a main cause of the failure of the Dorchester Company the fact "that no sure fishing place in the Land is fit for planting, nor any good place for planting found fit for fishing, at least neere the Shoare." (P. 74.)

27. Bradford, *History*, I, 320; Richard A. Preston, "The Laconia Company of 1629 . . . ," *Canadian Historical Review*, XXXI, no. 2 (June 1950), 136.

28. White, *Plea*, p. 70; see also Bradford, *History*, I, 235, 435.

29. The Pilgrims' debt to the New Plymouth Company merchants increased from £400 to £4,770 19s. 2d. between 1628 and 1631. Bradford, *History*, II, 40, 131; also I, 433, 448–449; II, 3, 43–44, 85; *Letter Book*, pp. 33, 54, 74; William Bradford and Isaac Allerton, Plymouth, Mass., to [New Plymouth Company], Sept. 8, 1623, in *A.H.R.*, VIII (1902–1903), 295; Francis X. Moloney, *The Fur Trade in New England 1620–1676* (Cambridge, 1931), pp. 26–27.

30. Bradford, *History*, I, 317; *The New English Canaan of Thomas Morton*, ed. Charles F. Adams (Boston, 1883), p. 206.

31. Friis, *Cockayne*, p. 370n; Bradford, *History*, I, 331; II, 83; *New English Canaan*, pp. 263–264; Charles E. Banks, "Thomas Morton of Merry Mount," *M.H.S. Procs.*, LVIII (1924–1925), 147–193.

32. John Josselyn, *An Account of Two Voyages to New England* (London, 1673), reprinted in M.H.S. *Colls.*, 3rd series, III, 352.

33. Bradford, *History*, II, 80–85; 18–19, 41, 43, 175; 17–18; Isaack de Rasieres to Samuel Blommaert, 1628, in *Narratives of New Netherlands 1609–1664*, ed. J. Franklin Jameson (New York, 1909), pp. 109–110; Preston, "Laconia Company," p. 137; Adams, *Three Episodes*, I, chaps. i–xix; Sabine, *Fisheries*, p. 106; Moloney, *Fur Trade*, p. 41.

34. In 1625 the Pilgrims sent home 800 pounds of furs besides a cargo of fish, and in 1628 their accounts show a credit of £659 16s. 11d. from fur sales. The few statistics left by the Dutch West India Company do not distinguish the fur cargoes by place of origin, but a good number of the 8,000 pelts sent to Holland in 1626 must have come from the beaver meadows of Connecticut and Rhode Island. Bradford, *History*, I, 345n, 435; "Plymouth Company Accounts," M.H.S. *Colls.*, 3rd series, I, 201.

CHAPTER II. ESTABLISHMENT OF THE PURITAN MERCHANTS

1. Frances Rose-Troup, *The Massachusetts Bay Company and Its Predecessors* (New York, 1930), pp. 19–21.

2. *D.N.B.*, IV, 1361; Frances Rose-Troup, *John White* (New York and London, 1930), pp. 58–59, 108. ·

3. Andrews, *Colonial Period*, I, 359–360; Frances Rose-Troup, "John Humfry," Essex Instit., *Hist. Colls.*, LXV (1929), 293–308.

4. Rose-Troup, *Bay Company*, p. 21.

5. *Records of the Governor and Company of the Massachusetts Bay in New England*, ed. Nathaniel B. Shurtleff (Boston, 1853–1854), I, 384, 386–398. (Hereafter referred to as *Mass. Records.*)

6. Compare, for example, John C. Hotten, *The Original Lists of Persons of Quality . . . and Others Who Went from Great Britain to the American Plantations 1600–1700* (London, 1874), xiv–xviii; Nellis M. Crouse, "Causes of the Great Migration, 1630–1640," *N.E.Q.*, V (1932), 3–36; George C. Homans, "The Puritans and the Clothing Industry in England," *N.E.Q.*, XIII (1940), 519–529.

7. Andrews, *Colonial Period*, I, 384.

8. *Mass. Records*, I, 49, 51.

9. *Mass. Records*, I, 62–66.

10. All of the undertakers who remained in England were merchants. Of the five who left for the New World only one was a merchant, and he, John Revell, returned to England in less than four weeks. Andrews, *Colonial Period*, I, 370; *Mass. Records*, I, 24–70; Thomas Dudley, Boston, to the Countess of Lincoln, March 12, 1631, in *Chronicles . . . of Massachusetts Bay*, ed. Alexander Young (Boston, 1846), pp. 315–316.

11. Edward Dering, *A Parte of a Register* ([Middleburg], 1593), p. 81, quoted in M. M. Knappen, *Tudor Puritanism* (Chicago, 1939), pp. 342–343.

12. *Winthrop's Journal*, ed. James K. Hosmer (New York, 1908), II, 238.

13. R. H. Tawney, *Religion and the Rise of Capitalism* (New York, 1926), pp. 40–42.

14. *Winthrop's Journal*, I, 317–318.

15. John Cotton, *An Abstract of the Laws of New England [Moses His Judicials]* (London, 1655), reprinted in *Hutchinson Papers*, ed. William H. Whitmore and William S. Appleton (*Publications of the Prince Society*,

Albany, 1865), I, 193–194. Compare Edgar A. J. Johnson, *American Economic Thought in the Seventeenth Century* (London, 1932), chap. vii.

16. Tawney, *Religion and the Rise of Capitalism*, pp. 102ff.; and his introduction to *A Discourse upon Usury* . . . [*1572*] by *Thomas Wilson* (London, 1925), pp. 16ff.

17. John Winthrop, "Modell of Christian Charity," *Winthrop Papers* (Boston, 1929–1947), II, 286. Compare Tawney, *A Discourse*, p. 118.

18. Cotton, *Abstract*, p. 194.

19. Johnson, *Economic Thought*, pp. 142ff.

20. *Winthrop Papers*, II, 111–112.

21. John White, Dorchester, England, to John Winthrop, Nov. 16, 1636, *Winthrop Papers*, III, 322. Compare *Winthrop Papers*, III, 133.

22. *The Diaries of John Hull, Mint-master and Treasurer of the Colony of Massachusetts Bay (Transactions and Collections of the American Antiquarian Society*, III, 1857), p. 168. (Hereafter referred to as Hull, *Diaries*.)

23. Bradford, *History*, II, 5, 6–7n, 29.

24. Roland G. Usher, *The Pilgrims and Their History* (New York, 1918), p. 220.

25. *Records of the Colony of New Plymouth*, ed. Nathaniel B. Shurtleff and David Pulsifer (Boston, 1855–1861), I, 119.

26. William B. Weeden, *Economic and Social History of New England 1620–1789* (Boston and New York, 1891), I, 38ff.; Moloney, *Fur Trade*, pp. 26–27; Bradford, *History*, II, 170, 170n.

27. John Winthrop, Boston, to Sir Nathaniel Rich, May 22, 1634, *Winthrop Papers*, III, 167.

28. Bradford, *History*, II, 268, 229; *Plymouth Records*, II, 4.

29. For example, John Howland left a farm and cattle worth £157 8s. 8d.; William Brewster left £150 7d., of which £42 19s. 11d. was in books; Myles Standish's property was estimated at £358 7s. *The Mayflower Descendant*, II (1900), 73–77; III (1901), 16–27, 155–156.

30. Bradford, *History*, II, 230–231.

31. Bradford, *History*, II, 299, 230, 229.

32. Bradford, *History*, II, 132.

33. Bradford, *History*, II, 206ff., 220, 245, 268–270; Andrews, *Colonial Period*, II, 71–72.

34. *Plymouth Records*, I, 62; II, 4; Edward Winslow, Plymouth, Mass., to John Winthrop, April 17, 1637, *Winthrop Papers*, III, 392. For subsequent developments, see Bradford, *History*, II, 314n.

35. Matthew Cradock, London, to John Winthrop, March 15, 1638, *Winthrop Papers*, III, 379; John Spenser, Robert Crane, and Others to the Governor and Assistants Massachusetts Bay, n.d. [ca. 1639], *Winthrop Papers*, IV, 91–92. Since the account books of the sub-company have not come to light one cannot entirely reject the possibility that the undertakers did profit to some extent by their fur franchise. But there is no evidence that they did. Mrs. Rose-Troup finds it difficult to trace the existence of the undertaking through its allotted seven years, and Moloney ignores it entirely. Rose-Troup, *Bay Company*, chap. xi.

36. Revell left in July 1630; Johnson died in September 1630, and Saltonstall left in April 1631. Above, n. 10; *Winthrop's Journal*, I, 52, 61.

37. *Mass. Records*, I, 388.

38. For example, Francis Kirby, London, to John Winthrop, Jr., Dec. 3, 1632, *Winthrop Papers*, III, 104.

39. Its slight economic vitality lay in a series of shifting independent partnerships formed under its auspices, the most important of which was that of Francis Kirby, a merchant experienced in the American fur commerce, Emmanuel Downing, a London lawyer, and his nephew, John Winthrop, Jr. Sharing costs and profits, they sent over goods which young Winthrop traded for furs. Other combinations attempted similar ventures, but these partnerships existed usually for a single voyage and together controlled but a small part of the early fur trade in the Puritan colonies. Kirby to Winthrop, Jr., *Winthrop Papers*, III, 150–151, 162–163; Winthrop, Jr. to Winthrop, *Winthrop Papers*, III, 170; Kirby to Winthrop, Jr., *Winthrop Papers*, III, 259.

40. Derived from "Pincheon Papers," M.H.S. *Colls.*, 2nd series, VIII, 231.

41. *Winthrop's Journal*, I, 110; Bradford, *History*, II, 229n.

42. Preston, "Laconia Company," p. 133.

43. *Winthrop's Journal*, I, 110.

44. *Mass. Records*, I, 394; Letters from Cradock to Winthrop and others, in *Winthrop Papers*, III, *passim*.

45. *Winthrop's Journal*, I, 86; *Mass. Records*, I, 108.

46. Joseph Willard, *Willard Memoir . . .* (Boston, 1858), p. 140; Moloney, *Fur Trade*, p. 68.

47. *Winthrop's Journal*, I, 83; Andrews, *Colonial Period*, II, 69ff.

48. Their reasons for moving were written in a letter from Davenport and Eaton to the Massachusetts General Court, March 12, 1638, *Winthrop Papers*, III, 18–20.

49. Isabel M. Calder, *The New Haven Colony* (New Haven, 1934), chaps. ii, iii.

50. *Johnson's Wonder-Working Providence*, ed. J. Franklin Jameson (New York, 1910), p. 171.

51. Calder, *New Haven*, p. 84; Oliver A. Roberts, *History of . . . the Ancient and Honorable Artillery Company of Massachusetts* (Boston, 1895), I, 33.

52. "Hopkins thou must, although weak dust, for this great work prepare,
     Through Ocean large Christ gives thee charge to govern his with care;
   What earthen man, in thy short span throughout the world to run
     From East to West at Christs behest, thy worthy work is done:
   Unworthy thou acknowledge now, not unto thee at all,
     But to his name be lasting fame, thou to his work doth call."
   Johnson's Wonder-Working Providence, p. 179.

53. Samuel Eliot Morison, "William Pynchon, The Founder of Springfield," M.H.S. *Procs.*, LXIV (1930–1932), 73; Willard, *Memoir*, p. 146; Anon., *History of the Town of Dorchester, Massachusetts* (Boston, 1859), pp. 46–47; Anon., *Historical Catalogue of the First Church in Hartford* (Hartford, 1885), pp. 10, 12. The only exception appears to be John Holman of Dorchester. It is interesting to note that unlike most of the other fur traders, Holman had been an apprentice to a city merchant before emigrating. *N.E. Register*, LXXII (1918), 190.

54. *Mass. Records*, I, 171, 321; Morison, "Pynchon," p. 81; *Winthrop Papers*, IV, 98–99.

55. *The Public Records of the Colony of Connecticut*, ed. James H. Trumbull and Charles J. Hoadly (Hartford, 1850–1890), I, 46.

56. Calder, *New Haven, passim;* Charles H. Walcott, *Concord in the Colonial Period* (Boston, 1884), pp. 43–44, 171; Samuel Eliot Morison, *Builders of the Bay Colony* (Boston, 1930), pp. 269–288.

57. *Mass. Records,* I, 81, 140, 96, 179; *Conn. Records,* I, 57.

58. For example, Simon Willard, whose father, Richard, was a well-to-do "Yeoman." Willard, *Memoir,* pp. 53–59.

59. Thus Pynchon wrote to Winthrop, Jr., "As for using ould traders to trade for you it is not the best way for your gaine: for they know how to save themselves but a trusty man that never was a trader will quickly find the way of trading and bring you best profitt." Pynchon, Roxbury, to John Winthrop, Jr., July 4, 1636, *Winthrop Papers,* III, 286.

60. The following paragraph is based mainly on Professor Morison's study of Pynchon cited in note 53 above.

61. Henry M. Burt, *The First Century of the History of Springfield . . .* (Springfield, 1898), I, 15.

62. *Mass. Records,* I, 100.

63. Thomas Shepard, *The Sincere Convert* (London, 1641), quoted in Andrews, *Colonial Period,* I, 480n.

64. The Company's plan had been to establish the familiar "magazine" as a store of goods sent to the colony by the undertakers for controlled sales. But the "magazine" was a failure. The undertakers' shipments proved to be too few and too irregular to fulfill the original plan of supply. Delays in England and the accidents of crossing reduced their occasional cargoes to rare though life-saving stopgaps. The result was a condition close to famine during the first years of settlement. Winthrop was forced to buy up for general distribution the whole of a number of cargoes of food as well as to send foraging expeditions to the surrounding Indian tribes. Virginia proved to be an excellent source of grain, far better than the other English settlements within reach — those of the fishermen and servants of commercial companies operating in Maine and New Hampshire. *Mass. Records,* I, 66; London Port Book Entries in *Winthrop Papers,* III; Thomas Dudley, Boston, to Countess of Lincoln, March 12, 1631, *Chronicles,* ed. Young, pp. 311–317; *Winthrop's Journal,* I, 64, 75, 76, 126, 131–132, 138, 176; Winthrop, Jr., London, to Winthrop, April 30, 1631, and Thomas Mayhew, "Meadeford," to Winthrop, Jr., April 22, 1636, *Winthrop Papers,* III, 30–31, 253.

65. *Mass. Records,* I, 74, 109, 111. For similar legislation in Connecticut, see *Conn. Records,* I, 52.

66. *Mass. Records,* I, 77, 92. The first law fixing grain prices at 6s. a bushel does not appear in the *Records.* It was repealed in April 1633. *Mass. Records,* I, 104.

67. *Mass. Records,* I, 160.

68. The question of grain prices was treated separately and answered by periodic lifting of the ceilings and the outright compensation of creditors injured by repayment in cheaper grain than that contracted for. *Mass. Records,* I, 104, 110, 115, 140, 142, 192, 206, 340; 200, 221, 238.

69. *Mass. Records,* I, 183.

70. *Mass. Records,* I, 223. It is interesting to note that the final solution hit upon, when the direction of the spiral was reversed, was what might be called a voluntary "escalator clause": ". . . workmen should bee content to abate their

wages according to the fall of the commodities wherein their labors are bestowed. . ." *Mass. Records*, I, 326.

71. *Winthrop's Journal*, I, 152.

72. For Plymouth's handling of a similar problem, see *Plymouth Records*, XI, 29.

73. *Mass. Records*, I, 142.

74. *Winthrop's Journal*, I, 152, 180; *Mass. Records*, I, 149, 159, 166.

75. *Note-Book Kept by Thomas Lechford, Esq. . . . from June 27, 1638, to July 29, 1641 (Transactions and Collections of the American Antiquarian Society*, 1885), VII, 74n, 75.

76. *Winthrop's Journal*, I, 120; *A Volume Relating to the Early History of Boston Containing the Aspinwall Notarial Records from 1644 to 1651 (Thirty-second Report of the Record Commissioners of the City of Boston*, Boston, 1903), pp. 215, 248. (Hereafter cited as *Asp. Records*.)

77. James Savage, *A Genealogical Dictionary of . . . New England . . .* (Boston, 1860–1862), II, 420; *Asp. Records*, p. 197.

78. *Mass. Records*, I, 163; *Lieutenant Joshua Hewes*, ed. and comp. Eben Putnam (New York, 1913), pp. 15, 22, 56–66.

79. *Boston Town Records (Second Report of the Record Commissioners of the City of Boston*, Boston, 1877), p. 40; William H. Sumner, *A History of East Boston* (Boston, 1858), pp. 187–191; *Asp. Records*, pp. 181, 410, 397, 398, 402, 404, 406.

80. *N.E. Register*, XIX (1865), 14–15; *Lechford's Note-Book*, pp. 87, 156. For other examples, see *Asp. Records*, p. 198 (Thomas Broughton); *N.E. Register*, VII (1853), 273–274 (John Wisswall).

81. Essex Instit., *Hist. Colls.*, XXVIII (1891), 84n; *Asp. Records*, p. 92; Brampton Gurdon, Sr., Assington, to Winthrop, June 6, 1649, *Winthrop Papers*, V, 36.

82. *N.E. Register*, LXVII (1893), 198–200; compare Bernard Bailyn, "The *Apologia* of Robert Keayne," *William and Mary Quarterly*, 3rd series, VII (1950), 568–577.

83. Essex Instit., *Hist. Colls.*, XXVIII (1891), 149.

84. Savage, *Dictionary*, I, 27.

85. *N.E.Q.*, IV (1931), 349.

86. Charles H. Pope, *The Pioneers of Massachusetts* (Boston, 1900), p. 436.

87. *N.E. Register*, XLI (1887), 363.

88. Calder, *New Haven*, p. 30.

89. Calder, *New Haven*, p. 75; Andrews, *Colonial Period*, II, 155, 174n.

90. Calder, *New Haven*, p. 30.

91. Charles E. Banks, *The Planters of the Commonwealth* (Boston, 1930), pp. 176–177, 198; John O. Austin, *The Genealogical Dictionary of Rhode Island* (Albany, 1887), p. 49.

92. Kenneth Rogers, *Old Cheapside and Poultry* (London, 1931), p. 6.

93. John Stowe, *A Survey of London* [London, 1603] (ed. Charles L. Kingsford, Oxford, 1908), I, 198.

94. Reginald R. Sharpe, *London and the Kingdom* (London, 1894–1895), II, chap. xxi.

95. Annie H. Thwing, *The Crooked and Narrow Streets of the Town of Boston, 1630–1822* (Boston, 1920), pp. 111ff.; Calder, *New Haven*, chap. i.

96. Roberts, *Artillery Company*, I, 7–12.

97. G. Goold Walker, *The Honourable Artillery Company* (London, 1926), chaps. i, ii; pp. 24, 26.

98. Keayne, Sedgwick, Weld, Savage, Hewes, Turner, Gibbons, Spencer, Harding, Holman, Collecott, and Upshall. Roberts, *Artillery Company*, I, 12ff.

99. Calder, *New Haven*, pp. 60, 124.

100. David Mathew, *The Age of Charles I* (London, 1951), p. 156; Friis, *Cockayne*, p. 236, chaps. iv–vi.

101. Thomas Hutchinson, *The History of the Colony and Province of Massachusetts-Bay* (ed. Lawrence S. Mayo, Cambridge, 1936), I, 73n. A complete listing of taxable estates in New Haven in 1643 will be found in *Records of the Colony and Plantation of New Haven, from 1638 to 1649*, ed. Charles J. Hoadly (Hartford, 1857), pp. 91–93. Eaton heads the list with £3,000.

102. Roberts, *Artillery Company*, I, 46.

103. Robert F. Seybolt, *The Town Officials of Colonial Boston 1634–1775* (Cambridge, 1939), pp. 3–10.

104. *Dorchester Town Records (Fourth Report of the Record Commissioners of the City of Boston*, Boston, 1880), p. 44.

105. James D. Phillips, *Salem in the Seventeenth Century* (Boston and New York, 1933), pp. 194–195.

106. William H. Whitmore, *The Massachusetts Civil List . . . 1630–1774* (Albany, 1870), pp. 16ff., 21.

107. For a moving example of this ideal in practice, see the Pilgrims' pledge of 1617 to remain as they were, "knite togeather as a body in a most stricte and sacred bond and covenante of the Lord . . . straitly tied to all care of each others good, and of the whole by every one and so mutually." Bradford, *History*, I, 76.

108. "THE LAST WILL AND TESTAMENT of me, Robert Keayne . . . 1653 . . . ," *A [Tenth] Report of the Record Commissioners of the City of Boston, containing Miscellaneous Papers* (Boston, 1886), pp. 47, 16.

109. For example, Edward Bendall, who crossed in the Winthrop Fleet, was fined and imprisoned for failure to "acknowledge the justice of the Court." *Mass. Records*, I, 176.

110. The crucial election of 1637 was held in Cambridge instead of Boston to reduce the effectiveness of the antinomian party. Andrews, *Colonial Period*, I, 482.

111. *Mass. Records*, I, 211–212; Howard M. Chapin, *Documentary History of Rhode Island* (Providence, 1916–1919), II, 16ff.

112. For a full account of Keayne and his troubles, see Bailyn, "Keayne."

113. "LAST WILL," p. 47; *Winthrop's Journal*, I, 215.

114. "LAST WILL," pp. 27, 34. *Mass. Records*, I, 281. The fine was later reduced to £80. *Mass. Records*, I, 290. Winthrop had little sympathy for Keayne: the "corrupt practice of this man . . . was the more observable because he was wealthy and sold dearer than most other tradesmen, and for that he was of ill repute for the like covetous practice in England . . ." *Winthrop's Journal*, I, 316.

115. "LAST WILL," p. 34; Records of the First Church of Boston (Handwritten copy in the Massachusetts Historical Society), pp. 12, 14.

116. Most of the documents bearing on this case, which resulted in the separation of the General Court into two houses, will be found in A. P. Rugg, "A Famous Colonial Litigation," *A.A.S. Procs.*, new series, XXX (1920), 217–250.

117. "LAST WILL," p. 34.

118. "LAST WILL," pp. 5, 42.

119. For other cases, see *Winthrop's Journal*, I, 77; *Mass. Records*, I, 163, 208, 279, 317; *Plymouth Records*, I, 137.

120. "LAST WILL," p. 15.

CHAPTER III. ADJUSTMENTS AND EARLY FAILURES

1. Hutchinson, *Massachusetts-Bay*, I, 82.

2. *Winthrop's Journal*, II, 31.

3. Francis Kirby, London, to John Winthrop, May 10, 1637, M.H.S. *Colls.*, 4th series, VII, 19–20.

4. John Tinker, "From the Downes" [England], to John Winthrop, May 28, 1640, *Winthrop Papers*, IV, 251.

5. John Winter, Richmond Island, to Robert Trelawny, June 27, 1640, *The Trelawny Papers*, ed. James P. Baxter (*Documentary History of the State of Maine . . . [Collections of the Maine Historical Society*, 2nd series, III, Portland, Maine, 1884]), p. 218. (Hereafter referred to as *Trelawny Papers.*)

6. *Winthrop's Journal*, II, 17, 31.

7. Marion H. Gottfried, "The First Depression in Massachusetts," *N.E.Q.*, IX (1936), 660.

8. *Mass. Records*, I, 307.

9. *Mass. Records*, I, 304; *Conn. Records*, I, 61.

10. *Mass. Records*, II, 3, 16–17, 80; III, 17.

11. *Winthrop's Journal*, II, 20.

12. Preston, "Laconia Company," p. 137; Letters of the Laconia Company, 1631–1637, *Provincial Papers: Documents and Records Relating to the Province of New-Hampshire*, comp. and ed. Nathaniel Bouton (Concord, N.H., 1867–1873), I, 61–80, 88–91, 93–94, 97, 98.

13. *N.H. Prov. Papers*, I, 61–62, 81–82; Preston, "Laconia Company," pp. 136, 140.

14. Letters of the Laconia Company, 1634, *N.H. Prov. Papers*, I, 89–92; *Capt. John Mason*, ed. John W. Dean (Boston, 1887), pp. 74ff.

15. *Winthrop's Journal*, II, 63; Amandus Johnson, *The Swedish Settlements on the Delaware 1638–1664* (Phila., 1911), I, 179–180; *Narratives of Early Pennsylvania, West New Jersey and Delaware*, ed. Albert C. Myers (New York, 1912), p. 47; Calder, *New Haven*, pp. 77–78.

16. *Winthrop's Journal*, II, 164; *Mass. Records*, II, 60.

17. Johnson, *Swedish Settlements*, I, 394–397; Arthur H. Buffinton, "New England and the Western Fur Trade, 1629–1675," *Pubs. C.S.M.*, XVIII (*Trs.*, 1915–1916), 174–175.

18. *Winthrop's Journal*, II, 191.

19. *Mass. Records*, II, 138–139; III, 53.

20. Moloney, *Fur Trade*, pp. 60–66.

21. Sylvester Judd, "The Fur Trade on Connecticut River in the Seventeenth Century," *N.E. Register*, XI (1857), 217–219. Compare, for example, *Johnson's Wonder-Working Providence*, p. 237.

22. William Pynchon, Record of Accounts with Early Settlers and Indians, 1645–1650 (MS in Forbes Library, Northampton, Mass.), *passim.*

23. *Conn. Records*, I, 496–498; compare the list of goods sold by Whiting

1650–1652, in Conn. Archives, Private Controversies, 1st series, I, 6a–f. Frances M. Caulkins, *History of New London, Connecticut* (New London, 1852), p. 101; Moloney, *Fur Trade*, p. 73; *Letters of John Davenport, Puritan Divine*, ed. Isabel M. Calder (New Haven, 1937), p. 90n; Roland M. Hooker, *The Colonial Trade of Connecticut (Publications of the Tercentenary Commission of the State of Connecticut*, L, 1936), p. 10.

24. Willard, *Memoir*, p. 157.

25. Samuel Eliot Morison, "The Plantation of Nashaway — An Industrial Experiment," *Pubs. C.S.M.*, XXVII (*Trs.*, 1927–1930), 208–209; Moloney, *Fur Trade*, pp. 74–75; *Mass. Records*, IV, part 1, 354.

26. *Mass. Records*, IV, 354.

27. Moloney, *Fur Trade*, pp. 114–117. Massachusetts' reopening of the trade under public auspices in Maine in the eighteenth century was an effort "to win the friendship of the Indians, rather than to earn a profit for the colony." Ronald O. Macfarlane, "The Massachusetts Bay Truck-Houses in Diplomacy with the Indians," *N.E.Q.*, XI (1938), 48.

28. Willard, *Memoir*, pp. 158–312, 325–333.

29. Calder, *New Haven*, p. 45.

30. Thomas R. Trowbridge, Jr., "History of the Ancient Maritime Interests of New Haven," *Papers of the New Haven Colony Historical Society*, III (1882), 93; Johnson, *Swedish Settlements*, I, 200ff., 208, 215; Calder, *New Haven*, pp. 185ff., 205.

31. Calder, *New Haven*, p. 57; Patrick Copeland [Bermuda], to John Winthrop, August 21, 1646, *Winthrop Papers*, V, 96; Trowbridge, "Maritime Interests of New Haven," pp. 96–98. Compare *New Haven Colony Records*, p. 91.

32. Letters from John Winter, Richmond Island, to Robert Trelawny, 1634–1640, *Trelawny Papers*, pp. 28, 53, 111, 171, 254; Moloney, *Fur Trade*, p. 125.

33. Samuel H. Brockunier, *The Irrepressible Democrat, Roger Williams* (New York, 1940), p. 5, chaps. i, xiv; Daniel B. Updike, *Richard Smith . . .* (Boston, 1937), pp. 15ff.; Howard M. Chapin, *The Trading Post of Roger Williams* (Providence, 1933), *passim;* "John Eliot's Description of New England in 1650," *M.H.S. Procs.*, 2nd series, II (1885–1886), 49; *Master John Cotton's Answer to Master Roger Williams*, ed. J. Lewis Diman [London, 1647] (*Publications of the Narragansett Club*, II, Providence, 1867), pp. 86, 87n.

34. Updike, *Smith*, pp. 16ff.; Chapin, *Trading Post, passim; Cal. S.P. Col.*, 1677–1680, §§1069, 1080, 1487, 1496 encl. 1.

35. Updike, *Smith*, pp. 65–66.

36. Buffinton, "Fur Trade," pp. 176–187; John B. Brebner, *New England's Outpost: Acadia before the Conquest of Canada* (New York, 1927), chaps. i, ii; *Cal. S.P. Col.*, 1574–1660, p. 441; 1661–1668, §111.

37. *Asp. Records*, pp. 11, 131.

38. *Asp. Records*, pp. 394–430.

39. *Mass. Records*, I, 28, 30.

40. *Mass. Records*, I, 327.

41. Alonzo Lewis and James R. Newhall, *History of Lynn . . .* (Boston, 1865), pp. 204–205.

42. Report of John Winthrop, Jr., on Possible Sites for Ironworks [ca. 1644], *Winthrop Papers*, IV, 424, 425; Petition of John Winthrop, Jr., to Parliament [ca. 1644], *Winthrop Papers*, IV, 424; *Winthrop's Journal*, II, 222. The company seems to have been formally organized in May 1645. *Suffolk*

Deeds, ed. William B. Trask *et al.* (Boston, 1880–1906), I, 229. For identification of these early investors, see Dissertation Copy, pp. 177–178.

43. Robert Child, Gravesend, to John Winthrop, Jr., March 1, 1645, *Winthrop Papers,* V, 11; *Asp. Records,* p. 15; Lynn Iron Works MSS (Baker Library, Harvard University), *passim.* (Hereafter referred to as Lynn MSS. The page numbers refer to the typescript copy.)

44. Report of John Winthrop, Jr., *Winthrop Papers,* IV, 425–426; *Boston Town Recs.,* p. 77; *Suff. Deeds,* I, 73.

45. Petition of John Winthrop, Jr., to the Massachusetts General Court [ca. 1644], *Winthrop Papers,* IV, 422–423; *Mass. Records,* II, 62, 81, 125–128.

46. *Winthrop's Journal,* II, 222; *Mass. Records,* II, 104, 126.

47. Report of John Winthrop, Jr.; Emmanuel Downing, London, to John Winthrop, Jr., Feb. 25, 1645; John Winthrop, Boston, to John Winthrop, Jr., Aug. 14, 1648; Certificate of John Winthrop, Jr., Aug. 6, 1649, *Winthrop Papers,* IV, 426; V, 6, 246, 369; E. N. Hartley, "Hammersmith, 1643–1675," *The Saugus Restoration* (n.p., 1951), p. 17.

48. The Promoters of the Ironworks, London, to John Winthrop, Jr., March 13, 1648, *Winthrop Papers,* V, 209.

49. Robert Child, Gravesend, to John Winthrop, Jr., March 1, 1645, *Winthrop Papers,* V, 11; *Mass. Records,* II, 104.

50. Emmanuel Downing, London, to John Winthrop, Jr., Feb. 25, 1645; Robert Child, Gravesend, to John Winthrop, Jr., March 1, 1645; Promoters of the Ironworks, London, to John Winthrop, Jr., June 4, 1645, *Winthrop Papers,* V, 7, 11, 27.

51. The undertakers' arguments have been reconstructed from the General Court's reply in *Mass. Records,* III, 91–93.

52. *Mass. Records,* III, 91–93; II, 85–86.

53. *Records and Files of the Quarterly Courts of Essex County Massachusetts,* ed. George F. Dow (Salem, 1911–1921), I, 294–295. (Hereafter referred to as *Essex Records.*)

54. *Suff. Deeds,* I, 80; *Essex Records,* I, 290–292; John Winthrop, Boston, to John Winthrop, Jr., Aug. 14, 1648; Richard Leader, Hammersmith [Lynn], to John Winthrop, Jr., Aug. 21, 1648; John Winthrop, Boston, to John Winthrop, Jr., Sept. 30, 1648, *Winthrop Papers,* V, 246, 248, 262.

55. Hartley, "Hammersmith," p. 20; *Suff. Deeds,* I, 217; Nicholas Bond *et al.,* London, to John Gifford, April 26, 1652, Lynn MSS, p. 31.

56. The exact number of prisoners used as laborers in the works is difficult to assign. But it is certain that in 1651 the company sent over 272 "passengers" on the *John and Sarah.* Their names are listed in *Suff. Deeds,* I, 5–6. Compare Dissertation Copy, p. 190n.

57. Hartley, "Hammersmith," p. 20; *Essex Records,* II, 89, 94, 88.

58. Nicholas Bond *et al.,* London, to John Gifford, April 26, 1652, Lynn MSS, p. 32. The commissioners were Robert Bridges of Lynn, William Tyng, Henry Webb, and Joshua Foote of Boston: pp. 35ff.; *Essex Records,* II, 88.

59. *Suff. Deeds,* I, 306; *Essex Records,* I, 293; II, 78.

60. William Hubbard, *A General History of New England, from the Discovery to MDCLXXX* (M.H.S. *Colls.,* 2nd series, V–VI), p. 374.

61. The commissioner was Henry Webb. *Mass. Records,* III, 351.

62. *Suff. Deeds,* II, 158–161; *Essex Records,* I, 401; II, 80, 81; III, 41–42; *Cal. S.P Col.,* 1661–1668, §50; *York Deeds* (Portland, Maine, 1887–1896), I, 103;

William Paine, Boston, to John Winthrop, Jr., Nov. 26, 1657, M.H.S. *Colls.*, 4th series, VII, 403.

63. *Essex Records*, VI, 235; VIII, 39; Hartley, "Hammersmith," p. 23.

64. *New Haven Town Records 1649–1662*, ed. Franklin B. Dexter (New Haven Historical Society, *Ancient Town Records*, I–II, New Haven, 1917–1919), I, 235, 260; Theophilus Eaton, New Haven, to John Winthrop, Jr., Jan. 4, 1655, M.H.S. *Colls.*, 4th series, VII, 477; Calder, *New Haven*, pp. 157–158.

65. *N.H. Town Records*, I, 321, 330–331, 349; II, 138; Letters of William Paine, Boston, to John Winthrop, Jr., 1657–1659; John Davenport, New Haven, to John Winthrop, Jr., June 22, 1663, M.H.S. *Colls.*, 4th series, VII, 402–410, 500, 524; Calder, *New Haven*, p. 160. On Clark's debts in the ironworks in 1678, see Conn. Archives, Private Controversies, I, 152.

66. J. Leander Bishop, *A History of American Manufactures . . .* (Phila., 1866), I, 478–483; *Mass. Records*, IV, part 1, 311, 429; Arthur C. Bining, *British Regulation of the Colonial Iron Industry* (Phila., 1933), pp. 11–13; Amos E. Jewett and Emily M. A. Jewett, *Rowley, Massachusetts* (Rowley, 1946), p. 214.

67. Hugh Peter [Salem], to John Winthrop [ca. April 10, 1639], *Winthrop Papers*, IV, 113; *Cal. S.P. Col.*, 1674–1675, §157; *Mass. Records*, I, 294, 303; *Winthrop's Journal*, II, 25; *Conn. Records*, I, 59–61.

68. *Mass. Records*, I, 320, 322; *Conn. Records*, I, 64, 75.

69. Jewett, *Rowley, passim*. See also *The Probate Records of Essex County Massachusetts* (Salem, 1916–1920), I, 93, 129, 251, 302.

70. Some children, the Court stated, whose parents could not furnish them with more substantial clothes, were "much scorched with fire, yea, divers burnt to death" as a result of the flimsiness of their garments. *Mass. Records*, II, 105–106.

71. *Mass. Records*, II, 251–252; III, 298; IV, part 1, 198, 256.

72. Hull, *Diaries*, pp. 179–180.

73. Ezekiel Rogers, Rowley, to William Sykes, Dec. 2, 1646, Jewett, *Rowley*, p. 33.

74. Jewett, *Rowley*, p. 171; *Asp. Records*, p. 414.

75. *Johnson's Wonder-Working Providence*, p. 211.

76. John Winthrop, Jr., Hartford, to Henry Oldenbourg, Nov. 12, 1668, M.H.S. *Colls.*, 5th series, VIII, 133–135; *Suff. Deeds*, II, 256–258; George H. Haynes, "The Tale of Tantiusques," A.A.S. *Procs.*, new series, XIV (1900–1901), 471–497.

77. *Mass. Records*, II, 137; III, 48.

78. John Winthrop [Boston], to John Winthrop, Jr., Sept. 30, 1648; Emmanuel Downing [Salem], to John Winthrop, Jr., Dec. 17, 1648, *Winthrop Papers*, V, 261, 289.

CHAPTER IV. THE LEGACY OF THE FIRST GENERATION

1. Smith, *Works*, I, 198–205; *Mass. Records*, I, 158, 230, 256, 326, 395, 403–404; Francis Kirby, London, to John Winthrop, Jr., Feb. 26 and April 11, 1634, *Winthrop Papers*, III, 151, 162; *Winthrop's Journal*, I, 310.

2. John Winthrop [Boston], to John White, July 4, 1632, *Winthrop Papers*, III, 87; London Port Book Entries, *Winthrop Papers*, III, 160, 171. Phillips, *Salem*, pp. 94, 111.

3. *Winthrop's Journal*, I, 169, 326; Matthew Cradock, London, to John Winthrop, Feb. 27, 1640, *Winthrop Papers*, IV, 208.

4. Harold A. Innis, *The C⌐⌐ Fisheries* (New Haven, 1940), p. 80; *Trelawny Papers*, pp. 66ff.; *Province and Court Records of Maine*, ed. Charles T. Libby *et al.* (Portland, Maine, 1928–1947), I, 44, 52. (Hereafter referred to as *Maine Court Recs.*) *Cal. S.P. Col.*, 1574–1660, §286.

5. Judah, *Fisheries*, pp. 90–91; Prowse, *Newfoundland*, p. 159. In December 1640, Winthrop wrote, "About the end of this month, a fishing ship arrived at the Isle of Shoals and another soon after, and there came no more this season for fishing." *Winthrop's Journal*, II, 19.

6. It was of the utmost importance to the success of the fishery that in the temperate climate of New England and on its relatively fertile shores men could be both farmers and fishermen at the same time. Fishermen in the winter and part of the spring, the settlers along the shores could attend to their crops during the summer and autumn months, deriving a livelihood from and protected against the insecurities of both. For a lyrical presentation of the significance of the permanently settled and fully employed fishing force made possible by the winter fishery, see Charles L. Woodbury, *The Relation of the Fisheries to the Discovery and Settlement of North America* (Boston, 1880), pp. 23–26. For inventories of the property of such fishermen-farmers, see *Ess. Probate Recs.*, I, 146–148, 454, 457.

7. *Mass. Records*, I, 326; II, 147; *Winthrop's Journal*, II, 178, 350; John S. Jenness, *The Isles of Shoals* (New York and Cambridge, 1875), pp. 82–97; Raymond McFarland, *A History of the New England Fisheries* (New York, 1911), pp. 60–64.

8. *Mass. Records*, II, 57; *Maine Court Recs.*, I, 119; *Winthrop's Journal*, II, 42, 321.

9. For example, *Maine Court Recs.*, I, 105n. *Winthrop's Journal*, II, 35–36, 62, 248, 255.

10. Ralph G. Lounsbury, *The British Fishery at Newfoundland 1634–1763* (New Haven, 1934), pp. 59ff.; Judah, *Fisheries*, p. 94; *Acts and Ordinances of the Interregnum 1642–1660*, ed. C. H. Firth and R. S. Rait (London, 1911), I, 912–913; II, 559–560.

11. *Asp. Records*, p. 24.

12. *Asp. Records*, pp. 218, 223, 305, 390; Waters, *Gleanings*, I, 48, 257–258.

13. Henry D. Sedgwick, "Robert Sedgwick," *Pubs. C.S.M.*, III (*Trs.*, 1895–1897), 161ff.; *Asp. Records*, pp. 78–79, 127.

14. *Asp. Records*, pp. 333, 418.

15. Such contracts are scattered through the *Asp. Records*. See, for example, pp. 217, 287–288, 305, 333, 361, 390, 392.

16. For example, *Asp. Records*, pp. 78–79, 180–181, 317–320; 79, 227; 217–218, 223–224.

17. For example, *Asp. Records*, pp. 217, 295; *Suff. Deeds*, II, 124ff., 279.

18. Invoices listed in *Asp. Records*, pp. 294–430.

19. The last English ship to engage in the New England fishery was said to have sailed in 1661. Innis, *Cod Fisheries*, p. 116.

20. *Asp. Records*, pp. 150, 197, 198; *Suff. Deeds*, I, 150–151; *York Deeds*, I, 91, 113; *Essex Records*, I, 215–217; Josselyn, *Two Voyages*, p. 351.

21. For example, *York Deeds*, I, 14.

22. Jenness, *Isles of Shoals*, pp. 86–87; John Winthrop, Jr., Hartford, to Fitz-John Winthrop, July 23, 1673, M.H.S. *Colls.*, 5th series, VIII, 149. For an indication of their wealth at the end of their careers, see the wills of John (1680) and Richard (1675), in Charles W. Brewster, *Rambles About Ports-*

mouth (Portsmouth, N.H., 1859–1869), 1st series, 30–38; and the estate of the least fortunate of the first generation Cutts, Robert, at his death in 1674 (estimated at £890 9s. 4d., including eight slaves), in Byron Fairchild, *Messrs. William Pepperell: Merchants at Piscataqua* (Ithaca, 1954), p. 9.

23. *Asp. Records*, pp. 71–72.

24. Hubbard, *General History*, p. 424; *Winthrop's Journal*, II, 89; *Asp. Records*, pp. 107–111.

25. *Winthrop's Journal*, II, 92–93, 152, 154, 157, 176; *Asp. Records*, pp. 91, 227.

26. Arthur P. Newton, *The European Nations in the West Indies 1493–1688* (London, 1933), p. 149, chaps. x, xi.

27. Bradford, *History*, I, 61–62; Henry Winthrop, Barbados, to John Winthrop, Oct. 15 [1627], M.H.S. *Colls.*, 5th series, VIII, 181.

28. *Winthrop's Journal*, I, 151; George Downing, Newfoundland, to John Winthrop, Jr., Aug. 26, 1645, *Winthrop Papers*, V, 43.

29. *Winthrop's Journal*, II, 252–253; *Mass. Records*, III, 58; *Asp. Records*, pp. 7, 19, 87.

30. James Parker, Barbados, to John Winthrop, June 24, 1646; Richard Vines, Barbados, to John Winthrop, July 19, 1647, *Winthrop Papers*, V, 83, 172; *Winthrop's Journal*, II, 345; *Asp. Records*, p. 220.

31. *Asp. Records*, p. 9; Stephen Winthrop [Teneriffe], to John Winthrop [1645], M.H.S. *Colls.*, 5th series, VIII, 203; Richard Blande, San Orotava [on Teneriffe], to John Winthrop, March 5, 1647, *Winthrop Papers*, V, 132; *Mass. Records*, II, 169.

32. *Asp. Records*, pp. 13–14, 31, 46, 100–101, 126, 145, 166–169, 175–177, 242, 245; *Winthrop's Journal*, II, 321; William Hyde, "Alexander Adams and his Relation to the Early Shipbuilders of Boston," *The Bostonian Society Publications*, II (1914), 86–96.

33. *Asp. Records*, pp. 70, 92; Brampton Gurdon, Sr., Assington [England], to John Winthrop, June 6, 1649; Thomas Fowle [Boston?], to John Winthrop, Jr., Sept. 20, 1642, *Winthrop Papers*, V, 351; IV, 355; Hermann F. Clarke, *John Hull* (Portland, Maine, 1940), pp. 102–103.

34. Thus Samuel Winthrop wrote to his father from Fayal in 1648 that he had been treated well in St. Kitts: ". . . likewise Captain Clement everet a Justice of peace, who being our country man and hearing our name used me verry Courtiously, and assisted me much in my law suites which were there verry many. Justice Froth, who was of your acquantance in England (as he informes me), was his Granfather. I have left in his handes my busines in St. Christpors. . ." Samuel Winthrop, Fayal, to John Winthrop, Jan. 10, 1648, *Winthrop Papers*, V, 196. Vines wrote that he had seen Samuel in Barbados, and added, "If the Lord please to send him here agayne or any other of your sonnes, I shall be ready to serve them in what I may." Richard Vines, Barbados, to John Winthrop, April 29, 1648, *Winthrop Papers*, V, 220. See also George Downing, Newfoundland, to John Winthrop [ca. March, 1646], *Winthrop Papers*, V, 43, 63–64; Samuel Winthrop, Rotterdam, to John Winthrop, Jr., Sept. 28, 1648, M.H.S. *Colls.*, 5th series, VIII, 241.

35. *Asp. Records*, p. 86; *Pubs. C.S.M.*, XXI (*Trs.*, 1919), 254–256; Vincent T. Harlow, *A History of Barbados, 1625–1685* (Oxford, 1926), p. 280.

36. *Asp. Records*, pp. 7, 31; Robert Keayne *et al.*, Boston, to Vincent Reyner, Nov. 26, 1646, *Winthrop Papers*, V, 225n.

37. Richard Vines, Barbados, to John Winthrop, July 19, 1647, and April

29, 1648, *Winthrop Papers*, V, 171–172, 219–220; *Asp. Records*, p. 177. Twelve hundred persons are said to have gone from Barbados to New England between 1643 and 1647. James Truslow Adams, *The Founding of New England* (Boston, 1921), p. 223n.

38. William Pead, Barbados, to John Winthrop, March 31, 1646, *Winthrop Papers*, V, 71; *Asp. Records*, pp. 290–294, 287, 300–301, 312; *Suff. Deeds*, I, 119, 254; Waters, *Gleanings*, I, 143–144.

39. Samuel's career may be most conveniently followed in his letters to his father and to his brother, John, Jr., 1646–1673, in M.H.S. *Colls.*, 5th series, VIII, 234–265.

40. The following section on the Hutchinsons is drawn from the correspondence in *The Letter Book of Peleg Sanford*, ed. Howard W. Preston *et al.* (Providence, 1928).

41. Peleg Sanford [Newport], to William Sanford, Dec. 28, 1668, *Sanford's Letter Book*, p. 69.

42. Beer, *Origins*, pp. 397–398.

43. For example, *Suff. Deeds*, I, 106; *Asp. Records*, p. 219.

44. *Asp. Records*, pp. 394–430.

45. Hull, *Diaries*, pp. 153, 159–160; Clarke, *Hull*, p. 43. Compare *Winthrop's Journal*, II, 253.

46. *Winthrop's Journal*, II, 184.

47. *Winthrop's Journal*, II, 185–186.

48. *Mass. Records*, III, 31–32.

49. *Mass. Records*, II, 69; III, 29; *Winthrop's Journal*, II, 255.

50. Beer, *Origins*, pp. 348–349; *Mass. Records*, III, 224, 240–241, 297; see also IV, part 1, 197; Mass. Archives, LX, 21; Hutchinson, *Massachusetts-Bay*, I, 428.

51. Beer, *Origins*, p. 409; Stephen Winthrop, Westminster, to John Winthrop, Jr., March 11, 1655, M.H.S. *Colls.*, 5th series, VIII, 216; *Cal. S.P. Col.*, 1574–1660, pp. 399, 431–432, 437–438; 1675–1676, §§202 and encls., 210, 213, 220–221, 224, 242, 245, 299, 313, 315.

52. *Winthrop's Journal*, II, 253–254; Calder, *New Haven*, pp. 206–208; Sedgwick, "Sedgwick," pp. 163ff.; Hutchinson, *Massachusetts-Bay*, I, 73n; *Davenport Letters*, p. 90n; M.H.S. *Colls.*, 5th series, VIII, xv; William L. Sachse, "The Migration of New Englanders to England 1640–1660," *A.H.R.*, LIII (1947–1948), 258, 270, 273–274; Charles M. Andrews, *British Committees, Commissions, and Councils of Trade and Plantations, 1622–1675 (Johns Hopkins University Studies in Historical and Political Science*, series XXVI, nos. 1–2–3, 1908), p. 40. For Bourne's farewell letter to Winthrop, Aug. 12, 1648, see *Winthrop Papers*, V, 243–245. For evidence of the use of his influence, see the documents cited in note 51 above. Hutchinson's will is printed in Waters, *Gleanings*, II, 1266.

53. Samuel Maverick, *A Briefe Discription of New England and the Severall Townes therein, together with the Present Government thereof* [ca. 1660] (reprinted in M.H.S. *Procs.*, 2nd series, I [1884–1885]), pp. 243, 236–239, 244–246.

54. For example, *Winthrop's Journal*, II, 341; *Asp. Records*, pp. 239ff.; Peleg Sanford [Newport], to [?], and to Daniel Burr, Dec. 9, 1667, *Sanford's Letter Book*, pp. 38–39; Bruce M. Bigelow, ed., "The Walter Newbury Shipping Book," *Rhode Island Historical Society Collections*, XXIV (1931), 73–91.

55. Maverick, *Briefe Discription*, pp. 236–237; Sylvester Judd, *History of Hadley* (Northampton, 1863), p. 80.

56. Maverick, *Briefe Discription*, p. 245; Leonard W. Labaree, *Milford, Connecticut (Publications of the Tercentenary Commission of the State of Connecticut*, XIII, 1936), pp. 15–16.

57. Phillips, *Salem*, pp. 194, 201; Essex Instit., *Hist. Colls.*, IX (1868), *passim;* Carl Bridenbaugh, *Cities in the Wilderness* (New York, 1938), chaps. i, ii, iii; Maverick, *Briefe Discription*, p. 237.

58. Maverick, *Briefe Discription*, p. 238; Bridenbaugh, *Cities*, p. 6.

59. For example, *Boston Town Recs.*, pp. 63–64, 76, 78–80, 84, 86, 87, 91, 102, 103, 107, 110, 112, 113, 119; Samuel C. Clough, "Cotton Hill and Adjacent Estates," *Pubs. C.S.M.*, XX (*Trs.*, 1917–1919), 264–266.

60. Maverick, *Briefe Discription*, p. 238.

61. Josselyn, *Two Voyages*, pp. 319–320.

62. The men appointed were Richard Parker, Nathaniel Duncan, Robert Keayne, William Tyng, Edward Tyng, Anthony Stoddard, and John Leverett. *Mass. Records*, III, 244.

63. Josiah H. Benton, *The Story of the Old Boston Town House, 1658–1711* (Boston, 1908), p. 51; John Winthrop, Jr., Hartford, to [?], Sept. 19, 1660, M.H.S. *Colls.*, 5th series, VIII, 67.

64. Adam Winthrop [Boston], to John Winthrop, Jr., Nov. 27, 1649, *Winthrop Papers*, V, 378; John Winthrop, Jr., Boston, to Fitz-John Winthrop, Sept. 12, 1658, M.H.S. *Colls.*, 5th series, VIII, 50.

65. *Maine Court Recs.*, I, 206.

66. Josselyn, *Two Voyages*, pp. 331, 349, 351–352.

67. *Records of the Colony of Rhode Island and Providence Plantation in New England*, ed. John R. Bartlett (Providence, 1856–1865), I, 398. (Hereafter referred to as *R.I. Records.*)

68. John Winthrop, Jr., Hartford, to William Brereton, Nov. 6, 1663, M.H.S. *Colls.*, 5th series, VIII, 86.

69. Everett S. Stackpole, *Old Kittery and Her Families* (Lewiston, Maine, 1903), pp. 128–129; Morison, *Builders of the Bay Colony*, pp. 178–180; Clarke, *Hull*, p. 91; *Asp. Records*, pp. 5, 9, 19, 20, 47, 143, 227, 337.

70. Sylvia L. Thrupp, *The Merchant Class of Medieval London* (Chicago, 1948), chap vi.

71. Mellen Chamberlain, *Documentary History of Chelsea* (Boston, 1908), I, chap. xix; Charles W. Tuttle, *Capt. Francis Champernowne . . . and other Historical Papers* (ed. Albert H. Hoyt, Boston, 1889), pp. 110–111; *Mass. Records*, III, 238.

72. For example, *Mass. Records*, III, 271, 330, 350, 429–430; IV, part 1, 65, 75, 147, 294–295, 304, 332, 355–356, 375, 398–402, 442–444.

73. For example, *Mass. Records*, III, 375; Roy H. Akagi, *The Town Proprietors of the New England Colonies* (Phila., 1924), pp. 44–49.

74. Seybolt, *Town Officials*, pp. 10–27; Phillips, *Salem*, chaps. xvi, xvii, p. 361; Richard Frothingham, *The History of Charlestown, Massachusetts* (Boston, 1845), chap. xiv.

75. Seybolt, *Town Officials*, pp. 12–27; Phillips, *Salem*, p. 358; *Mass. Records, passim;* Whitmore, *Civil List*, pp. 22–23.

76. *Mass. Records*, II, 48; III, 69; IV, part 1, 5–6; III, 221.

77. *Mass. Records*, IV, part 1, 10, 85–86, 246.

78. *Johnson's Wonder-Working Providence*, pp. 71, 35.

79. *Winthrop's Journal*, II, 259–260; *Mass. Records*, II, 141; III, 51.

80. *Mass. Records*, IV, part 1, 23; III, 245, 263, 291.

81. George Downing, Newfoundland, to John Winthrop, Jr., Aug. 26, 1645, *Winthrop Papers*, V, 42.

82. Stephen Winthrop, London, to John Winthrop, Jr., March 1, 1645; Hugh Peter, Gravesend, to John Winthrop, Jr., Sept. 4 [1646]; Hugh Peter [London?], to John Winthrop [ca. April 1647] and May 5, 1647, *Winthrop Papers*, V, 13, 102, 147, 158–159.

83. George L. Kittredge, "Doctor Robert Child the Remonstrant," *Pubs. C.S.M.*, XXI (*Trs.*, 1919), 70ff. The text of the Remonstrance is printed in *Hutchinson Papers*, I, 214–223.

84. Morison, *Builders of the Bay Colony*, pp. 245–247. Of the remonstrants, only Fowle is known to have been a recognized member of the New England Puritan church. Of the others, all but John Dand and John Smith are known *not* to have been members: p. 251; Kittredge, "Child," pp. 21–28.

85. *Hutchinson Papers*, I, 240, 223–247; Kittredge, "Child," pp. 50ff. Young Winthrop was quickly made to realize the cost of Child's treatment by the Puritans. Robert Child, Gravesend, to John Winthrop, Jr., May 13, 1648, *Winthrop Papers*, V, 221.

86. *Winthrop's Journal*, II, 271; Hutchinson, *Massachusetts-Bay*, I, 16n; Burt, *Springfield*, I, 81; *Mass. Records*, II, 200; III, 215, 240, 250; Hull, *Diaries*, p. 198.

87. *Cal S.P. Col.*, 1661–1668, §26; Richard P. Hallowell, *The Quaker Invasion of Massachusetts* (Boston, 1883), pp. 155, 156.

88. *Johnson's Wonder-Working Providence*, p. 254.

89. Hull, *Diaries*, pp. 211–212; *Winthrop's Journal*, II, 324.

90. *Mass. Records*, IV, part 1, 367.

91. Edward Howes [London], to John Winthrop, Jr., March 18, 1633, *Winthrop Papers*, III, 112; John Winthrop, Jr. [Boston?], to Fitz-John Winthrop, Feb. 8, 1655, M.H.S. *Colls.*, 5th series, VIII, 43.

92. Morison, *Builders of the Bay Colony*, p. 269. See also Burt's comparison of the two Pynchons: John, the settler's son, "was zealous in upholding the religion of his time, but he does not appear to have had any of the polemic or controversial spirit of his father. He was too eminently practical to enter into the discussion of the different points in theology, — possibly from the fact he was deeply concerned in trade, and in the accumulation of wealth. Whatever success came to him he evidently regarded as God given." Burt, *Springfield*, II, 627.

93. *Asp. Records*, pp. 137–142; Andrews, *Colonial Period*, I, 514.

94. [?], [Boston?], to John Davenport, July 5, 1662, *Davenport Letters*, pp. 201–202.

95. *Asp. Records*, pp. 137, 139, 141–142; Brebner, *N.E.'s Outpost*, pp. 32–35; Arthur H. Buffinton, "Sir Thomas Temple in Boston, a Case of Benevolent Assimilation," *Pubs. C.S.M.*, XXVII (*Trs.*, 1927–1930), 309–310; *Cal. S.P. Col.*, 1574–1660, p. 469.

96. Viola F. Barnes, "Richard Wharton, A Seventeenth Century New England Colonial," *Pubs. C.S.M.*, XXVI (*Trs.*, 1924–1926), 250.

97. Barnes, "Wharton," p. 249.

CHAPTER V. INTRODUCTION TO EMPIRE

1. Robert S. Bosher, *The Making of the Restoration Settlement* (London, 1951), p. 282.

2. Samuel Maverick [London?], to the Earl of Clarendon [ca. 1661], *The*

Clarendon Papers (Collections of the New York Historical Society for the Year 1869), pp. 23, 25.

3. Samuel Maverick [London?], to the Earl of Clarendon, March 28, 1663, *Clarendon Papers*, pp. 48, 50.

4. Buffinton, "Temple," pp. 310–313; *Cal. S.P. Col.*, 1574–1660, pp. 444–445, 466, 469–471, 474, 476, 478.

5. *Cal. S.P. Col.*, 1574–1660, p. 484; 1661–1668, §§ 225–226, 343; Brebner, *N.E.'s Outpost*, p. 26; *Acts of the Privy Council of England, Colonial Series*, ed. W. L. Grant *et al.* (Hereford and London, 1908–1912), I, 316, 322, 324. (Hereafter cited as *A.P.C., Col.*)

6. *Cal. S.P. Col.*, 1574–1660, pp. 490, 494, 496; 1661–1668, §§175, 189, 193; 1669–1674, §24; *A.P.C., Col.*, I, 330. See Dissertation Copy, pp. 298–300.

7. *N.Y. Col. Docs.*, III, 39–40.

8. *Cal. S.P. Col.*, 1661–1668, §80.

9. William D. Miller, "The Narragansett Planters," *A.A.S. Procs.*, new series, XLIII, part 1 (April 1933), 55.

10. *R.I. Records*, I, 403–404.

11. *The Records of the Proprietors of the Narragansett, otherwise Called the Fones Record*, ed. James N. Arnold (*Rhode Island Colonial Gleanings*, I, Providence, 1894), pp. 1–11. (Hereafter referred to as *Fones Record*.) *R.I. Records*, I, 421; The Rhode Island Assembly, Portsmouth, R.I., to the Commissioners of the United Colonies, Aug. 23, 1659. *The Trumbull Papers* (M.H.S. *Colls.*, 5th series, IX), pp. 10–12; Irving B. Richman, *Rhode Island, Its Making and Meaning* (New York, 1902), II, 237–238.

12. Daniel Denison *et al.* [Boston?], to John Winthrop, Jr. [ca. 1661]; Edward Hutchinson *et al.*, Boston, to John Winthrop, Jr., Sept. 24, 1661, *Trumbull Papers*, pp. 27–29, 30–31; John Winthrop, Jr., London, to John Mason *et al.*, March 4, 1663, M.H.S. *Colls.*, 5th series, VIII, 79.

13. John Clarke [London], to King Charles II, May 14, 1662, *Clarendon Papers*, p. 44; Agreement between John Winthrop, Jr. and John Clarke, April 7, 1663, M.H.S. *Colls.*, 5th series, VIII, 83.

14. John Scott, London, to Edward Hutchinson, April 29, 1663; King Charles II, Whitehall, to the New England Colonies, June 31, 1663, *Trumbull Papers*, pp. 53, 54; *Calendar of Treasury Books*, ed. William A. Shaw (London, 1904–1952), I, 220, 227, 519; compare pp. 116, 541. (Hereafter cited at *Cal. T. Bks.*)

15. *Cal. S.P. Col.*, 1661–1668, §§33, 50, 75, 78, 255, 899.

16. *Cal. S.P. Col.*, 1661–1668, §437; *N.Y. Col. Docs.*, III, 53, 55.

17. *Cal. S.P. Col.*, 1661–1668, §929; *Conn. Records*, I, 433, 439ff.; *N.Y. Col. Docs.*, III, 97.

18. *N.Y. Col. Docs.*, III, 55, 97; *Mass. Records*, IV, part 2, 175.

19. It was said that the commissioners intended to deny all liberty of conscience and that they came "to exact 12*d.* for every acre of land and 3,000*l.* a year besides." Attempts by the commissioners to scotch this rumor were to no avail, and the whispering campaign reached a crescendo with the allegation that one of the commissioners was a "papist" and "that Sir Rob. Carr kept a naughty woman." *Cal. S.P. Col.*, 1661–1668, §918; *Mass. Records*, IV, part 2, 184, 168; *N.Y. Col. Docs.*, III, 90–91, 94.

20. *N.Y. Col. Docs.*, III, 95–96; Thomas Deane, Boston, to the Earl of Clarendon, June 22, 1665, *Clarendon Papers*, p. 68.

21. Samuel Maverick, Boston, to the Earl of Clarendon, July 24 and Nov. 7,

1665, *Clarendon Papers*, pp. 70–71, 79–80; *Cal. S.P. Col.*, 1661–1668, §1020 encl. 2; *N.Y. Col. Docs.*, III, 136–137.

22. *N.Y. Col. Docs.*, III, 59, 65. Compare *Privateering and Piracy in the Colonial Period: Illustrative Documents*, ed. John F. Jameson (New York, 1923), pp. 27–46.

23. *N.Y. Col. Docs.*, III, 88; *Cal. S.P. Col.*, 1661–1668, §§917, 918, 921, 931, 933; Sir Richard Nichols, New York City, to the Earl of Clarendon, April 7 [1666], *Clarendon Papers*, p. 113.

24. The case started four years earlier when the French *Charles of Oléron* entered Boston harbor to trade. Denied this right according to the navigation acts, the ship had promptly departed. But several weeks later a small Massachusetts vessel arrived in Boston from Monhegan Island loaded with European goods consigned to the Boston merchant Joshua Scottow and his wife. Suspecting this cargo to be the French goods now being smuggled in, several young merchants and sailors led by Deane, Thomas Kellond, and Thomas Kirke boarded the vessel without a warrant and after seizing the goods demanded that the General Court punish the smugglers forthwith. This the Court attempted to do, but the case did not come to trial, though twice scheduled, because of insufficient evidence. It was then dropped and forgotten until the commissioners reopened the case as an instance of Massachusetts' refusal to abide by the navigation acts. *Mass. Records*, IV, part 2, 35–36, 218–219; Mass. Archives, LX, 127–129.

Such, at any rate, was Massachusetts' story, and the commissioners themselves later confessed that it was probably true. *Clarendon Papers*, p. 99. What the magistrates did not know was that between 1661 and 1665 Deane and his friends had been in London where they had recounted the tale before people interested in illustrating Massachusetts' recalcitrancy. It eventually came to the ears of Clarendon himself who instructed the commissioners to reopen the case in Boston. *N.Y. Col. Docs.*, III, 107. By 1665 it was out of Deane's hands and his efforts to keep the commissioners from attaching too much weight to the episode were to no avail. To them it was a useful focus for their controversy with Massachusetts, "which," Deane confessed to Clarendon, "I could have wished had been otherwise. . ." Thomas Deane, Boston, to the Earl of Clarendon, June 22, 1665, *Clarendon Papers*, p. 68.

25. Roberts, *Artillery Company*, I, 152–153; M.H.S. *Colls.*, 2nd series, IV, 100–101.

26. Savage, *Dictionary*, II, 30; Waters, *Gleanings*, I, 242–243; II, 1099.

27. *N.E. Register*, XIII, 237–238; Savage, *Dictionary*, II, 30.

28. *N.E. Register*, XLIII, 64–65; Sybil Noyes *et al.*, *Genealogical Dictionary of Maine and New Hampshire* (Portland, Maine, 1939), p. 614; William S. Southgate, *The History of Scarborough . . . (Collections of the Maine Historical Society*, III [1853]), chap. vii.

29. Joshua Scottow, *Old Men's Tears . . .* (Boston, 1749 ed.), p. 6.

30. Reprinted in M.H.S. *Colls.*, 4th series, IV, 279–330.

31. *Cal. S.P. Col.*, 1661–1668, §1171.

32. *Clarendon Papers*, pp. 132–134. For the complete list, see *Danforth Papers* (M.H.S. *Colls.*, 2nd series, VIII), pp. 105ff.

33. These occupational designations were flexible (for example, the merchant-cooper in *Mass. Records*, IV, part 2, 397–399), and all five of the nonmerchants probably engaged in trade.

34. For identification of the petitioners, see Dissertation Copy, pp. 319–320n.

35. *Cal. S.P. Col.*, 1661–1668, §§1009, 1010.

36. Samuel Maverick [Boston], to the Earl of Clarendon, July 24, 1665, *Clarendon Papers*, p. 72.

37. *Genealog. Dict. of Maine and N.H.*, pp. 330, 711.

38. *Cal. S.P. Col.*, 1661–1668, §§1015, 1024.

39. *Mass. Records*, IV, part 2, 293, 304–305, 317–318; Samuel Maverick [Newport], to George Cartwright [1666], *Clarendon Papers*, pp. 127–128.

40. *Cal. S.P. Col.*, 1661–1668, §§1829, 1835, 1848; *N.Y. Col. Docs.*, III, 170–171, 173–174; see also *N.Y. Col. Docs.*, III, 160–161.

41. *N.Y. Col. Docs.*, III, 69, 109, 115, 185; Sir Robert Carr, Boston, to the Earl of Clarendon, Dec. 5, 1665, *Clarendon Papers*, p. 81.

42. Though the act of 1660 clearly permitted such sales, the New England merchants and their English correspondents made doubly sure of the legality of this vital trade. In 1661 they petitioned for explicit permission to send their timber, fish, "and such other Gruff-commodityes" to continental Europe, agreeing to send the returns directly to England. The petition was granted. *A.P.C., Col.*, I, 304; *Cal. T. Bks.*, I, 206–207; *Cal. S.P. Col.*, 1661–1668, §28.

43. Compare *N.Y. Col. Docs.*, III, 45.

44. Andrews, *Colonial Period*, IV, 66–68, 110–113, 124ff.

45. *Suff. Deeds*, IV, 308–309.

46. Thomas Temple, Boston, to the Earl of Clarendon, Aug. 21 and 22, 1663, *Clarendon Papers*, pp. 50–56; *Cal. S.P. Col.*, 1669–1674, §§24, 32, 68, 95, 384; Buffinton, "Temple," p. 315.

47. Mass. Archives, LXI, 132.

48. *Cal. S.P. Col.*, 1661–1668, §1694 encl. 1; 1669–1674, p. 290. Compare Harlow, *Barbados*, chap. vi.

49. See the table of goods entered in customs from one plantation to another, Michaelmas, 1677–Michaelmas, 1678, in C.S.S. Higham, *The Development of the Leeward Islands under the Restoration, 1660–1688* (Cambridge, England, 1921), p. 210.

50. See above, p. 74.

51. *Mass. Records*, IV, part 2, 37, 344.

52. Lounsbury, *Fishery*, chap. vi, p. 192; Judah, *Fisheries*, p. 144.

53. Lounsbury, *Fishery*, chap. iv, pp. 190, 194ff.; Judah, *Fisheries*, pp. 116ff., 124, 126; *Cal. S.P. Col.*, 1669–1674, §616. If the volume of complaints is an indication of the extent of such smuggling, this clandestine trade was insignificant before 1675.

54. Lounsbury, *Fishery*, pp. 195, 191.

55. Wait Winthrop, Boston, to John Winthrop, Jr., Feb. 28, 1672, M.H.S. *Colls.*, 5th series, VIII, 389; *Cal. S.P. Col.*, 1669–1674, §§825 encl. 2, 883.

56. *Cal. S.P. Col.*, 1661–1668, §1255; Hull, *Diaries*, p. 237; Samuel Maverick [Boston], to John Winthrop, Jr., Aug. 29, 1666, M.H.S. *Colls.*, 4th series, VII, 314; Mass. Archives, LXI, 11–13; *N.Y. Col. Docs.*, II, 662–663, 715.

57. Mass. Archives, LX, 82; *Cal. S.P. Col.*, 1661–1668, §1271; 1669–1674, §§58, 82; *Mass. Records*, IV, part 2, 345, 423, 547–548.

58. Robert G. Albion, *Forests and Sea Power* (Cambridge, 1926), pp. 207, 213.

59. *Cal. S.P. Dom.*, 1661–1662, §§132, 400; 1663–1664, §§270, 395, 653; 1664–1665, §§250, 268, 303, 346, 402, 459, 477, 568; 1665–1666, §§71–72, 129–135, 223,

381; 1666–1667, §572; 1667, §§18, 107; 1667–1668, §260; 1670, §§58–59, 456–457; 1672, §§429–430; *Cal. S.P. Col.*, 1661–1668, §1149; *The Diary of Samuel Pepys*, ed. Henry B. Wheatley (Random House ed., New York, n.d.), I, 882, 884, 952; Arthur Bryant, *Samuel Pepys: The Man in the Making* (Cambridge, England, 1933), pp. 177, 218.

60. *Cal. S.P. Dom.*, 1666–1667, §325; *Pepys' Diary*, II, 366. Compare *Cal. S.P. Col.*, 1661–1668, §1333.

61. *Cal. S.P. Col.*, 1661–1668, §§1297, 1409, 1797; *Cal. S.P. Dom.*, 1668–1669, §7.

62. *Cal. S.P. Col.*, 1669–1674, §687; *Cal. S.P. Dom.*, 1670, §§58–59, 456–457; Albion, *Forests*, p. 218.

63. Albion, *Forests*, pp. 55ff.

64. George E. Hodgdon, *Reminiscences . . . of the Vaughan Family of New Hampshire* (Rochester, N.Y., 1918), p. 1.

65. So he referred to Child. *N.H. Prov. Papers*, I, 507, 527, 531.

66. *N.E. Register*, XIII, 237–238; XV, 14; *Cal. S.P. Dom.*, 1667–1668, §260; Jeffries Family Papers (MSS in the Massachusetts Historical Society), VI, 4.

67. Albion, *Forests*, p. 56.

68. Barnes, "Wharton," p. 242.

69. *Diary of Samuel Sewall*, July 31 and Nov. 11, 1675 (M.H.S. *Colls.*, 5th series, V, 10, 11.)

70. The following section is based on genealogical and biographical data too extensive to be footnoted in detail. The main sources, in which validation for the following statements will be found, are *N.E. Register*, I–L; Savage, *Dictionary*; Waters, *Gleanings*; Roberts, *Artillery Company*; *Genealog. Dict. of Maine and N.H.*

71. *Clarendon Papers*, p. 84.

72. Edmund S. Morgan, "A Boston Heiress and Her Husbands: A True Story," *Pubs. C.S.M.*, XXXIV (*Trs.*, 1937–1942), 499–513.

73. Henry W. Foote, *Annals of King's Chapel* (Boston, 1882–1896), I, 44–48.

74. E. Edwards Beardsley, *The History of the Episcopal Church in Connecticut . . .* (New York, 1868), I, 17.

75. George C. Mason, *Annals of Trinity Church, Newport, Rhode Island* (Newport, 1890–1894), 1st series, 34, 35; Wilfred H. Monro, *The Story of the Mount Hope Lands* [Bristol, R.I.] . . . (Providence, 1880), pp. 75–76.

76. Thus, when Henry Shrimpton's son Samuel, upon becoming a freeman in 1673, was elected constable of Boston, he announced in public meeting that he preferred to pay a fine of £10 rather than to serve in that office — "which was accepted by the town." Roberts, *Artillery Company*, I, 215.

77. Andrews, *Colonial Period*, I, 461n. Compare Rhode Island's handling of a similar problem of "persones [who] desire not to be made . . . freemen." *R.I. Records*, II, 357.

78. The subject of the following section has been discussed in detail by Perry Miller in his splendid essay, "Declension in a Bible Commonwealth," *A.A.S. Procs.*, new series, LI, part 1 (April 1941), 37–94, and at greater length in *The New England Mind from Colony to Province* (Cambridge, 1953), book I.

79. Thomas W. Higginson, *Descendants of the Reverend Francis Higginson* (n.p., 1910), pp. 8–11.

80. John Higginson, *The Cause of God and His People in New England* . . . (Cambridge, 1663), pp. 10–12.

81. Increase Mather, *An Earnest Exhortation to the Inhabitants of New-England* . . . (Boston, 1676), pp. 16–17; [Increase Mather], *Necessity of Reformation* . . . (Boston, 1679).

82. [Mather], *Necessity*, p. 6; Mather, *Exhortation*, pp. 17, 7.

83. John Oxenbridge, *New-England Freemen Warned and Warmede;* . . . ([Cambridge], 1673), p. 19.

84. Higginson, *Cause of God*, p. 14.

85. William Hubbard, *The Happiness of a People in the Wisdome of Their Rulers Directing* . . . (Boston, 1676), p. 55.

86. Hubbard, *Happiness of a People*, p. 58.

CHAPTER VI. ELEMENTS OF CHANGE

1. John Hull [Boston], to William Stoughton and Peter Bulkeley, Feb. 1, 1679, John Hull's Letter Book (MS in American Antiquarian Society, Worcester, Mass.), II, 411. (Page references are to the two volume typescript in the Society's library.)

2. Compare above, pp. 35ff., 79–82, 87–91.

3. Philip English MSS (Essex Institute, Salem, Mass.), I, 1.

4. English MSS, I, 1–50; Philip English Ledgers, 1678–1690, 1664–1708 (MSS in Essex Institute), *passim*.

5. English MSS, I, 50.

6. Henri Brunet, Boston, to "Mr. Faneuil," Feb. 4, 1675, Louis-André Vigneras, "Letters of an Acadian Trader, 1674–1676," *N.E.Q.*, XIII (1940), 106; see also Richard Wharton and Co., Boston, to Michel Boucher, Jan. 28, 1675, *Records of the Suffolk County Court, 1671–1680* (*Pubs. C.S.M.*, XXIX–XXX [*Collections*, 1933]), II, 667. (Hereafter referred to as *Recs. Suff. Ct.*)

7. For example, *Cal. S.P. Col.*, 1675–1676, §§840, 843; *Cal. T. Bks.*, V, part 1, 810.

8. Vigneras, "Letters," pp. 98–106; Henri Brunet, Boston, to "Mr. l'Intendant" [Colbert du Terron?], Feb. 5, 1675, Vigneras, "Letters," p. 109.

9. Henri Brunet, Boston, to "Mr. Faneuil," Feb 4, 1675, Vigneras, "Letters," p. 106.

10. *Records of the Court of Assistants of the Colony of the Massachusetts Bay, 1630–1692*, ed. John Noble (Boston, 1901–1928), I, 129. (Hereafter referred to as *Ass. Ct. Recs.*): Barnes, "Wharton," pp. 240–241.

11. Roberts, *Artillery Company*, I, 217; *A.P.C., Col.*, I, 885; *Recs. Suff. Ct.*, I, 141, 175; Richard Wharton and Thomas Bendish, Boston, to James Elson, Nov. 12, 1674, *Recs. Suff. Ct.*, II, 661–662.

12. Roberts, *Artillery Company*, I, 451–455; Stewart L. Mims, *Colbert's West India Policy* (New Haven, 1912), pp. 184–185, 208–211, 318ff.; Richard Wharton and Co., Boston, to Michel Boucher, Jan. 28, 1675, *Recs. Suff. Ct.*, II, 665–666.

13. *Recs. Suff. Ct.*, II, 661ff.

14. Richard Wharton and Co., Boston, to Michel Boucher, Jan. 28, 1675, *Recs. Suff. Ct.*, II, 667.

15. *Recs. Suff. Ct.*, II, 665–666.

16. Wesley F. Craven, *The Southern Colonies in the Seventeenth Century,*

1607–1689 (*A History of the South*, ed. Wendell H. Stephenson and E. Merton Coulter [Baton Rouge, 1949], I), pp. 319, 408–409; Robert Holden, Boston, to commissioners of customs, June 10, 1679, Gay Collection of Transcripts (Massachusetts Historical Society), State Papers, II, 69.

17. See, for example, John Hull [Boston], to John Alden, Sept. 18, 1671, and to John Winsley, Dec. 6, 1672, Hull's Letter Book, I, 26, 86; Theodora Keith, *Commercial Relations of England and Scotland, 1603–1707* (Cambridge, England, 1910), p. 118. *Cal. S.P. Col.*, 1675–1676, §816; 1677–1680, §802.

18. Stock, *Proceedings*, I, 310. In 1686 the Attorney General of England himself made the point: ". . . I am of opinion that the exporting of commodities from the Canaries which are out of Europe, to New England is no offence within that [Act of 1673] or any other Act that I know of." *Cal. T. Bks.*, VIII, part 2, 957–958.

19. Andrews, *Colonial Period*, IV, 118ff.

20. George L. Beer, *The Old Colonial System, 1660–1754* (2nd ed., New York, 1933), I, 81ff.; Lawrence A. Harper, *The English Navigation Laws* (New York, 1939), pp. 163–164, 175, 397.

21. See Sir Joseph Williamson's Notes on the New England Trade, April 24, 1676, *Cal. S.P. Col.*, 1675–1676, §900 (p. 381).

22. John Hull [Boston], to William Stoughton and Peter Bulkeley, Dec. 22, 1677, Hull's Letter Book, II, 365; *Cal. S.P. Col.*, 1677–1680, §747.

23. Beer, *Colonial System*, II, 196, 198. For Culpeper's fate in England, see *Cal. S.P. Col.*, 1677–1680, §§1017, 1236, 1274, 1288–1290.

24. John Hull [Boston], to William Stoughton and Peter Bulkeley, Dec. 22, 1677, Hull's Letter Book, II, 365.

25. John Hull [Boston], to William Stoughton and Peter Bulkeley, Feb. 1, 1689, Hull's Letter Book, II, 411.

26. *Cal. S.P. Col.*, 1675–1676, §§405 (pp. 156ff.), 881; *Cal. S.P. Col.* 1676–1677, §§586–587; Mass. Archives, CVI, 210.

27. *Cal. S.P. Col.*, 1675–1676, §§889, 898, 900.

28. *Cal. S.P. Col.*, 1661–1668, §§1485, 1588; 1669–1674, §§150, 184, 439, 583, 651, 860, 907, 1247; 1675–1676, §§545, 506, 563, 568.

29. *Cal. S.P. Col.*, 1675–1676, §§ 797, 800, 803, 813.

30. *Edward Randolph*, ed. Robert N. Toppan and Thomas S. Goodrick (Boston, 1898–1909), I, 1ff.; VI, 1–8. (Hereafter referred to as Toppan, *Randolph*.)

31. Toppan, *Randolph*, II, 196–199, 203; Edward Randolph, Boston, to "Mr. Sec: Coventry," June 17, 1676, Toppan, *Randolph*, II, 203–204.

32. Toppan, *Randolph*, II, 205, 207.

33. Toppan, *Randolph*, II, 203–209.

34. Toppan, *Randolph*, II, 207; Edward Randolph [London], to King Charles II, Sept. 20, 1676, Toppan, *Randolph*, II, 221–222.

35. Edward Randolph [London], to the Privy Council, Oct. 12, 1676, Toppan, *Randolph*, II, 235, 255.

36. Toppan, *Randolph*, II, 241, 249, 250; Edward Randolph's Representation of New England, received May 6, 1677, Toppan, *Randolph*, II, 266.

37. *Mass. Records*, V, 200, 201.

38. Toppan, *Randolph*, II, 277; William Stoughton [London?], to [Massachusetts General Court], Dec. 1, 1677, quoted in Hutchinson, *Massachusetts-Bay*, I, 270.

39. Toppan, *Randolph*, II, 277–279; *Cal. S.P. Col.*, 1677–1680, §§653, 691, 695, 705; 1675–1676, §556.

40. *Cal. S.P. Col.*, 1677–1680, §787.

41. *Mass. Records*, IV, part 2, 117–118. Compare George H. Haynes, *Representation and Suffrage in Massachusetts, 1620–1691* (*Johns Hopkins University Studies in Historical and Political Science*, 12th series, VIII–IX, Baltimore, 1894), pp. 57–59.

42. Whitmore, *Civil List*, pp. 16–17, 21ff.

43. Toppan, *Randolph*, II, 287; III, 5–6, 19–30. The agents claimed that Randolph was not only "a person of a very indigent fortune and soe not likely to continue unbiassed in this the employment designed him." They were undoubtedly behind his sudden arrest on June 11, 1679, for a 300 shilling debt he had incurred in Scotland ten years earlier. Toppan, *Randolph*, VI, 75–77, 81–82.

44. Edward Randolph [London], to [William Stoughton?], July 18, 1678, Toppan, *Randolph*, III, 31.

45. Edward Randolph [London], to Lords of Trade, ca. Feb. 22, 1679, Toppan, *Randolph*, III, 39–40; *Cal. S.P. Col.*, 1677–1680, §§996, 1036, 1041.

46. *Cal. S.P. Coll.*, 1677–1680, §§1053, 1058.

47. Toppan, *Randolph*, III, 34–38, 41, 47.

48. Toppan, *Randolph*, I, 121.

49. Edward Randolph, Boston, to Josiah Winslow, Jan. 29, 1680, Toppan, *Randolph*, III, 64; 104–105.

50. Toppan, *Randolph*, III, 61, 63, 69.

51. *Ass. Ct. Recs.*, I, 176; Edward Randolph, Boston, to the commissioners of customs, June 7, 1680, Toppan, *Randolph*, III, 70–73.

52. The case of the two sloops, and the *St. John* of Dublin, Toppan, *Randolph*, III, 85, 86. Compare Toppan, *Randolph*, VI, 109–111.

53. Case of the *Expectation*, Toppan, *Randolph*, III, 84; Edward Randolph, Boston, to the commissioners of the customs, June 9, 1680, Toppan, *Randolph*, III, 73–76. See also Toppan, *Randolph*, VI, 105.

54. Toppan, *Randolph*, III, 85. The ruling of the Massachusetts court of assistants in this case was emphatically supported by the commissioners of the customs. *Ass. Ct. Recs.*, I, 176–177; Toppan, *Randolph*, VI, 106.

55. Toppan, *Randolph*, III, 85.

56. *Ass. Ct. Recs.*, I, 177; Toppan, *Randolph*, VI, 106–107. Compare below, pp. 165–166.

57. *Ass. Ct. Recs.*, I, 149, 170–171; Edward Randolph, Boston, to the commissioners of the customs, June 7, 1680, Toppan, *Randolph*, III, 71–72.

58. Oliver M. Dickerson, *The Navigation Acts and the American Revolution* (Phila., 1951), chap. ix.

59. Edward Randolph, Boston, to the commissioners of the customs, June 7, 1680, Toppan, *Randolph*, III, 72.

60. Toppan, *Randolph*, VI, 101, 106.

61. Toppan, *Randolph*, VI, 101, 109, 110.

62. Toppan, *Randolph*, VI, 101, 106–107. Compare Joseph R. Frese, Writs of Assistance in the American Colonies 1660–1776 (Unpublished Ph.D. Dissertation, Harvard University, 1951), chap. v.

63. Toppan, *Randolph*, VI, 101–102, 111–112.

CHAPTER VII. THE MERCHANT GROUP AT THE END OF THE SEVENTEENTH CENTURY

1. John Hull [Boston], to Peleg Sanford, July 7 and Aug. 21, 1679, Hull's Letter Book, II, 420–422, 426; *Cal. S.P. Col.*, 1677–1680, §§1496, 1537. Compare *Cal. S.P. Col.*, 1677–1680, §§1102, 1247.

2. Fitz-John Winthrop [New London], to [?], Nov. 22, 1680, M.H.S. *Colls.*, 5th series, VIII, 293; *Cal. S.P. Col.*, 1681–1685, §88; *Fones Record*, pp. 38–39.

3. Toppan, *Randolph*, III, 110; *Cal. S.P. Col.*, 1681–1685, §§636, 1039.

4. Gertrude A. Jacobsen, *William Blathwayt* (New Haven, 1932), pp. 186–189; Toppan, *Randolph*, VI, 170n.

5. Edward Cranfield, Portsmouth, N.H., to William Blathwayt, Feb. 20, 1683; Edward Cranfield, Great Island [N.H.], to William Blathwayt, Oct. 5, 1683, Toppan, *Randolph*, VI, 138–139, 148. For the commission's report, see *Cal. S.P. Col.*, 1681–1685, §1986.

6. *Cal. S.P. Col.*, 1685–1688, §1414 encl. 5.

7. Barnes, "Wharton," pp. 248–249, 266; Joseph Dudley and Samuel Shrimpton [Boston], to William Blathwayt, Jan. 18, 1686, Jeffries Papers, IV, 108.

8. Barnes, "Wharton," pp. 243, 246–248, 266–268.

9. Edward Randolph [London], to Sir Robert Southwell, Aug. 8 and Oct. 23, 1685, Toppan, *Randolph*, IV, 34, 63; V, 71.

10. Edward Cranfield, Boston, to William Blathwayt, June 19, 1683, Toppan, *Randolph*, VI, 144.

11. *Mass. Records*, V, 517; [Robert N. Toppan, ed.], "Dudley Records," M.H.S. *Procs.*, 2nd series, XIII (1899–1900), 234–235, 246–247, 252, 260–261, 264, 279–280, 283.

12. Richard Pares, *King George III and the Politicians* (Oxford, 1953), pp. 5ff.; Whitmore, *Civil List*, pp. 30–31; *Cal. S.P. Col.*, 1685–1688, §1197 encl. 1.

13. Edward Randolph, Boston, to John Povey, June 21, 1688, Toppan, *Randolph*, IV, 227.

14. See also below, pp. 191–192; *Cal. S.P. Col.*, 1689–1692, §261 encl. 3; *The Andros Tracts*, ed. William H. Whitmore (Boston, 1868–1874), I, 20.

15. *The Acts and Resolves . . . of . . . Massachusetts Bay . . .* (Boston, 1869–1922), I, 1–20; Kenneth B. Murdock, *Increase Mather* (Cambridge, 1925), pp. 249–250; Viola F. Barnes, *The Dominion of New England* (New Haven, 1923), pp. 269–270.

16. Jeremy Belknap, *The History of New-Hampshire* (ed. John Farmer, Dover, N.H., 1831), I, 148ff.; *N.E. Register*, XXIII (1869), 411.

17. Toppan, *Randolph*, I, 146–149; IV, 49–50, 58, 67–68.

18. *Mass. Records*, V, 337–338.

19. Toppan, *Randolph*, III, 128–129, 135, 139, 167ff., 205, 346.

20. Bernard Randolph, Boston, to Edward Randolph, June 13, 1683, Toppan, *Randolph*, III, 249; 181–183, 284.

21. Edward Randolph, Whitehall, to Sir Robert Southwell, Jan. 29, 1685, Toppan, *Randolph*, IV, 5.

22. Edward Randolph, Whitehall, to Sir Robert Southwell, Aug. 19, 1683, Toppan, *Randolph*, III, 264; 173, 175; I, 208; Barnes, *Dominion*, pp. 195–198.

23. Toppan, *Randolph*, I, 187–188; III, 285, 269–270; Bernard Randolph, Boston, to Edward Randolph, June 13, 1683; Edward Randolph, Whitehall, to Samuel Shrimpton, July 18, 1684, Toppan, *Randolph*, III, 249–250, 311.

24. Toppan, *Randolph*, I, 252, 262; IV, 51ff.; Edward Randolph [Whitehall], to Joseph Dudley, Jan. 9, 1685, Toppan, *Randolph*, IV, 13; *Cal. S.P. Col.*, 1685–1688, §384.

25. Edward Randolph, Boston, to Sir Robert Southwell, July 10, 1686, Toppan, *Randolph*, IV, 92; Edward Randolph [Boston], to the Bishop of London, May 29, 1682, Toppan, *Randolph*, III, 145; IV, 121, 141.

26. Edward Randolph, Boston, to the Lord Treasurer, Aug. 23, 1686; to William Blathwayt, July 28, 1686; and to the Archbishop of Canterbury, Aug. 2, 1686, Toppan, *Randolph*, IV, 114, 98, 105; VI, 18; Barnes, *Dominion*, p. 65.

27. *N.Y. Col. Docs.*, III, 283, 302ff.; Edward Randolph, Boston, to John Povey, Jan. 24, 1688, Toppan, *Randolph*, IV, 198; II, 69; Hutchinson, *Massachusetts-Bay*, I, 305.

28. *Andros Tracts*, I, 14, 40.

29. Sewall, *Diary*, I, 340; Austin, *Gen. Dict. of R.I.*, p. 252; *Cal. S.P. Col.*, 1693–1696, §689 encl. 1; Toppan, *Randolph*, II, 141n; V, 71–72; Harper, *Navigation Laws*, p. 214; Winslow Warren, "The Colonial Revenue Service in Massachusetts in Its Relation to the Revolution," M.H.S. *Procs.*, XLVI (1912–1913), 461–462.

30. Edward Randolph, [London and] Boston, to Sir Robert Southwell, July 30, 1685; and to William Blathwayt, Nov. 23, 1687, Toppan, *Randolph*, IV, 27; VI, 235; Johnson, *Economic Thought*, p. 174; M.H.S. *Procs.*, LII (1918–1919), 335–340.

31. John Hull [Boston], to Henry Ashurst, Dec. 17, 1679, Hull's Letter Book, II, 438–439.

32. *Colonial Currency Reprints 1682–1751*, ed. Andrew M. Davis (Boston, 1910–1911), I, 109–111.

33. *Currency Reprints*, I, 114, 116; Andrew M. Davis, *Currency and Banking in the Province of the Massachusetts-Bay, Part II—Banking* (New York, 1901), p. 72. (Hereafter referred to as Davis, *Banking*.) Andrew M. Davis, "Boston 'Banks' — 1681–1740 — Those Who Were Interested in Them," *N.E. Register*, LVII (1903), 274–275.

34. Nathaniel Mather [Dublin], to Increase Mather, Dec. 31, 1684, *The Mather Papers* (M.H.S. *Colls.*, 4th series, VIII), p. 60; Davis, *Banking*, pp. 77–78.

35. "Dudley Records," p. 272; also pp. 248–249. Davis, *Banking*, pp. 75ff.

36. Davis, "Boston 'Banks,'" p. 275.

37. Johnson, *Economic Thought*, pp. 171ff.; Curtis P. Nettels, *The Money Supply of the American Colonies Before 1720* (*University of Wisconsin Studies in the Social Sciences and History*, no. 20, Madison, Wisc., 1934), pp. 232–233; Hull, *Diaries*, p. 301.

38. Nettels, *Money Supply*, p. 236n; Johnson, *Economic Thought*, p. 172.

39. Mass. Archives, C, 350–351, 388; "Dudley Records," p. 244; Barnes, *Dominion*, p. 162.

40. Mass. Archives, C, 162–163. On the identification of the draft of Wharton's proposal, see Barnes, *Dominion*, p. 163n.

41. Robert N. Toppan, ed., "Andros Records," A.A.S. *Procs.*, new series, XIII (1899–1900), 252.

42. "Andros Records," pp. 262–263.

43. Edward Randolph, Boston, to John Povey, Jan. 24, 1688 and May 21, 1687, Toppan, *Randolph*, IV, 199, 163; Nettels, *Money Supply*, p. 237; *Currency Reprints*, I, 154–187.

44. *Currency Reprints*, I, 22ff.; Andrew M. Davis, *Currency and Banking in the Province of the Massachusetts-Bay, Part I — Currency* (New York, 1901), pp. 15–19.

45. Compare, for example, *Cal. S.P. Col.*, 1685–1688, §§1878, 1879; *Mather Papers, passim;* Edward Randolph, Boston, to Sir Leoline Jenkins, June 14 and Nov. 13, 1682, Toppan, *Randolph*, III, 160, 215; see also Toppan, *Randolph*, III, 284.

46. Letters from Hull and Sewall to Papillon are scattered through Hull's Letter Book. See A. F. W. Papillon, *Memoirs of Thomas Papillon of London, Merchant (1623–1702)* (Reading, England, 1887), chap. xi.

47. *Cal. S.P. Col.*, 1689–1692, §305; Foote, *King's Chapel*, I, 44ff., 48n; Barnes, "Wharton," p. 239.

48. *Cal. S.P. Col.*, 1689–1692, §§741, 883, 1390, 1439. A photostat of the last document, "An Account of the Persons who have Subscribed the New England Address with the value of their Estates according to Common Estimation," will be found among the Burbank Papers, Baker Library, Harvard University.

49. Dickerson, *Navigation Acts*, pp. 209, 233ff.; Hutchinson, *Massachusetts-Bay*, I, 317. See Charles Lidget, London, to Francis Foxcroft, Nov. 5, 1690, *N.E. Register*, XXXIII (1879), 406–408.

50. *Cal. S.P. Col.*, 1689–1692, §§1390, 1393; "An Account of the Persons who have Subscribed . . . ," Burbank Papers.

51. See Charts A, B, C in Dissertation Copy, pp. 473–475, based on "Tax List and Schedules. — 1687," *First Report of the Record Commissioners of the City of Boston, 1876* (Boston, 1876), pp. 91–133. Shrimpton was the highest taxpayer on all three lists. See Sumner, *East Boston*, chap. ix.

52. Sewall, *Diary*, I, 110–111, 128ff., 139.

53. See for example, Samuel Sewall's Business Journal, Sept. 18, 1685–July 19, 1689 (MS in Baker Library, Harvard University).

54. Sewall, *Diary*, I, 132, 150–151, 217, 228, 338.

55. Wait Winthrop, Boston, to Fitz-John Winthrop, June 2, 1679 and Nov. 28, 1684, M.H.S. *Colls.*, 5th series, VIII, 418, 447; Sewall, *Diary*, I, 102, 158. Compare Sewall, *Diary*, I, 95.

56. Sewall, *Diary*, I, 162, 164; Edward Randolph, Boston, to John Povey, May 21, 1687, Toppan, *Randolph*, IV, 163; Barnes, *Dominion*, pp. 199–200.

57. Sewall, *Diary*, I, 263.

58. *The Journal of Madam Knight* (New York, 1935), p. 40; *Cal. S.P. Col.*, 1712–1714, §520.

59. *Conn. Records*, II, 279, 284, 292, 322, 379, 399, 409, 432, 463; Conn. Archives, Court Papers, p. 124b; Nettels, *Money Supply*, p. 69; Bridenbaugh, *Cities*, pp. 185, 196, 252–253; M.H.S. *Procs.*, LII (1918–1919), 337; *Cal. S.P. Col.*, 1700, §354 encl. 19.

60. *Cal. S.P. Col.*, 1700, §592; *Boston News-Letter*, Feb. 18, 1712, June 15, 1713.

61. Belknap, *New-Hampshire*, I, 224, 231; see also *Cal. S.P. Col.*, 1728–1729, §§998, 1046, 1050; Ralph G. Lounsbury, "Jonathan Belcher, Junior, Chief Justice and Lieutenant Governor of Nova Scotia," *Essays in Colonial History Presented to Charles McLean Andrews by His Students*, ed. Viola F. Barnes et al. (New Haven, 1931), pp. 169–197. See also the correspondence between Jonathan and Jonathan, Jr. in *The Belcher Papers* (M.H.S. *Colls.*, 6th series, VI–VII).

62. Belknap, *New-Hampshire*, I, 187, 262ff.; Lawrence S. Mayo, *John Went-*

worth, Governor of New Hampshire, 1767–1775 (Cambridge, 1921), *passim;* Albion, *Forests,* p. 253.

63. William T. Baxter, *The House of Hancock* (Cambridge, 1945), pp. 101, 122.

64. Thomas Hancock [Boston], to [John] Thomlinson, Nov. 6, 1761, quoted in Baxter, *Hancock,* p. 145.

65. James B. Hedges, *The Browns of Providence Plantations: Colonial Years* (Cambridge, 1952), chaps. i–x; William E. Foster, *Stephen Hopkins . . . (Rhode Island Historical Tracts,* no. 19, Providence, 1884), chaps. v, vii.

Bibliographical Note

It is not the purpose of this note to list all the materials used in preparing this account of the New England merchants. Such a compilation will be found in the Dissertation Copy, pp. 476ff. Also, a convenient bibliography of early New England history will be found in *Harvard Guide to American History*, ed. Oscar Handlin *et al.* (Cambridge, 1954), sections 83–86, 88, 90, 99. The following is meant to be a brief guide to the records and writings which were of particular importance for this book and which illustrate the types of material useful for such a study.

PRIMARY SOURCES

MANUSCRIPTS

Though historians and antiquarians have brought to print most of the literary sources of early American history, there remain valuable materials in manuscript, especially business records, which throw light on more than economic or entrepreneurial problems. Of particular interest in the case of New England are the business papers of the Hull-Sewall family (John Hull's Letter Book, 1670–1685 [original and also a two-volume typescript in the American Antiquarian Society, Worcester, Mass.], and Samuel Sewall's Business Journal, 1685–1690 [Baker Library, Harvard Graduate School of Business Administration, Boston, Mass.]). The Pynchon business records, though composed mainly of messy day books difficult to use, illustrate the transformation of Connecticut Valley commerce in the course of the seventeenth century (William Pynchon's Record of Accounts with Early Settlers and Indians, 1645–1650 [Forbes Library, Northampton, Mass.], and John Pynchon's Account Books, 1661–1694 [6 vols. in the Connecticut Valley Historical Society, Springfield, Mass.]).

The Essex Institute of Salem, Mass., has an extensive collection of family business records. Though relatively few of the voluminous Corwin Papers were found useful for this study, attention should be called to George Corwin's Letters, Bills, Ledgers, and Day Books, 1651–1684 (12 scrapbook vols.), and Jonathan Corwin's Ledgers and Day Books, 1676–1714 (5 vols.). The earliest of the many Philip English papers (especially the Day Books and Ledgers, 1664–1718 [6 vols.]) show in some detail the commercial settlement of a mid-century newcomer. Useful material for the seventeenth century will also be found in the first (1661–1730) of sixteen volumes of the Hathorne Family MSS; John Higginson, Jr.'s Ledger, 1678–1689; Thomas Maule's Receipt Book, 1681–1701; the first box of the Pejebscott Papers, 1664–1885; and the first of the three typed volumes of Abstracts of English Shipping Records, 1686–1775.

Among the massive manuscript resources of the Massachusetts Historical Society in Boston, the most valuable single collection for this study is the thirty-three-volume Jeffries Family Papers, of which the following are of particular importance: volumes 1–4, 15, 29 (John Usher Papers); 5 (Benjamin Davis Papers); and 6 (Lidget Papers). Lawrence Hammond's Diary and Commonplace Book, 1677–1691, contains an "Account of my severall Marriages."

The Massachusetts State Archives are well enough indexed to allow convenient use; the Connecticut Archives are excellently preserved and catalogued. Most documents in these collections relate to the period after 1700, but of the Massachusetts Archives (State House, Boston, Mass.) volumes 7, 60–62, 100, 106, and 119 contain relevant information. Volume 7, which includes a registry of Massachusetts shipping, 1696–1714, invites statistical analysis. Of the Connecticut Archives (Connecticut State Library, Hartford, Conn.), the volumes entitled Private Controversies and Court Papers contain pertinent documents.

In a special category are the Lynn Iron Works Papers, 1650–1685 (originals and typescript copy in the Baker Library), which form the basis for a reconstruction of the ironworks episode.

PRINTED MATERIAL: PUBLIC RECORDS

The published public records of the various colonial governments are too familiar to be commented on. They should be supplemented, however, by "The Andros Records," A.A.S. *Procs.*, new series, XIII (1899–1900), 237–268, and "Dudley Records," M.H.S. *Procs.*, second series, XIII (1899–1900), 226–286, both edited by Robert N. Tappan. The legal records are indispensable; they contain important information on all aspects of colonial society. For this study the most valuable ones are *The Records and Files of the Quarterly Courts of Essex County, Massachusetts*, ed. George F. Dow (8 vols., Salem, 1911–1921); *Records of the Suffolk County Court 1671–1680*, ed. Samuel Eliot Morison (*Pubs. C.S.M.*, XXIX–XXX, Boston, 1933); *Records of the Court of Assistants of . . . Massachusetts Bay, 1630–1692*, ed. John Noble (3 vols., Boston, 1901–1928); *Suffolk Deeds*, ed. William B. Trask *et al.* (14 vols., Boston, 1880–1906); *York Deeds* (11 vols., Portland, Maine, 1887–1896); *The Probate Records of Essex County Massachusetts* (3 vols., Salem, 1916–1920); and *Province and Court Records of Maine*, ed. Charles T. Libby *et al.* (3 vols., Portland, Maine, 1928–1947).

To the separately printed volumes of TOWN RECORDS, such as the carefully edited *New Haven Town Records 1649–1662*, ed. Franklin B. Dexter (New Haven Historical Society, *Ancient Town Records*, I–II, New Haven, 1917–1919), should be added those that appear among the *Reports* of the Boston Record Commissioners: especially the *Boston Town Records (Second Report*, Boston, 1877); *Charlestown Land Records (Third Report*, Boston, 1878); *Dorchester Town Records (Fourth Report*, Boston, 1880).

On the ENGLISH side, the *Calendars of State Papers*, domestic as well as colonial series, should be supplemented by *The Calendar of Treasury Books*, ed. William A. Shaw (25 vols., London, 1904–1952); *The Acts of the Privy Council of England, Colonial Series*, ed. William L. Grant and James Monro (6 vols., Hereford and London, 1908–1912); and *Proceedings and Debates of the British Parliaments respecting North America*, ed. Leo F. Stock (5 vols., Washington, 1924–1941).

OTHER PRINTED SOURCES

The writings of the first three American generations of Winthrops touch on all aspects of early New England life. Portions of their letters and papers have been published in three main groups: *Winthrop's Journal*, ed. James K. Hosmer (2 vols., New York, 1908); *Winthrop Papers* (5 vols., Boston, 1929–1947); and *Winthrop Papers* (M.H.S. *Colls.*, 4th series, VI, VII; 5th series, I, VIII; 6th series, III, V). Other standard literary sources contain information about the merchants. William Bradford's *History of Plymouth Plantation 1620–1647*, ed. Worthington C. Ford (2 vols., Boston, 1912), Edward Johnson's *Wonder-Working Providence 1628–1651*, ed J. Franklin Jameson (New York, 1910), Samuel Maverick's *A Briefe Discription of New England . . .* [ca. 1660] (M.H.S. *Procs.*, 2nd series, I [1884–1885], 231–249), and John Smith's *Works*, ed. Edward Arber (2 vols., Westminster, 1895) are particularly useful.

A number of collections of less familiar documents illuminate dark corners. The economic history of the pre-Puritan period may be reconstructed from the documents contained in *Forerunners and Competitors of the Pilgrims and Puritans*, ed. Charles H. Levermore (2 vols., Brooklyn, N. Y., 1912); *The Story of the Pilgrim Fathers . . .*, ed. Edward Arber (London, 1897); *Chronicles of the First Planters of . . . Massachusetts . . .* (Boston, 1846); Miller Christy, ed., "Attempts toward Colonization: The Council for New England and the Merchant Venturers of Bristol, 1621–1623," *A.H.R.*, IV (1898–1899), 678–702; Charles Deane, ed., "Records of the Council for New England," *A.A.S. Procs.*, 1867, 51–131; *The Sagadahoc Colony . . .*, ed. Henry O. Thayer (Portland, Maine, 1892); and the correspondence in *Sir Ferdinando Gorges . . .*, ed. James

P. Baxter (3 vols., Boston, 1890). Other documents edited by Baxter contain sources of seventeenth-century Maine history: *Christopher Levett . . .* (Portland, Maine, 1893), *George Cleeve . . .* (Portland, Maine, 1885), and *The Trelawny Papers* (*Collections of the Maine Historical Society*, 2nd series, III, Portland, Maine, 1884). *The Farnham Papers 1603–1688*, ed. Mary F. Farnham (*Documentary History of the State of Maine*, VII, Portland, Maine, 1901); and *Capt. John Mason*, ed. John W. Dean (Boston, 1887) should also be consulted.

Prominent collections of documents relating to the history of the merchants in the southern New England colonies are *The Records of the Proprietors of the Narragansett . . . The Fones Record*, ed. James N. Arnold (*Rhode Island Colonial Gleanings*, I, Providence, 1894); *The Letter Book of Peleg Sanford*, ed. Howard W. Preston *et al.* (Providence, 1928); Bruce M. Bigelow, ed., "The Walter Newbury Shipping Book," *Rhode Island Historical Society Collections*, XXIV (1931), 73–91; *The Clarendon Papers* (*Collections of the New York Historical Society for the Year 1869*, New York, 1870); *Documents Relative to the Colonial History of the State of New York*, ed. E. B. O'Callaghan, comp. John R. Brodhead (11 vols., Albany, 1853–1861); and *The Hutchinson Papers*, ed. William H. Whitmore and William S. Appleton (2 vols., Albany, 1865).

Two volumes of notarial records are of unique significance for the history of the merchants, for the agreements and notices they contain not only show in precise terms business devices frequently used, but also make clear the personal nature of commercial relationships. These are *A Volume . . . Containing the Aspinwall Notarial Records from 1644–1651* (*Thirty-Second Report of the Record Commissioners of the City of Boston*, Boston, 1903), and *Note-Book Kept by Thomas Lechford, Esq., Lawyer, in Boston, Massachusetts Bay, from June 27, 1638, to July 29, 1641* (*Transactions and Collections of the American Antiquarian Society*, VII, Cambridge, 1885).

Important collections for the later seventeenth century are *Colonial Currency Reprints*, ed. Andrew M. Davis (4 vols., Boston, 1910–1911), *Edward Randolph*, ed. Robert N. Toppan and Thomas S. Goodrich (7 vols., Boston, 1898–1909), and *The Andros Tracts*, ed. William H. Whitmore (3 vols., Boston, 1868–1874). The "Tax List and Schedules—1687," *The First Report of the Record Commissioners of the City of Boston, 1876* (Boston, 1876), contains material for an economic profile of the Massachusetts metropolis.

In a few fortunate cases the literary remains of the merchants have survived and have been published. Foremost among these are *The Diaries of John Hull . . .* (*Transactions and Collections of the American Anti-*

quarian Society, III, Boston, 1857); *Diary of Samuel Sewall, 1674–1729* (M.H.S. *Colls.*, 5th series, V–VII [1878–1882]), and his *Letter Book* (M.H.S. *Colls.*, 6th series, I–II [1886–1888]); and Robert Keayne's extraordinary 50,000 word apologia in the form of a will, printed in the [*Tenth*] *Report of the Boston Record Commissioners* (Boston, 1886).

The Diary of Samuel Pepys, ed. Henry B. Wheatley (2 vols., New York [1946]), and Louis-André Vigneras, ed., "Letters of an Acadian Trader, 1674–1676," *N.E.Q.*, XIII (1940), 98–110, contain information on English and French connections.

SECONDARY WORKS

GENEALOGICAL

Since personal relationships played such an important role in the economic and political lives of the merchants, much use must be made of genealogical and biographical writings. Notable among the genealogical works is Henry F. Waters, *Genealogical Gleanings in England* (2 vols., Boston, 1901), in which are published *verbatim* innumerable wills and records pertaining to colonial Americans and their English connections. James Savage's pioneer reference work, *A Genealogical Dictionary of New England* ... (4 vols., Boston, 1860–1862), has been corrected and supplemented by later findings, many of which will be found in the 108 volumes of *The New England Historical and Genealogical Register* (Boston, 1847–   ). Since the general index to this treasury of genealogical lore covers only the first fifty volumes, the others must be checked individually.

The northern New England colonies are well served by *The Genealogical Dictionary of Maine and New Hampshire*, ed. Sybil Noyes *et al.* (Portland, Maine, 1939), as is Rhode Island by *The Genealogical Dictionary of Rhode Island*, ed. John O. Austin (Albany, 1887). The many writings of Charles E. Banks on New England, especially Massachusetts, genealogy should be used with caution.

Besides such general works there is, of course, an extensive library of studies of individual New England families, such as George E. Hodgdon, ... *Vaughan Family* (Rochester, N. Y., 1918), and Thomas W. Higginson, *Descendants of Reverend Francis Higginson* (n.p., 1910). The most complete collection of such writings will be found in the library of the New England Historic Genealogical Society, 9 Ashburton Place, Boston, Massachusetts.

BIOGRAPHICAL

The handiest compilations of biographical sketches, aside from the *Dictionary of American Biography*, ed. Allen Johnson *et al.* (21 vols.,

New York, 1928–1944), are Charles H. Pope, *Pioneers of Maine and New Hampshire* (Boston, 1908) and *Pioneers of Massachusetts* (Boston, 1900), and Oliver O. Roberts, *History of the . . . Honorable Artillery .Company of Massachusetts* (4 vols., Boston, 1895–1901). Sketches of the pre-Puritan personalities are in Charles K. Bolton, *The Real Founders of New England* (Boston, 1929). Outstanding among the few full accounts of early seventeenth-century merchants are Samuel Eliot Morison's essay on William Pynchon (*M.H.S. Procs.*, LXIV [1930–1932], 67–107) and his chapters on John Hull, Robert Child, and John Winthrop, Jr., in *Builders of the Bay Colony* (Boston, 1930). On Hull, see also Hermann F. Clarke, *John Hull . . .* (Portland, Maine, 1940), and on Child, George L. Kittredge's article in *Pubs. C.S.M.*, XXI (*Trs.*, 1919), 1–146. Henry W. Belknap, *Traders and Tradesmen of Essex County, Massachusetts* (Salem, 1929) has scattered information on early Salemites.

Other studies of first generation merchants are Bernard Bailyn, "The *Apologia* of Robert Keayne," *William and Mary Quarterly*, 3rd series, VII (1950), 568–587; *Lieutenant Joshua Hewes*, ed. and comp. Eben Putnam (New York, 1913); Henry D. Sedgwick, "Robert Sedgwick," *Pubs. C.S.M.*, III (*Trs.*, 1895–1897), 156–173; Charles W. Tuttle, *Capt. Francis Champernowne . . .* ed. Albert H. Hoyt (Boston, 1899); Daniel B. Updike, *Richard Smith . . .* (Boston, 1937); and Joseph Willard, *Willard Memoir . . .* (Boston, 1858).

Writings on later seventeenth-century merchants are Viola F. Barnes, "Richard Wharton . . . ," *Pubs. C.S.M.*, XXVI (*Trs.*, 1924–1926), 238–270; Henry W. Belknap, "Philip English . . . , " *A.A.S. Procs.*, new series, XLI (1931), 17–24; Ralph B. Harris, "Philip English," Essex Instit., *Hist. Colls.*, LXVI (1930), 273–290; and Arthur H. Buffinton, "Sir Thomas Temple . . . ," *Pubs. C.S.M.*, XXVII (*Trs.*, 1927–1930), 308–319. Kenneth B. Murdock has included a short section on Samuel Sewall in *Literature and Theology in Colonial New England* (Cambridge, 1949). Byron Fairchild, *Messrs. William Pepperell* (Ithaca, 1954), which concentrates on the early eighteenth century, is an excellent account of the rise of a merchant family.

ECONOMIC

One path to a deeper understanding of colonial commerce lies in closer examination of the details of business organization and of the social and political context. Thus K. G. Davies' valuable essay, "The Origins of the Commission System in the West India Trade," *Transactions of the Royal Historical Society*, 5th series, II (1952), 89–107, suggests the social importance of a change in business arrangements, and Oliver Dickerson has pointed the way toward a reconsideration of the relationship between trade and politics in *The Navigation Acts and the American Revolution* (Phila., 1951). One focus for further study along such lines is the operation of the customs service in the colonies. Lawrence A. Harper, *The English Navigation Laws* (New York, 1939) considers the problem from the administrative point of view. The political implications, clearly illuminated by Dickerson, may also be seen in Winslow Warren, "The Colonial Revenue Service in Massachusetts in Its Relation to the Revolution," *M.H.S. Procs.*, XLVI (1912–1913), 440–474, which deals with the late seventeenth and early eighteenth centuries.

Much can be derived from the available work treating particular types of economic activity. FUR TRADE: Francis X. Moloney, *The Fur Trade in New England 1620–1676* (Cambridge, 1931), covers a good deal of ground but leaves out details of business organization and also ignores certain regions. Particular portions of the New Englanders' fur trade are discussed in Arthur H. Buffinton, "New England and the Western Fur Trade, 1629–1675," *Pubs. C.S.M.*, XVIII (*Trs.*, 1915–1916), 160–192; Sylvester Judd, "The Fur Trade on Connecticut River in the Seventeenth Century," *N. E. Register*, XI (1857), 217–219; Howard M. Chapin, *The Trading Post of Roger Williams . . .* (Providence, 1933); Richard A. Preston, "The Laconia Company of 1629 . . . ," *Canadian Historical Review*, XXXI (1950), 125–144; Thomas R. Trowbridge, Jr., "History of the Ancient Maritime Interests of New Haven," *Papers of the New Haven Colonial Historical Society*, III (1882), 85–204; and Amandus Johnson, *The Swedish Settlements on the Delaware 1638–1664* (2 vols., Phila., 1911).

FISHERIES: Raymond McFarland, *A History of the New England Fisheries* (New York, 1911) treats the period superficially, but sections of Harold A. Innis, *The Cod Fisheries* (New Haven, 1940) cover the seventeenth century in detail. Relations with the northern grounds are also discussed in Ralph G. Lounsbury, *The British Fishery at Newfoundland 1634–1763* (New Haven, 1934), and in Daniel W. Prowse, *A History of Newfoundland* (London, 1895). Lounsbury is also concerned with the political implications of the fisheries, which is the major interest of Charles B. Judah, Jr., *The North American Fisheries and British Policy to 1713* (*Illinois Studies in the Social Sciences*, XVII, nos. 3–4, Urbana, 1933). Lorenzo Sabine's outdated *Report on the Principal Fisheries of the American Seas . . .* (Washington, 1853) is still useful for certain statistics. Particular controversies are discussed by Arthur H. Buffinton, "John Nelson's Voyage to Quebec in 1682: A Chapter in the Fisheries Controversy," *Pubs. C.S.M.*, XXVI (*Trs.*, 1924–1926), 427–437; and Richard A. Preston, "Fishing and Plantation: New England in the Parliament of 1621," *A.H.R.*, XLV (1939), 29–43. Charles L. Woodbury,

The Relation of the Fisheries to the Discovery and Settlement of North America (Boston, 1880) discusses the importance of farming in the lives of the early fishermen.

Other aspects of economic history have received less extensive treatment. Transitions in the INLAND TRADE are made clear in Roland M. Hooker, *The Colonial Trade of Connecticut*, and Leonard W. Labaree, *Milford, Connecticut*, both *Publications of the Tercentenary Commission of the State of Connecticut* (New Haven, 1936). Roy H. Akagi, *The Town Proprietors of the New England Colonies* (Phila., 1924) contains material on the merchants' involvement in LAND SPECULATION. Information on the TIMBER TRADE is found in Robert G. Albion, *Forests and Sea Power* (Cambridge, 1926). SHIPBUILDING is touched on in William Hyde, "Alexander Adams . . . , " *The Bostonian Society Publications*, XI (1914), 85–101. Deane Phillips, *Horse Raising in Colonial New England* (Cornell University Agricultural Experiment Station, *Memoir*, no. 54, Ithaca, 1922) is useful, but does not go beyond the obvious sources.

Seventeenth-century INDUSTRY is dealt with superficially in J. Leander Bishop, *A History of American Manufactures from 1608–1860* . . . (3 vols., Phila., 1861–1868), and is touched on in Victor S. Clark, *History of Manufactures in The United States* (Washington, 1916). Arthur C. Bining, *British Regulation of the Colonial Iron Industry* (Phila., 1933) includes a brief survey of the early period. There is as yet no full account of the Lynn Iron Works. Sketches are "The First Iron Works in the Colonies," *Bulletin of the Business Historical Society*, I (1927), 1–12, and E. N. Hartley, "Hammersmith, 1643–1675," *The Saugus Restoration* (n.p., 1951).

The MONETARY PROBLEM is treated fully by Curtis P. Nettels, *The Money Supply of the American Colonies Before 1720* (*University of Wisconsin Studies in the Social Sciences and History*, no. 20, Madison, Wisc., 1934). Among the numerous writings of Andrew M. Davis on financial problems, the most comprehensive is *Currency and Banking in the Province of the Massachusetts Bay* (2 parts, New York, 1901). The indispensable works on ECONOMIC THOUGHT are Edgar A. J. Johnson, *American Economic Thought in the Seventeenth Century* (London, 1932), and R. H. Tawney, *Religion and Rise of Capitalism* (New York, 1926).

LOCAL HISTORIES can form the basis for important generalizations about social trends. At best, as in the case of Isabel M. Calder, *The New Haven Colony* (New Haven, 1934), they can make general developments vivid and concrete. Occasionally they yield unsuspected information. Amos E. and Emily M. A. Jewett, *Rowley* . . . (Rowley, 1946) contains material on early textile manufactures, and Henry M. Burt, . . . *Spring-field, Mass.* (2 vols., Springfield, 1898–1899) includes large portions of William Pynchon's *The Meritorious Price of Our Redemption.* But though there are many histories of New England towns, few rise above the antiquarian level. Distinguished exceptions are Samuel Eliot Morison, "The Plantation of Nashaway . . . ," *Pubs. C.S.M.,* XXVII (*Trs.,* 1927–1930), 204–222; Mary J. Lanier, The Earlier Development of Boston as a Commercial Centre (Unpublished Ph.D. Dissertation, University of Chicago, 1924); David L. Babson, Maritime History of Gloucester, 1600–1807 (Unpublished Washburn Prize Essay, Harvard University, 1932); and James D. Phillips, *Salem in the Seventeenth Century* (Boston and New York, 1933).

Among the CHURCH HISTORIES, those relating to the episcopal institutions are especially important for the social history of the merchants. E. Edwards Beardsley, *The History of the Episcopal Church in Connecticut* . . . (2 vols., New York, 1869), Henry W. Foote and John C. Perkins, *Annals of King's Chapel* (3 vols., Boston, 1882–1940), and George C. Mason, *Annals of Trinity Church, Newport, Rhode Island* (2 series, Newport, 1890–1894) are the most prominent for the early period and contain sketches of leading personages. Some church histories, like Hamilton H. Hill, *History of the Old South Church* (2 vols., Boston, 1890), are as valuable for the incidental material they contain, such as membership lists and quotations from church records, as they are for the central historical account.

The exact nature of the all-important connections between the colonial and the ENGLISH MERCHANTS is difficult to establish, especially since so little has been written on the history of the English business community. Nothing exists for the seventeenth and eighteenth centuries comparable to Sylvia L. Thrupp, *The Merchant Class of Medieval London* (Chicago, 1948). The most comprehensive view for this period is Ray B. Westerfield, *Middlemen in English Business . . . 1660–1760* (*Transactions of the Connecticut Academy of Arts and Sciences,* XIX, New Haven, 1915), which discusses business organization in a variety of trades. Of the more specialized works, Astrid Friis, *Alderman Cockayne's Project and the Cloth Trade* (Copenhagen and London, 1927), and William R. Scott, *The Constitution and Finance of English, Scottish and Irish Joint-Stock Companies to 1720* (3 vols., Cambridge, England, 1910–1912) are outstanding. Full examination has not been made of the role of the London merchants in the Civil War and the Revolution of 1688.

Index